The Phoenix Rises

A Portrait of Coventry University in its City

The Phoenix Rises:
A Portrait of Coventry University in its City

First published in 2009 by
Third Millennium Publishing Limited,
a subsidiary of Third Millennium Information Limited.

2–5 Benjamin Street
London
United Kingdom
EC1M 5QL
www.tmiltd.com

ISBN (Hardback): 978 1 906507 05 3
ISBN (Paperback): 978 1 906507 16 9

British Library Cataloguing in Publication Data
A CIP catalogue record for this book is available from the British Library.

Text by Paul Cheeseright and Nick Stokes
Book design: Matthew Wilson
Cover design: Marketing & Communications, Coventry University
Production: Bonnie Murray

Printed by Butler Tanner & Dennis

The Phoenix Rises

A Portrait of Coventry University in its City

Paul Cheeseright

Contents

4

5

6

Foreword

SIR JOHN EGAN, CHANCELLOR

As Chancellor I am privileged to be a part of the many exciting initiatives that take place within Coventry University; none more so than this. *The Phoenix Rises* is a significant milestone in the University's history. It's a record of the University's past, present and future and a celebration of everything that the University embodies.

This institution has been shaped by some of the most innovative thinkers in education and produced graduates who have succeeded in some of the most sought-after positions in the world. The physical presence of the University has made a significant contribution to the city of Coventry and its residents.

The Phoenix Rises manages to capture the culture, the people and the University in all its various forms. It's not only a great read, but also a great resource and I thank all those who have contributed to its creation. This book is testimony to my pride in being Chancellor of Coventry University.

Left: *View of William Morris Building (W Block) past the Lanchester Library.*

Right: *The School of Art and Design, Graham Sutherland Building (M Block).*

VENTRY SCHOOL OF
ART AND DESIGN
Coventry
University

Introduction

Coventry University's history spans three centuries. In that time it has shaped the future of hundreds of thousands of people and brought millions of pounds worth of investment to the city of Coventry and its community. Throughout it has forged enduring links with business and industry within the region and beyond, placing emphasis on the practical value of work-related learning and encouraging a study culture which supports external organizations as a logical outcome of academic research. *The Phoenix Rises* captures the highlights – the good times and the bad, the anecdotes, the imagery and the plans for the future of this great institution.

It has been known in many guises; the College of Art and Design, the Lanch, the Poly and most recently, Coventry University. But what's in a name? The purpose has always remained consistent – to provide students with an excellent education founded on the acquisition of advanced skills, knowledge and experience that have practical relevance in the working world. As memories of the University's predecessor institutions begin to fade, it has become more and more important to produce a record and celebration of all the great achievements that have been made since the first students walked through the door. By capturing first-hand testimonials of the culture embedded in the memories of staff and students who shaped the organization in its formative days, *The Phoenix Rises* will help the story of the University to live on.

The physical form of the University has developed hand-in-hand with Coventry – giving both a reputation for reinvention and innovation. The University lies in the heart of the city and its buildings are as much a part of the landscape as the distinctive Cathedral spires. The University has attracted investment to the city through research and collaboration with industry – helping to foster strong relationships between town and gown.

The book captures it all: the buildings, the people, the research, the community, the partnerships, and the international perspective. Find out more about how this institution has impacted on so many, and follow its footprint to the present day and beyond.

Below: *The James Starley Building (D Block).*

Opposite: *Informal study facilities within the Lanchester Library enable students to benefit from comfortable surroundings and access to digital technology while working on team projects.*

Campus Map

Building	Key
Alan Berry Building (F Block) (oldest library)	1
Alma Building	A
Armstrong Siddeley Building (N Block)	2
Bugatti Building	3
Charles Ward (A Block)	4
Design Hub	5
Ellen Terry Building (Odeon/Gaumont Cinema)	6
Enterprise Centre	7
George Eliot (B Block)	8
Graham Sutherland Building (M Block)	9
Health Design & Technology Institute (completed 2009)	10
Hillman/Humber Lecture Theatres	11
Innovation Village	B
Institute for Creative Enterprise (ICE)	12
Jaguar Building (Q Block)	13
James Starley Building (D Block)	14
Lanchester Library	15
Maurice Foss Building (T Block)	16
Priory Hall (G, H and J Blocks)	17
Richard Crossman Building (L Block) (Old Library)	18
Singer Hall	C
Sir Frank Whittle Building (C Block) (former site)	19
Sir John Laing Building (K Block)	20
Sports Centre	21
Student Enterprise Building (new site)	22
Student Centre (and site for new Engineering and Computing Building)	D
Students' Union – Cox Street	23
Students' Union – Priory Street (E Block)	24
TechnoCentre and	25
Conference Centre	26
Whitefriars Building	27
William Lyons Building	E
William Morris Building (W Block)	28

17
24
4
1
8
19
11
18
22
14
6
3
16
23
A
20
27
9
C
21
2
E
13
28
D
15

1 THE FIRST 180 YEARS

Lineage of a City and its University

Coventry University is the child of its city. Its lineage reflects the changes and the evolution of Coventry at a number of different levels over nearly 200 years. The University and its predecessors have been a key driver in these changes as the University and the city have responded to the cultural, social, and economic challenges of the time.

The practical strand weaves in and out of the institutional changes covering 163 years, up to the designation of Coventry University in 1992, and beyond. The genealogy (see opposite) shows four lines of change.

The first line started when local residents formed a Mechanics Institute in 1829. They were responding both to

Previous pages: *Official opening of the Lanchester College of Technology, May 1961. On the platform (left to right) are the Lord Mayor, Alderman H. Stanley; the Rt Hon. Sir David Eccles MP, Minister of Education; The Chair of the Board; and Alan Richmond, Principal. Holding bouquets in the background are the Lady Mayoress, Mrs H. Stanley (left) and Mrs F.W. Lanchester (right).*

Left: *J.J. Cash's ribbon-weaving factory, 19th century. In 1821 there were 5,000 ribbon weavers in Coventry out of a population of 21,000. In 1841 the industry employed 30,000 people, but by the 1860s ribbon weaving had crashed in the face of cheap imports.*

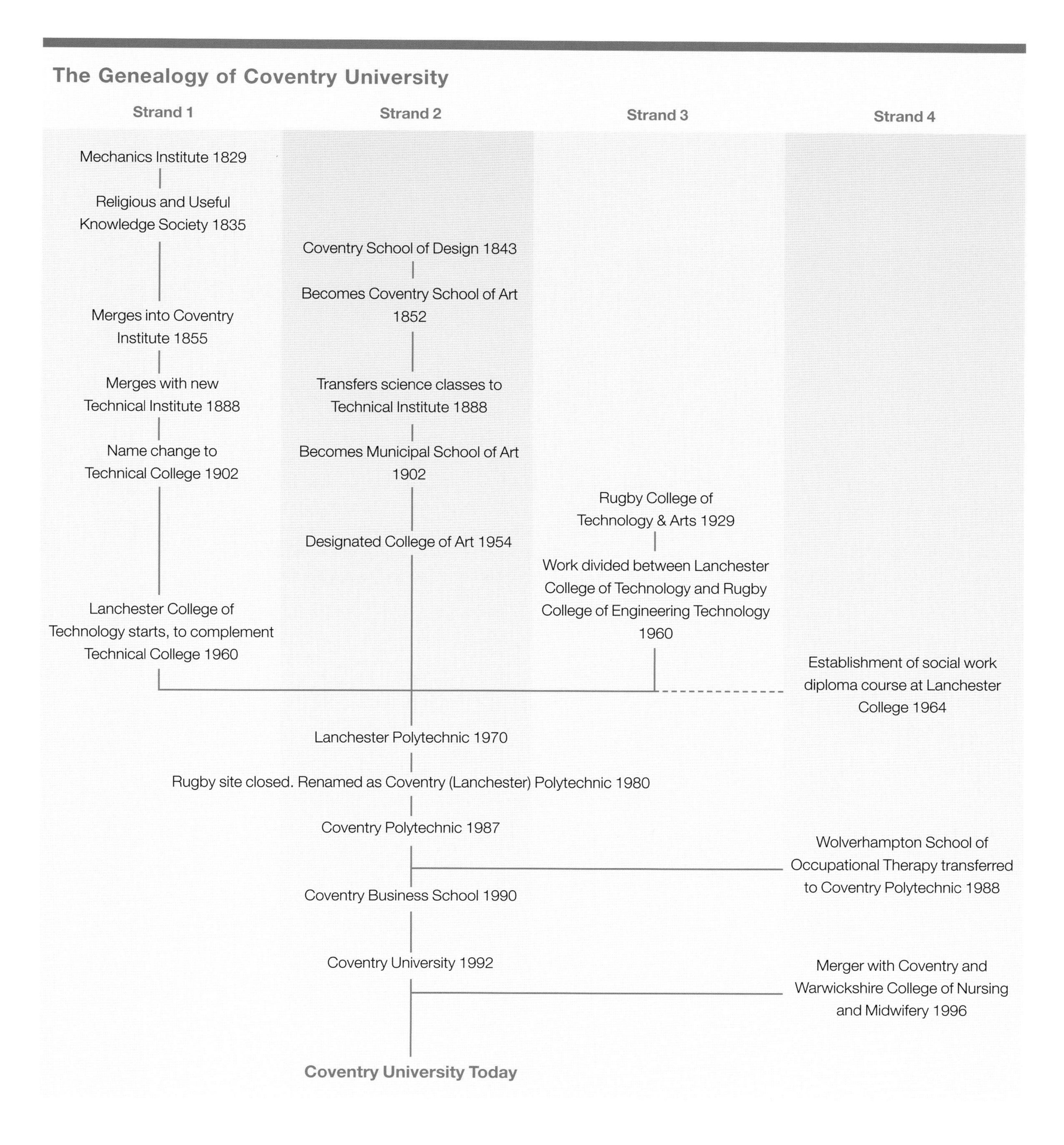
The Genealogy of Coventry University
Strand 1
Strand 2
Strand 3
Strand 4
Mechanics Institute 1829
Religious and Useful Knowledge Society 1835
Merges into Coventry Institute 1855
Merges with new Technical Institute 1888
Name change to Technical College 1902
Lanchester College of Technology starts, to complement Technical College 1960
Coventry School of Design 1843
Becomes Coventry School of Art 1852
Transfers science classes to Technical Institute 1888
Becomes Municipal School of Art 1902
Designated College of Art 1954
Rugby College of Technology & Arts 1929
Work divided between Lanchester College of Technology and Rugby College of Engineering Technology 1960
Establishment of social work diploma course at Lanchester College 1964
Lanchester Polytechnic 1970
Rugby site closed. Renamed as Coventry (Lanchester) Polytechnic 1980
Coventry Polytechnic 1987
Wolverhampton School of Occupational Therapy transferred to Coventry Polytechnic 1988
Coventry Business School 1990
Coventry University 1992
Merger with Coventry and Warwickshire College of Nursing and Midwifery 1996
Coventry University Today

Above: *A distant view of Coventry in the early Victorian period.*

Left: *An example of Coventry ribbonwork, 1851.*

individual requirements for technical education and learning, and to business requirements for a workforce of at least some educational attainment. The urge for improvement could only be met by private initiative; there was no public provision for education.

The initiative linked Coventry into a wider movement. Mechanics Institutes proliferated so that, by the middle of the 19th century, more than 700 had started in the UK and overseas. In some cases they proved to be the start of an historical process; just as that in Coventry became a university, so one in Manchester became the University of Manchester Institute of Science and Technology, another in London became Birkbeck College, University of London.

For Coventry, the Mechanics Institute started a trend. It showed that education and learning could be coupled with a job. Indeed, it could offer relief from day-to-day learning and could open up new prospects. It also introduced students to the discipline of learning and teaching, which is so well documented in books like *Tom Brown's Schooldays*, set within Rugby School just a few miles away. It was classroom-based and intense with little or no time for social life – rather it was an extension of school life.

Industrialization, sweeping across the Midlands of England, led to rapid but agitated expansion of Coventry. The population roughly doubled to more than 30,000 in the first 40 years of the 19th century. Cholera, strikes, and riots punctuated growth as workers coped with harsh conditions, and industrialists grappled with competition and suspicions about the employment effects of new machinery.

Left: *The Coventry School of Design. The School was opened in 1843 as part of a campaign to support the ribbon industry. Appropriately, it was housed in a former ribbon factory.*

Ribbon weaving and manufacture, started incidentally in a part of Coventry now adjacent to the University, initially made up the core of the city economy. The products had a measure of protection but not enough to blunt the threat of French sales in the British market. The need to enhance the ability of the local industry to hold its own in the marketplace led directly to the start, in 1843, of the Coventry School of Design, which would later call itself the Coventry School of Art.

This marked the start of the second line in the Coventry University genealogy. Just as the institution of the first line linked into a wider national movement, so too did the School of Design. Five years before, the government, through the Board of Trade, had opened a school of design, to better equip British industry for international competition: better designs from workers of higher skill could equal higher sales. Coventry was the fifth such school.

Since then the government and Coventry have moved on roughly parallel courses in design. There has been a long line of government reports, reviews and exhortations to promote better design, the 21st-century version being the report of Sir George Cox, chairman of the Design Council. His concern echoed the reports of the past: the UK is not making the best use of its creative talent.

The renamed Coventry School of Art rapidly consolidated its local place and, in one guise or another, has been a feature of Coventry life ever since. The parallel courses merged when Cox opened, in 2007, the University's Design Hub, created as one response to his injunctions, with the purpose of nurturing and supporting local designers and entrepreneurs. The then Dean of the school, Professor Mike Tovey, explores the thinking behind these developments further on page 40.

The Design Hub holds the promise of expansion. By contrast, the moves in the mid-19th century had a defensive quality. Weakened in the domestic market by industrial disputes, the ribbon weavers watched their customers disappear and their industry collapse, when, in 1860, the government removed duties on foreign ribbons. By this time, in any case, Coventry's fortunes had started to rely on watchmaking: one economic phase ended, another began.

Far right: *A Coventry watchmaking factory, late 19th century. Watchmaking and clockmaking boomed in Coventry between 1850 and 1890, before falling victim to mass-produced foreign imports. However the skills won later transferred to cycle manufacture and later still to automobile components, contributing greatly to prosperity in the early 20th century.*

Right: *View of Coventry pre-World War Two, dominated by the famous twin spires.*

Left: *Early days in the Coventry motor industry, showing vehicle frames made from wood.*

Below: *Art School diploma, 1930.*

Bottom: *The Rover Safety Cycle, manufactured by John Starley, was first exhibited in 1885. Coventry became a leading cycle manufacturer, many of its cycle companies going on to become makers of cars and commercial vehicles after the introduction of the internal combustion engine.*

Watchmakers, in turn, had already taken the first tentative steps to create a local system of technical education when they set off the movement for a new Coventry Institute which, in an extension of the first line of genealogy, absorbed during 1855 the Mechanics Institute and the Religious and Useful Knowledge Society. By 1872 the science classes of the Institute were taking place in the School of Art and would do so for 16 years, the first indication that the two genealogical lines would, in time, also merge.

For Coventry and other British manufacturing centres, economic conditions in the last quarter of the 19th century were gloomy. Britain was in depression, which meant that companies had a continuing battle with falling prices. The watchmakers faced the same sort of competitive pressures which had brought down the ribbon weavers. The local plea for more technical education pushed the city authorities to give financial support for a new technical college.

Inauspiciously, in 1887, the Technical Institute opened its doors to students in two donated old ribbon-weaving factories and took over the work of the Coventry Institute. But it had no full-time staff and, in those early days, employers supervised the work. It is clear now that this humble start evoked three themes. Firstly, it drew the city authorities into the educational system and set them on a course of support and occasional control that would last a century. Secondly, it emphasized the concern of industrialists about the shortage of qualified and skilled personnel, a complaint then and a complaint still in the 21st century. And, thirdly, it also prompted those working in the Institutes and Colleges to see that there was a role, not just for teaching but for working with local industry, and in helping to shape it. This theme has been fundamental to the operation and development of the University, and its predecessors, ever since.

Hence the Technical Institute became the Technical College. The School of Art became the Municipal School of Art, acknowledging that, under the 1902 Education Act, the City Council assumed responsibility from a group of

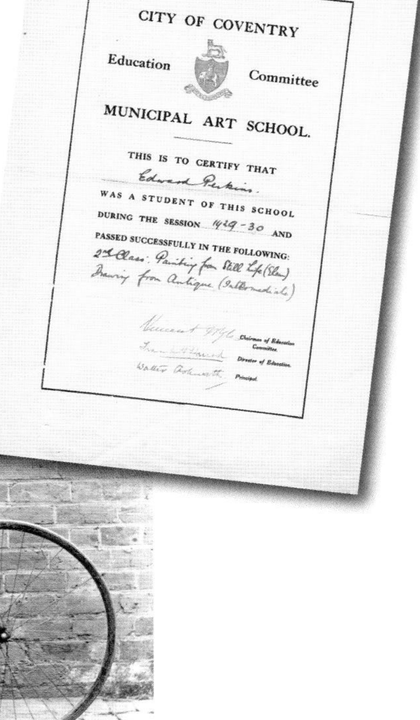

CITY OF COVENTRY

Education Committee

MUNICIPAL ART SCHOOL.

THIS IS TO CERTIFY THAT

Edward Perkins.

WAS A STUDENT OF THIS SCHOOL

DURING THE SESSION 1929-30 AND

PASSED SUCCESSFULLY IN THE FOLLOWING:

2nd Class: Painting from Still Life

Drawing from Antique

Chairman of Education Committee

Director of Education

Principal

Alan Richmond

Sir Alan Richmond dominated the College of Technology. Those who worked for him recalled his ruthless efficiency, his capacity for work, his demand for quality, and his readiness to sack staff who failed to meet his standards. He advocated risk: no success would come without it.

He was not a man for small talk: 'We never had a normal conversation. It was all business', remembered Norman Bellamy, who joined the staff at about the time Richmond had hit his full stride.

Bellamy, though, wondered what sort of a place he had joined when, shortly after his arrival, Richmond called an urgent departmental meeting for an inquest into the throwing of a paper dart out of a fifth floor window. Richmond used his power to inculcate exactitude, and that excluded litter. 'It was the fear factor', said Bellamy, 'but it became the tidiest place in Coventry'.

Top right: *The Technical College, Coventry, known to generations as 'Cov Tech'. Opened in 1935 this iconic building served until 2008, when staff and students moved to new premises in Swanswell as part of City College, Coventry.*

Above: *The opening of the Technical College, 1935.*

local supporters. Inside the Technical College, important changes took place. The demands of the horological industry waned as the industry itself waned. By the end of the first decade of the 20th century, the most important work centred on mechanical engineering. This reflected changes in the city, with the College helping to lead the way.

John Starley, whose uncle James is commemorated on a University building, invented the Rover Safety Cycle in 1885, and started to manufacture it. Dunlop patented the pneumatic tyre in 1889. Daimler established the founding factory of the British car industry in 1896. Alfred Herbert started what would become the largest machine tool company in the UK. The late 19th and early 20th centuries, in short, saw a burgeoning of mass manufacture. The days of the early small craft factories had finished. The new developments would flourish mainly in large factories. Coventry had started another economic phase, and it would last for about 70 years. Cycles begat motor cars, motor cars begat aircraft. The College and School quickly adapted

Left: *Bomb damage from the series of Nazi air raids beginning in July 1940, and culminating in the massive raid on the night of November 14th and morning of the 15th which left much of the city centre in ruins.*

Below: *Coventry Cathedral in the wake of the November raid.*

to these developments, by widening their teaching provision and offering new and relevant disciplines and skills.

This was despite the fact that the basic structure of adult technical education remained the same, based on the Technical College and the Municipal School of Art. There was one exception. The Warwickshire Local Education Authority founded the Rugby College of Technology & Arts in 1929, primarily to service the companies which later became GEC, the leading British electrical engineering group until the 1990s. This was the third line of the University's genealogy.

Although the Technical College moved into new premises during 1935, the privations of the 1930s followed by the World War of 1939–45 caused massive disruption to an educational system which, in any case, did not have enough facilities for those who wanted to use them. Even as the City Council grappled with the physical rebirth of Coventry after bombing, it worked on plans for the expansion of adult education. It envisaged three institutions: a college of technology which would take over some of the work of the Technical College, the School of Art, and a new associated college of general education.

All of that eventually took place, but not in the form first conceived by the City Council. The proposed college of general education was overtaken by notions of a new university, and this emerged in the 1960s as the University of Warwick, oddly named for an institution on the south side of Coventry and on land partly provided by the City Council. Yet, well before then, in the mid-1950s, the Coventry Technical College was full to overflowing with nearly 9,000 students, and

'I certainly hope that, within the national policy framework, the Lanchester Polytechnic will be a college of individual policy and attributes, based on the collective realization by staff and students alike of a community of interest in reputable academic standards, in diversification of educational opportunities, in innovatory developments and concepts, and in genuine consultation based on democratic principles between all the groups which comprise the Polytechnic community.'

Alan Richmond, 1970

Left: *View of Coventry Cathedral from the top of the George Eliot Building (B Block).*

Below: *Construction of F Block, now the Alan Berry Building.*

'I was headhunted by Dr Richmond and appointed Head of Production Engineering in August 1959, this being the first academic post filled, although the Registrar, Alan Bonner, beat me by two days but resigned after a short time. The first of us had to serve a year at The Butts as Lanchester College of Technology was still being built. Only C Block, the engineering workshops, labs, and offices were completed – although the toilets were not connected, so one went out to the public facilities. In fact Richmond had stopped the work on B Block, the teaching block, because he insisted on non-loadbearing plaster partitioning so that future changes of room size and purpose could be easily made. This block contained at this early stage the Principal's office, the library, and the canteen. It was when I was with Richmond in his office that we saw the steel girders for the Admin Block F slowly collapse and crash to the ground, carrying one of the workmen with it – he survived. The outcome of the re-design was that classrooms were to hold 25, rather than the conventional number the council architect had provided. All the windows had Venetian blinds fitted and we eventually received an edict from the City Architect's department that the blinds were to be kept down but open, "to preserve the appearance of the façade".'

Robert I. Aston, M.Phil.

'The interview, in March 1960, for the post of Senior Lecturer in Metallurgy at Lanchester College of Technology had gone well. Dr Alan Richmond offered me the post and asked when I wished to start. Cheekily I suggested 1 July, which would give me two months to write lecture notes before lecturing commenced in that September. Dr Richmond agreed, adding that it would be better for me to start as a member of the Lanchester staff – everyone else, including himself and Dr Foss, being transferred from the Coventry Technical College payroll on 1 September (the official starting date for the Lanchester). Hence I became Lanchester's first official employee and started a career that has now lasted almost half a century.'

Professor David Kirk, Materials Science, joined 1960

Below: *Construction of F Block – a fine example of an exoskeleton steel structure.*

Right: *Alan Richmond with a model of the site c.1960.*

the need for full-time courses as well as those traditionally offered for part-time students had become paramount.

When the Ministry of Education mooted the idea of a diploma in technology at degree level, the college of technology, first suggested by the City Council in 1948, began to take shape. It opened in 1960 with new buildings within the City Centre as Lanchester College of Technology, a homage to one of the founders of the motor industry, and giving rise to a diminutive, 'the Lanch', which is still in use. The first principal was Sir Alan Richmond, a formidable and respected educator, whose academic rigour and vision provided the grounding from which the later Polytechnic and University would grow.

During the 1960s, Coventry had become accepted as a leading regional college, with a range of courses aligned to industry and the professions, and with a stiffening backbone of research. As Richmond wrote in the union handbook of 1966–7:

'Lanchester was noted as an engineering college. I was on the first social science course that was run and, to put it bluntly, people at the college had never seen so many female students before. It took them some time to get used to the idea. Next, the Lanch absorbed Rugby College of Technology, the School of Physiotherapy and the Art College. This was another shock. The college was full of arts' students with long hair and coloured shirts, who sat around in studios thinking creatively all day long. The colleges may have merged but engineering and art students didn't seem to mix in my day. Lastly, there was the ring road. Neither the students nor the citizens of Coventry seemed to think that it was necessary, but the authorities forged ahead with it.'

Chris Hutchinson, Applied Social Science, 1973

'Important developments are constantly taking place in research activities...extension of the boundaries of knowledge is an important and inseparable function ... an increasing number of research projects are directly related to problems which have arisen in industry or in other organizations.'

Richmond had the wind behind him. The Labour government of 1964–70 presided over a ferment of activity in higher education, pressing for more places for more people, for greater opportunities across the spectrum. One channel in that ferment was the thought that regional colleges of art and technology could work together in the form of polytechnics, acting as a complement to the expanding university sector. The polytechnics would offer a full range of courses in science and technology; they would cater for full- and part-time students; they would be controlled by local authorities. So Lanchester Polytechnic emerged in 1970, bringing together the College of Technology, the College of Art (as it had become) and the Rugby College of Technology & Arts.

At this point the first three lines of Coventry University's genealogy became one. The institution had begun to assume its modern shape. But Richmond did not stay long to mould the new institution. In 1972 he left for the quieter environment of Strode Further Education College in Somerset.

He left behind a flourishing institution with over 4,000 students and 500 academic staff, with a growing reputation in engineering and design. This was driven in particular by the close links between business and the college. Many of the students were funded for sandwich degrees by their employers, who, in turn, influenced the nature and form of the teaching. These courses were accredited by the professional bodies and the CNAA (Council for National Academic Awards), and the awarding of full degrees was dependent upon their agreement. Roger Medwell (Engineering, 1968) was one such student; he recalls two happy years learning theoretical and practical skills to enable him to develop his career in his chosen profession, up to his present role as the Chief Executive of NP Aerospace, still based in Coventry.

However, at the same time, Richmond also departed from a city where assurance of growth, ingrained for 70 years, had faded. As the UK economy fell into recession, this student intake from employers was, by no means, the certain funding source it had been.

Far left: *New Street, early 20th century.*

Opposite: *New Street, 2008, with the Frank Whittle Building (C Block) on the left (prior to its removal) and F Block ahead.*

More and More from Less and Less:
The Holroyde Years, 1975–87

The period 1972–5 was a turbulent time in education. Uncertainty about funding, a difficult economic and political climate, and a militant student base made life difficult for Alan Richmond's successor, Keith Legg, a distinguished engineer from Loughborough University. His style was very different from Richmond, who pulled all the strings, and was the centralizer par excellence. Legg wanted more democracy, and a much greater level of staff involvement in the running of the Polytechnic.

To this end, he set up a network of committees, such as one for finance, in which elected staff and students had a

Left: *Richmond Crossman extension (L Block) – see text below.*

Far left: *Geoffrey Holroyde, 1975.*

'The photo above was taken from Jordan Well, close to the Odeon cinema (now the Ellen Terry Building) looking towards the old library building opposite John Laing. The person closest to the camera is the then SU President of Lanchester Poly, cutting the first sod with the help of Geoffrey Holroyde – Director of the Poly. The building about to be started was the then library extension which fronts Jordan Well, which at the time had an open flight of steps. Access to the library used to be from the doorway under the Lanchester sign.'

Diane Edwards, Geography, 1979

Above: *The Directors of Lanchester Polytechnic, 1976.*

presence. This led to an uncertain balance between leadership exercised at the centre, and direction provided at a lower, delegated level. It also created a vacuum which the Students' Union, following examples set by other institutions such as the Polytechnic of North London, was quick to exploit. A disillusioned Legg, frustrated by his development plans being turned down by the City Council, left.

Hence, when his successor, Geoffrey Holroyde, arrived at Lanchester Polytechnic as the new Director in 1975, he found an organization at odds with itself, a strained relationship with the controlling City Council, stretched finances, an unfriendly political environment, and a regional economy moving towards crisis. 'Managing was not easy in this period', he recalled.

Indeed, the President of the Students' Union, who had the right to address the degree ceremony, disrupted the first of Holroyde's era in 1975. He took advantage of the first degree ceremony for two years, as the previous year was cancelled due to fears of IRA activity. 'He put out an ultra-left view, which caused the audience of graduates and guests in the Cathedral to boo and stamp', Holroyde remembered. Dissident students found allies among some of the Polytechnic staff, making a combination which further stifled the network of committees.

Any new director would have found this sort of inheritance to be troublesome. Holroyde more than most. He arrived accompanied by suspicion. Neutral academics worried because he had an unorthodox background for his post: a first degree to be sure, but he followed that with ten years at sea, ten years in engineering, and five years as head of a community college. Those opposed to authority saw him as a tool of the City Council, brought in to wield a retrenching axe.

'My decision ultimately to choose Coventry was probably as a result of an Open Day visit that I made on a glorious spring day. I vividly remember walking down towards the Polytechnic past the tables and parasol umbrellas outside the Golden Cross Pub and the cherry blossom trees, between the two Cathedrals and down to the Polytechnic, and I remember thinking what a beautiful environment it was. Although I was naturally keen to learn more about the mathematics programme, I am sure that this first exposure to Coventry had a major influence upon my decision to study there.'

Professor Graham Henderson
BSc Honours in Mathematics, 1975
Vice-Chancellor, University of Teesside

Above: *The Graham Sutherland Building (M Block), seen in the 1970s. It is named in honour of Graham Sutherland OM (1903–80), who as an official War Artist in World War II recorded mining, industry and bomb damage in Britain during the war years. He designed the tapestry Christ In Glory (1962), for the reconstructed Coventry Cathedral.*

'It was a great course. The Lanch was much smaller than many more respected institutions, but that was an advantage because everybody knew each other and the staff were young (ish) and enthusiastic. Also there was a good emphasis placed on mooting, which is the best preparation you can have for a career in advocacy.'

Rick Pratt QC, Law Graduate, 1978

In fact, there was little choice but to retrench. High levels of inflation during the mid-1970s, and the government's chronic problems with its own finances fed through to Holroyde and all other academic administrators.

'My arrival coincided, for the first time since World War II, with a reduction of expenditure in real terms for higher education, almost for the first time in living memory. So my first budget enabled the dissidents to convince people that I was just a City Council plant, to cooperate in a budget squeeze.'

This set a tone for the whole of Holroyde's tenure. On the one hand, central government policy demanded greater and greater access to higher education. On the other, there was less and less financial scope to manage it. The Polytechnic was in the odd position of having had generous capital provision, so that all its buildings were bespoke in the city centre, but not of having an adequate revenue provision to maintain them. This problem did not go away.

The City Council could have topped up central government funding but was not in a strong position to do so. The city's population was not large enough for an extended local tax base, and in any case had started to fall; after topping 335,000 in 1971, it had dropped to 310,000 by 1996. Coventry had ceased to draw in employment. First the aerospace plants closed and then, after 1972, the motor industry went into sharp decline. Industry departed and so did a portion of local finance.

Across the manufacturing spectrum, companies closed, rationalized, or clung to survival. Between 1974 and 1982, 46 per cent of manufacturing jobs disappeared. One of the most prosperous towns in the UK in the early 1960s, Coventry had hit the doldrums, and, hovering over the descent, was the same phenomenon as that which hit the

Right: *The Duke of Kent visits, 1981.*

Far right: *The Rugby College of Engineering, which became part of Lanchester Polytechnic.*

Bottom right: *Holroyde with a Chinese delegation, 1984.*

ribbon weavers a century before: products which ceased to attract the market, and which were too expensive.

The main responsibility for financing the Polytechnic rested with central government, but the Department of Education and Science channelled its funds and its policy pronouncements through the City Council. While the Polytechnic was supposed to be independent, with a board of governors to which the Director reported, the City Council and Warwickshire County Council, in effect, had control over the Polytechnic's internal affairs.

Holroyde thus had to balance ensuring that he had the support of the City Council before he made recommendations to the governors or, indeed, took major measures in the Polytechnic. But it was not all gloom.

'When I first began work in December 1978 in the library at 'the Lanch', it was housed in one wing of the Richard Crossman building. Engineering occupied the other wing. When they moved out, that section of the building was gutted and refurbished and fitted out with beautiful wooden library shelving. We then moved the entire stock across, while our old home was similarly refurbished, and then moved everything again as we expanded into our huge new premises. Our proud boast was that during all this time we knew exactly where every book could be found, and that, like the Windmill Theatre, we never closed.'

Mrs Sally Patalong, Subject Librarian

Holroyde inherited many able and committed academic staff and a strong academic base.

Over the years, therefore, Holroyde made the system work, helped by two factors. First, he set about streamlining the Polytechnic's organization, cutting back committees, and pushing towards the door recalcitrant staff. Initially, as a Polytechnic, the Lanchester was very student-focused, with high class contact, small lecture sizes, and individual one-to-one tutorials being a timetabled activity. The student to

'I was not really sent to Coventry – I wanted to go – Lanchester Polytechnic was only one of three places in the country that offered a Social Work degree, so here I was. I wan't sure what to expect in September 1969. My family lived in semi-rural Gloucestershire and the first and only time I had seen Coventry was the day my father drove me to the "Lanch" for the interview. On arrival Coventry seemed fun; I loved the Cathedral, and never tired of looking at it; reflecting within its walls; and the modern postwar architecture / design of the city was certainly different and stimulating – there was this strange thing called a pedestrianized precinct which none of us students (even those who had moved from other cities) had seen before!

Coventry was booming; the car industry dominated the city (and the Poly in the early days); and there was wealth; the shops were shining and new; things cost more than they had in Bristol (especially before a kind 2nd year student showed me where the market was hidden) and we seriously thought that Coventry students should have been eligible for the higher level of grant given to students in London and Oxbridge.

Our lecturers were generally young and enthusiastic (only fairly recent graduates had studied such areas), and the whole thing felt like an adventure. In 1969, the move from a Gloucestershire bedroom with Che Guevara on the wall to studying sociology in what was still the "industrial" and well-unionized Midlands felt fine.'

Chris Player (née Collins)
Applied Social Sciences, 1972

Left: *Construction of the Maurice Foss Building (T Block), 1986.*

Bottom left: *Geoffrey Holroyde with an experimental electrically powered car at the Jaguar factory, Coventry, mid-1970s.*

staff ratio was as low as 7:1. These costs could not be sustained. There was a steady reduction in the unit of resource for teaching, leading to larger lecture groups and the removal of separate tutorials.

Second, power ebbed away from local authorities and trades unions after the arrival of the Thatcher government in 1979. The Polytechnic quietened. 'The institution had survived on its momentum for a few years, driven by committed academics,' as Holroyde put it, while senior staff worked to put in place more coherent internal management.

With much of his time absorbed by external work, not least working for the real independence of polytechnics, Holroyde relied heavily on his deputy, Maurice Foss, to run the institution internally. (His success in that is enshrined in the naming of one of the campus buildings after him.)

One of the early tasks was accommodating the students from Rugby College, after the Warwickshire County Council decided to relinquish interest since the Coventry site was both overcrowded and in urgent need of investment. This was helped by a government grant for a new block to ease space constraints (see campus development section – page 84).

The government then decided that all the freestanding colleges of education should be absorbed into universities or

Above: *Demolition of the Rolls Royce Parkside site for the Technology Park.*

> *'Higher education has a hierarchy of priorities ... It must provide ideas and people which can a) develop and exploit science and technology for the benefit of mankind, b) develop new social systems and skills, and attitudes in people, so that the technology can be exploited for the benefit of everyone on a more acceptable basis than hitherto, c) guarantee our continuing prosperity as a trading nation, d) enhance the quality of life, the result of our understanding, our acceptance of each other, our beliefs and moral codes, and our capacity to enjoy the creative arts and the new leisure.'*
>
> Geoffrey Holroyde, 1982

polytechnics. Warwick University and the Polytechnic were put into the ring to fight for the Coventry College and its valuable resources. Ultimately, the City Council recommended to the government that the University should adopt the College – on the casting vote of the Lord Mayor.

Internally, Holroyde and Foss slimmed the clumsy Academic Board, where everything, down to emptying waste bins, had been discussed. Professor Morris, subsequently Head of the Faculty of Business and Management Studies in the 1990s, recalls two such examples. A policy on tea and biscuits, and which meetings qualified for which, was only agreed after some discussion, and, on one particularly famous occasion, nine senior managers spent 40 minutes deciding whether or not it was appropriate for the part-time contract for the nude life model in the art and design school to be increased from six to eight hours per week!

They delegated power to the deans, in charge of the faculties, but, in order to hold back empire building and foster a common approach, established a directorate in which each had responsibilities across the institution.

The shape of the academic organization stayed much the same as it had been under Richmond. There were four faculties, three of which reflected traditional strengths and the regional economic background: engineering, science, and art and design. Social sciences with business studies rounded the portfolio, helping to create what Holroyde called in 1982 'a mix not unlike that found in many of the newest universities, but distinguished from any university by the presence of art and design, and paramedical subjects'. There was little or no provision for mainstream arts or humanities courses such as English, history or the languages. To study these, students had to go to the mainstream universities.

As Holroyde's term drew to a close, the student roll had risen to 6,000, marking precisely the expansion of opportunities which had been behind the establishment of polytechnics during the 1960s. In many cases they offered similar education to the universities, but with closer links to employers, and with flexible modes of attendance. As Holroyde pointed out, they provided it at two-thirds of the unit cost; more and more students for relatively less cost.

He and his fellow directors felt like poor cousins. They began to press for independence and freedom from local authority control. Having played a leading role in this campaign, in the last months of his tenure, Holroyde had his wish. That closed an era of expansion on the one hand, but unrest and stringency on the other, probably the most testing time in the history of the institution. Holroyde's achievement was to have guided the Polytechnic through to independence from city control, and to have provided a legacy on which his successor could build.

A Change in Name but not in Style:
The Goldstein Years, 1987–2004

Michael Goldstein followed Geoffrey Holroyde in seamless succession. His promotion to Director of what had then become Coventry Polytechnic had been carefully planned: 'a prime duty of any leader is to find the best successor', Holroyde wrote later. Goldstein came to the Polytechnic as Deputy Director in 1983, after the retirement of Maurice Foss, so that, by the time he stepped up four years later, he knew the institution in detail. He had not been part of the 1970s turmoil, but rather of the growing success of the 1980s.

He had firm ideas about the direction in which the institution should move:

> *'The driving force for me was making quality higher education available to as many people as can benefit. Higher education has to be relevant to the needs of the people. I was committed to an institution linked to industry and business. You need that on the doorstep to provide for local people.'*

This was a view influenced by his own background. Passing the 11+ gave him a route out of a deprived background in Stoke Newington, north London. Northern Polytechnic, as it then was, provided him with a BSc and a PhD in chemistry, and then the opportunity to research and teach. The Polytechnic took him out of the shoe shop which otherwise might have been his destiny.

Goldstein took this commitment to a local and expansive role significantly further than his predecessors. His personal background was a driving force and compelling passion. He also had a much greater measure of freedom to make it happen. The removal of polytechnics from local government control gave Coventry Polytechnic greater independence.

Financial pressures, however, did remain. Central government, of course, remained overwhelmingly the main source of funding. The new institution confronted a major backlog of repairs and maintenance, and a massive

Left: *Michael Goldstein.*

Above: *The site for the TechnoCentre, late 1990s.*

'When I was at Coventry, we were just starting to use computers. I see the work students are doing now and it's fantastic. We had to present our designs on A2 paper – that was the biggest you could get! Coventry is still by far one of the best universities training up future graduates in this industry. There's robustness in the graduates; they're informed and rounded. The bar is getting higher and higher and the skill sets students are learning at Coventry are really needed to get into the industry.'

Richard Shaw, Transport Design 1988
Chief Designer, GM Europe

programme of organizational development to make it fit for purpose. Bridges needed to be built with the City Council.

For all that, the Polytechnic could organize its own internal affairs without the fear of local intervention which had dogged Holroyde's days. Here Goldstein seized the opportunity. His first strategic plan, for 1989–90 to 1991–2, showed how he intended to grasp it for the longer term.

The plan outlined an extensive programme, opening up access to the Polytechnic across the curriculum, widening the income base, extending the Polytechnic's international work, and fostering relations with further education institutions across the region. It stressed the importance of research and committed two per cent of revenue to support it.

Outside the Polytechnic, the wider economic and social trends cried out for what the Polytechnic was trying to do. Goldstein recognized that economic advance for Coventry could spring out of the Polytechnic, and the strategic plan reflected that:

> *'The powerful economic and industrial base of the Midlands, and of Coventry in particular, now recovering rapidly from the traumas of the early 1980s, has been a major influence on the Polytechnic's development.'*

Above: *The Lanchester Library in the early stages of construction.*

The local economy, in any case, desperately needed to enter a new phase. Unemployment was at unprecedented levels. The future lay, not in the large-scale manufacture which had given Coventry 70 years of prosperity, but in diversification through smaller, high-technology companies placing a premium on innovation. This was a need to which the institution could provide a major part of the solution. The change in designation, from Polytechnic to University during 1992, did not alter that: the name changed but the style and purpose remained the same.

Indeed, in 1995, Goldstein noted that the government's greater emphasis on regional and sub-regional development played to the University's strengths and commitment to applied education and development. He cited the bringing into higher education of the education and training of health-related professions, the growing importance of start-up enterprises, and working more closely with business.

In practical terms, the Polytechnic first and the University later were changing quickly. One fundamental way was through the development of a new area of expertise for the University – healthcare. This is where the fourth line in the University's lineage joins in. The Polytechnic had been offering a social work diploma since 1964. In 1980, the Faculty of Social, Biological and Health Sciences was established, with the addition of physiotherapy. This expanded in 1988 with the transfer of

'The main contrast is in numbers of students in classes. In the late 1980s "Bob's Full House" created a shock when I recruited 100 first-year students onto the Law degree. Nowadays, 100 students is unthinkably small given that we normally enrol 250 students to the programme.'

Bob Gingell, Senior Lecturer in Law, joined 1975

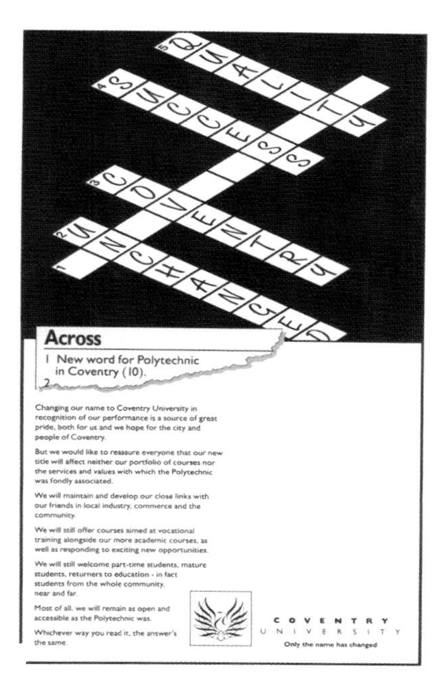

Left: *Elements of the re-branding campaign supporting the change of name from Lanchester Polytechnic to Coventry University.*

the Wolverhampton School of Occupational Health, so that by 1993, degrees in both occupational therapy and social work were offered.

However, the real change took place in 1996 when the Warwickshire College of Nursing and Midwifery merged with the University, bringing with it around 800 students and 70 staff. It led to the establishment of various nursing and physiotherapy programmes within the School of Health and Life Sciences, under Professor Donald Pennington, and then from 2002, Dr Linda Merriman. This part of the School was initially located at the Walsgrave Hospital in Coventry, but quickly moved to the Gulson Hospital site on the edge of the main campus, and then to the Richard Crossman Building, which remains the headquarters of the Faculty of Health and Life Sciences today.

The Faculty has grown rapidly since 1996, as illustrated by the timeline (see page 36), so that today, it is responsible for the initial education and training of 13 health and social care professions, with more than 4,000 students and staff, three times the number in 1988. It plays a prominent role in the regional and local healthcare community, but is increasingly developing a national and international profile in a number of niche areas such as neonatal, teenage, and young adult cancer care. This is explored further in the section on healthcare and the community, pages 121–3.

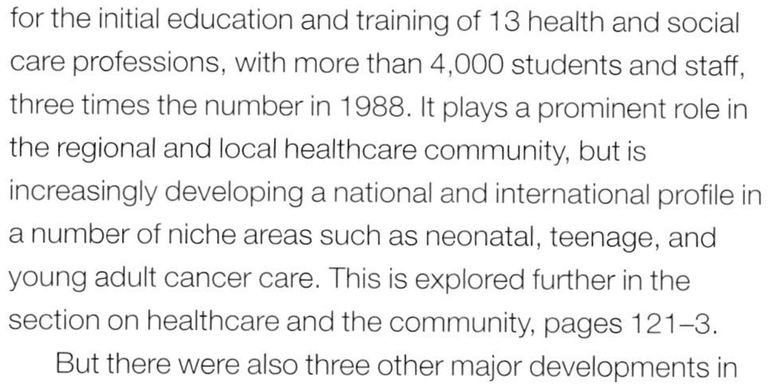

But there were also three other major developments in the late 1980s and 1990s that dramatically changed the look of the new Coventry University.

Right: *University construction in the shadow of Coventry Cathedral.*

First, there were the changes taking place in terms of business and management provision. Economics had been offered alongside social studies since the 1960s. In 1984, the departments of Business and Management Studies, Economics, and Law had been merged into the School of Business and Management Studies. This structure lasted until 1990 when the Coventry Business School was created, led by Professor David Morris, with a post substantially funded by Peugeot. This reflected the growing need for a more rounded education to be available to students at more higher education institutions, and for the University to rebuild business partnerships by offering more than the specialist skills it had before. Under the direction of Professor Morris, the Business School broadened its portfolio through the 1990s, moving into areas such as leisure, sport and tourism, and developing new modes of delivery through early versions of online and distance learning courses with support from industry – such as Cable and Wireless.

Second, there was the change in teaching methodology with the development of modular-based teaching. While this enabled the University to establish close collaboration with industry, given the need for project work and industrial input into course development, it also reduced teaching flexibility and meant that the University depended more on its partners for the practical experience to balance the theory. There was a suggestion to reduce laboratory activity in engineering, for example. Peter White, one of the Faculty's Associate Deans, recalls: 'This led to a move to reduce and remove high-cost laboratories with the advent of cheaper computing, allowing for more simulation. However, the experience of conducting a laboratory experiment on a gas turbine is far more memorable and educational than a small simulation. Therefore the faculty resisted this move and Coventry University has continued to use laboratories for project work.' The benefit of this can now be seen in the activity-led learning initiative which is described on page 109.

Timeline for the development of health and social care at Coventry University

Year	Activity
1964	Establishment of Social Work at the University – diploma course
1980	Faculty of Social, Biological and Health Sciences set up; Physiotherapy established.
1988	The then Wolverhampton School of Occupational Therapy transferred to the Coventry Polytechnic in September 1988. It was established as the regional school of OT.
1990	Established first honours degree in Occupational Therapy in the UK.
1993	Degree in Social Work launched – 10 years before social work became a graduate profession.
1994	School of Health and Social Sciences established.
1996	Merger with the Coventry and Warwickshire College of Nursing and Midwifery on the 1st March 1996. Nursing became part of the School of Health and Social Sciences.
1998	Establishment of Child Nursing course Establishment of Clinical Psychology
1999	Establishment of the BSc Hons Dietetics course
2004	Establishment of Operating Department Practice course Establishment of paramedic courses
2005	Faculty of Health and Life Sciences established Establishment of Learning Disability Nursing course
2007	Establishment of Youth Work course

Above: *Geoffrey Holroyde, Michael Goldstein and partners with Maurice Foss (right) at the official opening of the Technology Park in May 2007.*

Opposite: *Frederick William Lanchester (1868–1946), the engineering genius who came to be identified with the Midlands motor industry in general, and the Coventry-based Daimler company in particular.*

Third, the demise of the Council for National Academic Awards also now meant that the University could validate its own degrees. Practically, this made little difference as the institution already had robust methods of quality assurance.

'I applied to Coventry's Business School because I got a positive response from the British Council about the quality of education at Coventry. I enjoyed both campus and city life. The deep sense of tradition, history, and culture make it a unique city. The diversity of cultures also make it one of the most cosmopolitan cities in the UK. The attraction of studying in Coventry was its unrivalled role in the world of business. My MBA has helped me a lot in building my career in the teaching and research field. It provided opportunities, resources, and expertise to help me achieve academic, personal, and career goals within a stimulating and supportive environment. I have developed interpersonal communication and leadership skills to work effectively with others and lead teams to accomplish objectives.'

Mokhdum Morshed, MBA 1999, is from Bangladesh and is now a Senior Lecturer in the School of Business at North South University in the capital, Dhaka

But the composition of degrees changed with the introduction of the modular system, adding flexibility and variety to single-subject course degrees.

The introduction of modular structures came in the late 1980s. A student could build up a degree by accumulating modules containing a short but specific programme of work – thus extending the range of degrees available beyond those based on a single subject. This gave students many more options. It encouraged part-time and mature student study because it did not tie a student to a defined duration for the attainment of a degree, and it allowed entry based on experience and prior learning.

Norman Bellamy, then Pro-Vice-Chancellor, spent a year reviewing the scheme created by Goldstein and his previous Deputy Director, Mike Fitzgerald, and conceded that not all staff favoured the introduction. One of the problems was that modules needed a common set of rules; staff, in short, could not simply structure courses the way they wanted.

But the introduction of the modular structure, allied to the greater availability of part-time opportunities and the enlarging portfolio of courses which Coventry could offer, took the institution further and further into the community. Until the 1970s there had been a tendency for the institution to present itself as a training facility for companies. Now the University, alert to market trends, could adapt to what both students and companies required.

With these initiatives, links with business gradually took on a different tone. Instead of being largely a provider of services, responding to industry needs, the University became a partner, opening up specialist expertise to the commercial world through focused, relevant programmes, and through research and consultancies. The creation of Coventry University Technology Park to provide facilities for start-up, small- and medium-sized enterprises was a major achievement in this regard. The institution also established its own centres of excellence related to local industry need, such as in technology and automotive

Above: *HRH The Princess Royal opens the Lanchester library on 27 September 2001. A pre-war Lanchester sedan can be seen in the foreground.*

design. The University also expanded its expertise into new areas – for example the Centre for Local Economic Development (now SURGE) and the provision of MBA programmes (initially in partnership with Warwick) within the Business School; Geography, Disaster Management and Sociology were incorporated within Environmental Sciences, and the various developments listed on page 36 within Healthcare.

Similarly, Goldstein substantially improved the tone of relations with the city. The cutting of the umbilical cord meant that the Polytechnic and then the University could be a partner with Coventry Council rather than just another department.

'The University is totally a part of everything in Coventry', as Goldstein said. Students and staff engage in voluntary projects, there are effective links with colleges and schools, and there is a real engagement in civic endeavours to, for example, encourage inward investment, and to enhance the quality of life for all those who live, work, or play in the city and its region.

The University, in any case, dominates the city centre. The Goldstein years saw the refurbishment of hurriedly built 1960s properties, rehabilitation of earlier historic buildings, such as the Business School's William Morris Building, a former factory, and new construction like the library named after Frederick Lanchester. The estate trebled in 20 years. The nature of the city campus is discussed on page 78, but the importance of the property work done in these years strengthened the University and revitalized the city centre. Because the work took place on a controlled rather than a speculative basis, with little debt incurred, it increased the value of the University's assets.

This took place as the University's income rose. In the first 11 years of the University's existence, total income grew to over £93m in 2002–3 from £56.6m in 1992–3. This ran in parallel with the rise in student numbers, more than doubling to 17,000 from the time Goldstein arrived in Coventry. Running costs were held down and devolved budget holders worked within their own, approved, business plans. Because borrowing was minimal, Goldstein left for his

'Research and international activity are fundamental to our role as a high-quality and progressive higher education institution. But we are at pains to emphasize that these dimensions to our function and purpose will not in any way lessen our commitment, either as a teaching institution or as an organization which puts local responsibilities to the fore. Our research enhances and enlivens teaching; our internationalism enriches and informs our local impact.'

Michael Goldstein, 1992

Above and below right: *Foundations are laid in 1957 for what would later become the Charles Ward Building (A Block).*

successors a sound financial position, not the least benefit of his legacy. Unusually, he ran a university without debt.

For Goldstein personally, the finances were a concomitant of the central desire, the one he set out at the start, that of opening up higher education. The numbers showed success: nearly two-thirds of Coventry's students when he left came from within the region, a fine record of widening participation. 'There is now', he said, 'a wider range of quality opportunities for people who deserve the life-enhancing possibilities that higher education provides.'

Developments in the School of Art and Design

'Industrial Design had fourteen students and seven staff when I joined.' Professor Michael Tovey was the seventh in a department which, he recalled, had a remarkable feature: 'seniority was defined exactly by height.' These staff laid the grounds for the emergence of Coventry as a prominent centre of design expertise and, in the case of automotive design, *the* prominent centre of expertise nationally.

Professor Tovey saw it all and participated in most of it as a senior player. When he arrived in 1973, there was a prototype course in automotive design. He became the course director, shepherding the work to full degree status. First as Head of Department, then as Dean of Art and Design for 18 years, and latterly Director for Design, he and Coventry grew together in design reputation.

The initial steps were not easy. The early automotive coursework showed strong awareness of the ethics of design, to meet need in a way which was socially acceptable and sustainable, but it did not necessarily make the graduates employable. Professor Tovey saw that this approach demanded even more academic rigour, and it had to be brought closer to the motor industry. The Polytechnic, as it then was, had to identify what the industry needed from new employees.

Gradually the shift took place, helped not least by bringing to the staff people with an industrial background. 'Initially it was tough; we had to build a good name. The breakthrough came in the mid-1980s as design directors in the industry took us seriously and we won Department of Trade and Industry awards,' Professor Tovey explained. Indeed, Coventry graduates began to spread through the industry, and the department became the biggest of its type in the UK. Links with industry, then and now, are a fundamental part of the Coventry approach to academic work. Success in the motor sector encouraged expansion into other areas, both internally and externally.

Internally, Coventry began to meld automotive design with engineering, and to extend the scope of its undergraduate

Left: *Professor Michael Tovey.*

Below: *Michelle Steel (Surface Decoration, 2008) exhibiting her work as part of the Art and Design Degree Show 2008 in the Lanchester Gallery within the Graham Sutherland Building*

offering from car design to ergonomics, and from ergonomics to fashion. It introduced Europe's first postgraduate course in electronic graphics in 1986.

Externally, Professor Tovey was instrumental in attracting funds for research. The government-funded Science and Engineering Research Council at the end of the 1980s invited Coventry to explore how computer-aided design could work in industrial design. It wanted to examine the crossover from art and design to engineering; Professor Tovey took a place on the Council's design and engineering committee.

Below: *Performing arts students rehearsing in the Theatre Studio in the Ellen Terry Building.*

Above: *Students practising in the dance studio in the Ellen Terry Building.*

'Having established a reputation for transport design, with good research rankings, the University was able to bid for public funding. This resulted in the development of the Bugatti Building, as a facility matching the highest professional standards in full scale automotive design. These facilities also benefitted from generous support from the Bugatti Trust (marked by a prominent annual Bugatti Lecture) and demonstrated the growing economic importance of cultural activity'.

Professor Tovey led the negotiations which resulted in the 1995 incorporation of the Coventry Centre for the Performing Arts, until then run by the City Council.

He suggested to Vice-Chancellor Michael Goldstein, that the University should acquire the nearby unused Odeon cinema. He then supervised its conversion into a centre for media, communications and the performing arts, 'a fraught process', he recalled: 'a new concrete box in the skin of the building, just keeping the original rooms at the front.' Operations scattered around Coventry came under one roof.

In like vein, he was one of the originators of the Institute for Creative Enterprise (ICE), which opened during 2008 in a converted stationery warehouse next to the University's Technology Park. ICE is a postgraduate centre specializing in media, digital design and performance, with space for practitioners and small-scale companies in the creative industries sector.

Coventry
University

New Emphases:
The Atkins Years, 2004–

When Madeleine Atkins arrived at Coventry in 2004 from Newcastle University she came with a mission to prove that a modern university is a learning environment striving for excellence and capable of not only engaging with emerging trends but also of shaping the future economy.

Her first task was to review the curriculum to make sure it was fit for the 21st century. 'We spent a lot of time examining what knowledge and skills were going to be needed in the economy and society, both in the region and further afield,' she recalls. 'Then we compared these with our current courses and discovered where the gaps were.'

Much was to change. In her first three years, the faculties brought in more than 30 new courses as a direct result of this exercise. Professor Atkins was determined that Coventry University was going to offer what employers most valued. Out, for example, went single honours chemistry. In came environmental and health technologies, new media, and up-to-the minute IT courses.

As well as anticipating changes in the economy, Professor Atkins was also concerned to make sure that students were getting what they wanted from the University. An extensive student feedback programme was put in place, asking students in great detail every two years about everything from the food on offer to the standard of their teaching. The feedback determines what improvements are made to student services and to the learning experience.

Staff surveys also became a biennial exercise, and the University sought the views of organizations in the public and voluntary sectors, including schools in the region, to

'Our core values are: commitment to academic freedom; contributing to economic and social prosperity; fostering innovation, creativity, and enterprise; sustained partnerships and teamwork; client-focused, continual improvement with modern IT; valuing diversity, fairness, and equality of opportunity; encouraging our staff to make decisions and contribute positively; caring for, and valuing our staff, and encouraging their development; caring for the environment and the communities within which we operate.'

Madeleine Atkins, 2006

'I have worked at other UK universities, and at two in Asia, and I have found a kind of openness, flexibility, and sense of innovation at Coventry that has been lacking in some of the others. Here, I feel able to bring out a sometimes outrageous idea, and say "How about it?" Some work, some don't, and some should never get approved; but there is generally a healthy acceptance of innovation and change. In this spirit, I designed the University's first distance-learning programme, a Certificate in Peace and Reconciliation Studies. It has been running successfully for many years now, with students from all around the world learning about peace and reconciliation without ever coming to the city which promotes it: a virtual Coventry.

I am sure that Coventry provides a first-class education for students from all kinds of backgrounds, from the UK, from continental Europe, and from a wide range of other countries. It is a real pleasure to walk into the classrooms, libraries, and social spaces and see the productive interaction of people of all ages, backgrounds, ethnicities, and professions. I never found any sense of snobbery, exclusiveness, or prejudice. I think that is quite an achievement.'

Alan Hunter FRSA, Professor of Asian Studies
Director for Centre of Peace and Reconciliation Studies

gauge perceptions of Coventry University. 'Our aim is to make sure that our quality is driven not by fashions or fads, or by what other people are doing, but by the needs and perceptions of those who matter to us,' she says. 'This is our niche, because we understand how strongly the University is connected to the business world, the professions, and the voluntary sector, and we need to keep going back to our roots in order to be innovative and creative, and alive to emerging trends.'

Academic courses have not been the only aspect of Coventry's work which has been updated. Research has been through a similarly robust overhaul, to shift the emphasis firmly in the direction of solving real-world

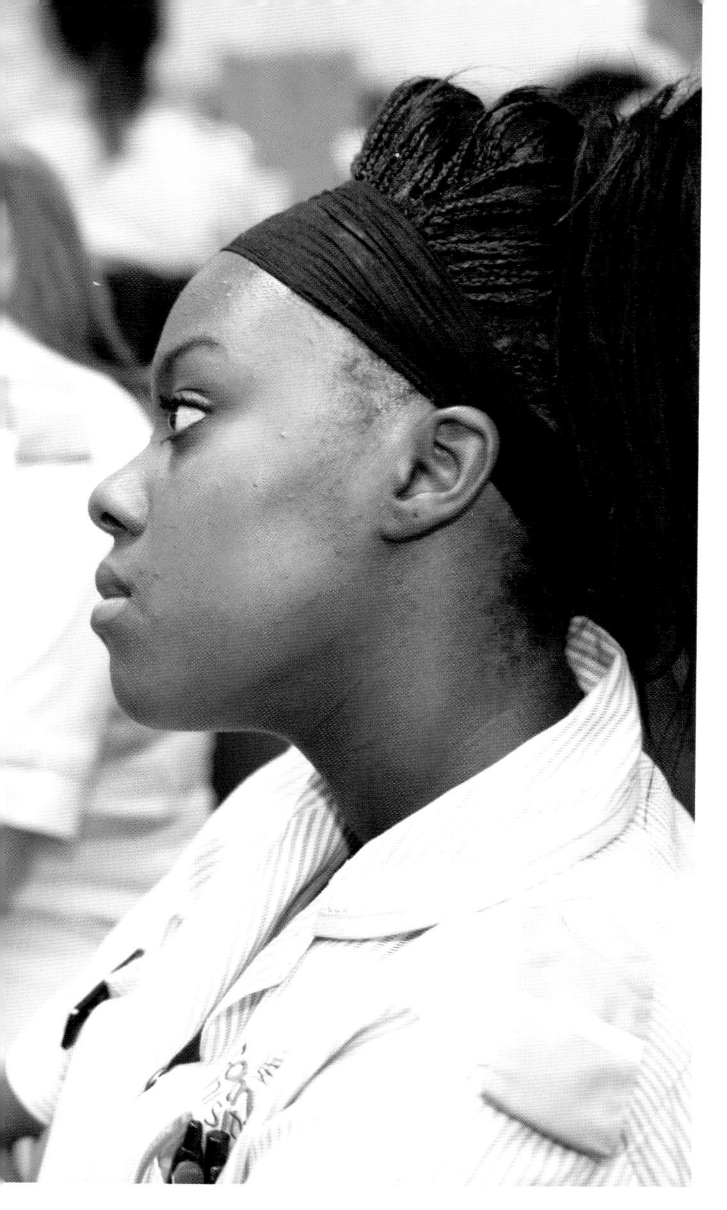

Left: *A wide range of age groups pass through the University's Nursing, Midwifery and Healthcare course, ensuring that skillsets are up to date.*

Below: *Students study on one of the 350 computers available in the Lanchester Library.*

Opposite: *The Queen's Anniversary Prize for Higher & Further Education for the University's work in automotive design was presented to the Vice-Chancellor, Professor Madeleine Atkins and Professor Jill Journeaux, Dean of the School of Art and Design, by Her Majesty The Queen and HRH The Duke of Edinburgh at a ceremony in Buckingham Palace on Thursday 14 February, 2008.*

Right: *Total University income from all sources since foundation in 1992.*

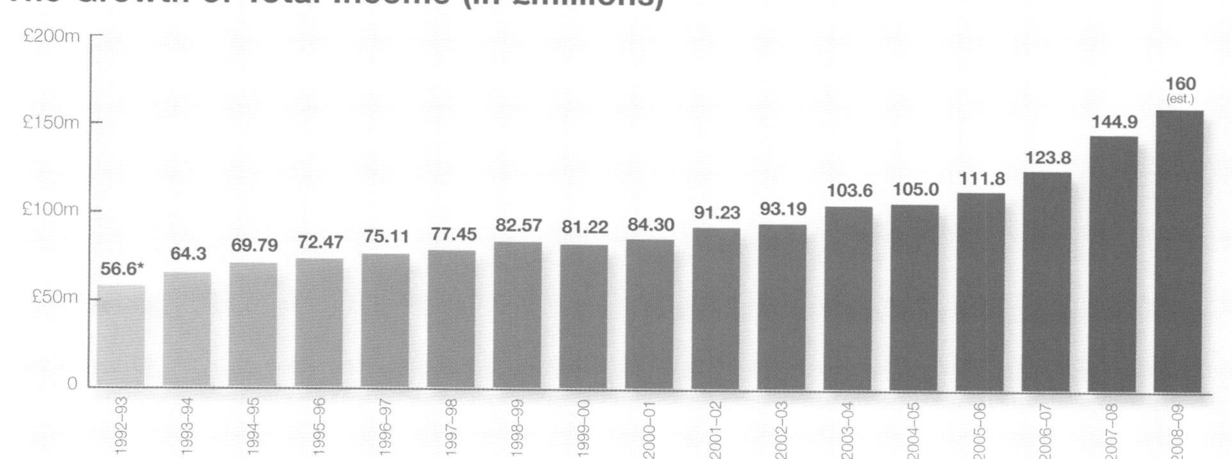

*1992–3 comprised a 16-month period to bring all University years in line with each other. The figure stated was calculated as pro rata of the £75.46m for the 16 months.

Source: Coventry University Annual Reviews, Corporate Plans

'My favourite memories relate to the time I spent with other students from different cultures. I made so many good friends, and they are sweet memories I will have forever.'

Jaiganesh Kandaswamy, Engineering Management, 2006

problems. A number of research institutes have been established on the University's Technology Park to support a unique combination of commercial activity, academic research, and postgraduate teaching. These institutes are pioneering new models of higher education, and have been generously supported as pilots by the Higher Education Funding Council for England (HEFCE) and by the Regional Development Agency, Advantage West Midlands.

'We wanted every member of academic staff to be involved in some aspect of applied research, which is ambitious I know, but our lecturers are brilliant and have become thoroughly engaged with this agenda.' The proportion undertaking applied research has rocketed from 35 per cent to 84 per cent, a shift which not only benefits the outside organizations they are working with, but their students as well, as the research is translated into case studies, or into project work in the curriculum.

And a pilot programme which Professor Atkins believes has great potential for the future, is currently testing a completely new type of tailored course, delivered for private and public sector organizations on their own premises. Known as the Employers Engagement Programme, it has clients including the AA, Caterpillar, and various Trusts in the NHS. It is also funded by HEFCE.

'Our teaching really is informed by all of the work we do with external organizations, so when we say our courses are vocational, we really mean it!' she says.

Graduates leave Coventry ready to enter the employment market with relevant knowledge, up-to-date skills, and an enterprising outlook that is so valued by employers. Almost all students undertake the 'Add+vantage Scheme' as part of their degree, to enhance their employability. They can, for example, learn some Mandarin or Arabic from scratch, and they will usually have some leadership training, and some volunteering or work experience under their belt. Overseas work or study placements are also a growing trend at Coventry, thanks to increasingly deep partnerships being created with international organizations.

The campus itself is also going through a process of renewal under a £160m development plan which will see the creation of iconic, contemporary buildings and more pedestrianized green spaces growing up in the City Centre location. The shift will please students who will have access to the very latest teaching facilities and laboratories, as well as organizations across the region who will be encouraged to use the University's specialist facilities much more than ever before.

The plans contribute to a wider £9.4bn redevelopment of the City Centre of Coventry, including a new Learning Quarter encompassing the University, City College (its neighbouring further education college), and a new City Academy which will be sponsored by the University. As Professor Atkins says, 'As we break down the old image of Coventry as a concrete city, a new vision is emerging which includes more friendly spaces, green roofs with grass and trees, and more water features. Our campus development supports this vision and is all part of our wider work in raising aspirations and creating a learning environment of the highest quality – which is at the very core of what we do.'

'I remember being in a business class with several young men from different firms within the motor industry, who were highly competitive, yet banded together instantly, when anyone was dismissive of the industry as a whole. Graduating in such a lovely venue as Coventry Cathedral, is a special memory.'

Jo Hibbard (née Saxelby), Business Administration MBA, 2001

Opposite: *View past the Bugatti Building towards the Maurice Foss Building (T Block).*

Coventry
University
Coventry
University

Coventry People: Starting, Passing, Living

Coventry is proud of the famous people who have associations with the city. In an ongoing project, Coventry's Walk of Fame, residents vote each year for Coventarians to be immortalized by having their names set into the flooring in Priory Place in the form of a Hollywood-style star. From literature and the arts to engineering and invention, Coventry can claim a vibrant tradition.

POLITICS

1 **Richard Crossman**: MP for Coventry East.

2 **Mo Mowlam**: Head Girl at Coundon Court School.

3 **Henry Parkes**: born in a cottage in Canley.

UNIONS

4 **Jack Jones**: helped keep the city's munitions industry working through WWII as an official (and later General Secretary) of the TGWU.

5 **Tom Mann**: born in a cottage in Grange Road, Longford.

THEATRE/BOOKS

6 **George Eliot** (Mary Ann/Marian Evans) was at school in Warwick Row.

7 **Nigel Hawthorne**: Born in a house on the Binley Road, now demolished.

8 **Philip Larkin**: lived in Manor Road near Coventry Railway Station as a boy and went to Henry VIII School nearby.

MUSIC

9 **Rajinder Singh Rai** (Panjabi MC): resident in the Holbrooks area of Coventry.

10 **Pete Waterman**: grew up in the Stoke Heath area of the city and was a DJ at the old Locarno Ballroom, now Coventry's Central Library.

SPORT

11 **David Duckham**: site of the former Coventry Rugby Club ground in Coundon Road.

12 **Jimmy Hill**: lived on the Kenilworth Road.

13 **David Moorcroft**: site of the Butts Stadium, former home of Coventry Godiva Harriers.

CITY

14 **Cuthbert Bardsley**: Bishop of Coventry Cathedral, 1952–76.

15 **Lady Godiva**: said to be buried in a church she founded on this spot.

16 **Alfred Herbert**: the gallery and museum that bears his name.

17 **Basil Spence**: architect of the new Coventry Cathedral, consecrated in 1962.

18 **James Starley**: Coventry Transport Museum, which has a major collection of his machines.

19 **Arnold Wesker**: at least two of his plays were premiered at the Belgrade Theatre.

20 **Frank Whittle**: his birthplace was in the Earlsdon area.

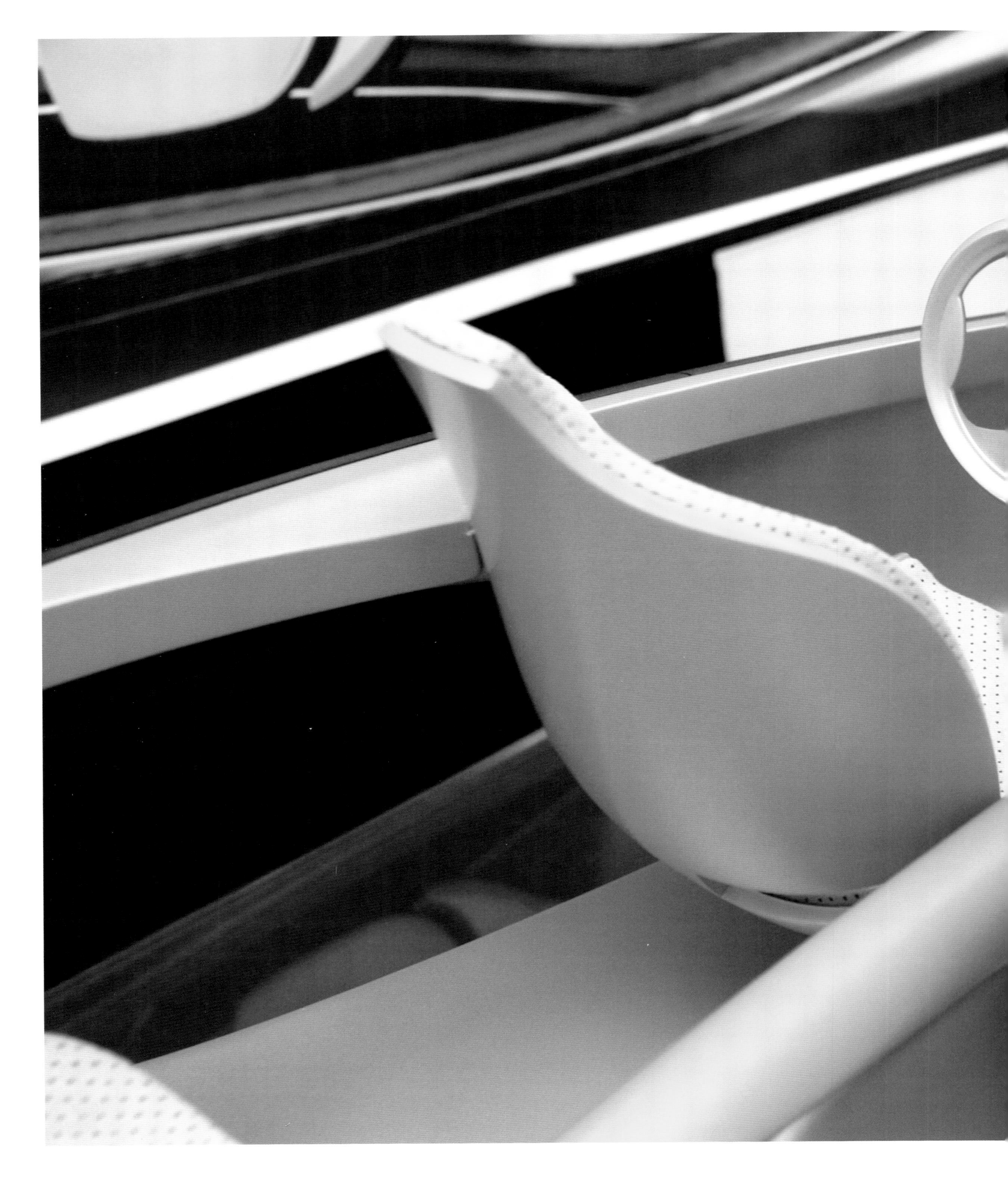

2 COVENTRY REACHES OUT TO THE WORLD

Learning and the Working Environment

Through each phase of its history the relationship between learning and the experience of working has been central to the story of Coventry University's success.

Local industry played a vital role in the foundation of the Mechanics Institute in Coventry in 1829, and the needs of industry and business have impacted on choices made and avenues pursued at Coventry University ever since. The fact that Coventry offered only limited provision for teaching in the arts and humanities until the 1990s demonstrates the determining strength of the relationship with industry.

From the perspective of the student, the experience of learning is one that has always connected to the realities of the workplace.

In the 1930s and 1940s many students attending the Rugby College of Technology and Arts were apprenticed to leading engineering firms, most notably the British Thomson-Houston (BTH) Company based in Rugby, which manufactured a wide array of electrical systems and steam turbines.

Jack Osbourne (Engineering, 1938) and John Hull (Engineering, 1938) are friends who met through the BTH apprenticeship programme, working for the company during an exciting era when, among other activities, it was involved in building the world's first prototype jet engine for Frank Whittle's Power Jets company.

'Twenty years ago, first year engineering students were scheduled for approximately 26 hours per week. Much of this time was spent in practical laboratory situations, team building, presentation and communication exercises in addition to formal lectures. Most of us had never heard of pedagogy let alone what it meant! We produced some excellent students and were on first name terms with over 300 students.'

Jon Baxter, Associate Head of Department, Engineering Manufacturing and Management, joined in 1989

Previous pages: *Interior of Transport Design student's work at Degree Show, 2008.*

Below: *Postgraduate students in the graduate CPD Centre.*

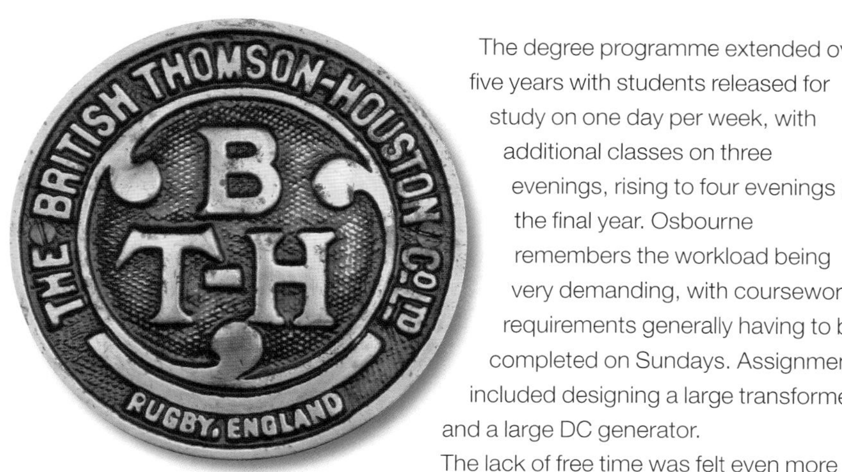

Above: *The British Thomson-Houston company of Rugby was one of a number of local industries that took engineering students from Rugby College of Technology and Arts in the 1930s and 1940s.*

The degree programme extended over five years with students released for study on one day per week, with additional classes on three evenings, rising to four evenings in the final year. Osbourne remembers the workload being very demanding, with coursework requirements generally having to be completed on Sundays. Assignments included designing a large transformer and a large DC generator.

The lack of free time was felt even more acutely by another student. Maurice Banks (Engineering, 1942), who studied during the war years, remembers only seeing daylight at weekends for most of the academic year. Banks was also apprenticed to BTH, spending some of his apprenticeship working on the early stages of radar development. Like the others, his ambition, duly achieved, was to secure membership of the Institution of Electrical Engineers as a chartered engineer.

Lectures and demonstrations tended to focus on issues of engineering theory, with the learning of practical skills located in the workplace. All three students found their degrees to be extremely practical, and of direct relevance to the workplace, remarking that they often felt themselves better equipped than university graduates who generally joined the company with little or no workplace experience.

Around half of the 14 or so students in Osbourne and Hall's year succeeded in completing the full five-year course, the rest withdrawing due to work pressures. Their degrees were formally awarded by the University of London at a ceremony in the Royal Albert Hall.

Much had changed when Ray Owen joined Lanchester College on a four-year sandwich course in Business Studies in 1966. However, the aspect of industrial experience remained as integral to the learning experience as before. Owen's degree involved a work placement with British Leyland at their Preston plant. He was only the second student to be taken on by British Leyland in a non-engineering capacity. Although formally specializing in the marketing option within his Business Studies degree (other options were accounting and purchasing), he spent much of his placement getting involved in personnel related issues, an experience which led to a subsequent career in that area.

Like many of his contemporaries, Owen graduated onto the sandwich course programme after passing the National Diploma. He had several friends from his native Liverpool who went to Lanchester, and recalls a cosmopolitan community of students drawn from all parts of the UK. On arriving in Coventry he was among the very first cohort to move into the much-loved Priory Hall residence, at that

'The greatest memory I have is of all the people I met at the College. It was the time when I had the greatest freedom to grow my mind and explore not only the subjects I was taking, but also life. It set me up to be independently minded and not to be the same as everyone else, but to reason what is my position on this topic/situation. This stayed with me all my life, as during my working career in computer business systems I was always challenging the way a company/country did business. I was at the forefront of the use of computers in business, the start of online systems and the use of the web.'

Derek Ward, Lanchester College of Technology, 1966–69

'Students who had not performed well within the traditional education system and A level examinations benefited from the former polytechnics' approach where additional staff attention was offered. With this personalised care students could excel and go on to achieve successful PhD outcomes at what are now Russell Group Universities.'

Peter White, Engineering, 1973

'I remember visiting the Social Work Educational Institution in Finland with Bill Smith (now retired), and we were shown the 'wonders of how email worked' and were impressed that you could send messages to people! When I started in 1991, I had to handwrite messages to people, as even the use of computers was very limited. Once we did get the first version of email, Pegagus I think (snail mail as we used to call it), we did not trust it and had to go and ask people whether they really got the email. So technologywise we have really developed in the last 10 years, and I would have never anticipated where we are now.'

Ms Sonna Odedra, Associate Head of Department, Social and Community Care, joined in 1991

stage still being fitted out. Opportunities to enjoy a social life had clearly grown since the 1940s, and Owen recalls attending many gigs at the Students' Union by leading bands of the era, such as Cream.

Stephen Kingswell (Business Administration 1995, Communication 1997) came to Coventry University as a mature student aged 35, having already attained the position of company director in an HR executive and technical recruitment company.

Like Osbourne and Hull, his experience of learning was concentrated in workday evenings and weekends, including a number of weekend residential programmes.

Despite the everyday pressures of running a successful company, Kingswell enjoyed 'losing himself' in studies as a break from the boardroom table. In fact the theoretical aspect of his studies provided him with new tools to take into his workplace. Where previously he might have made decisions on the basis of instinct, his studies enabled him to rationalize decisions in terms of a learned model – though very often the outcome of the decision would be the same.

The degree's curriculum was modular, although a core group of perhaps 20 part-time students took the same options and became a close-knit group, socializing in Cork's Wine Bar after (and occasionally before) classes most weeks. The camaraderie was not merely social, since the group of mainly mature students established informal study partner arrangements, ensuring that notes from missed lectures could be shared and assignments discussed.

With his background in running a company Kingswell was able to share some expertise of his own, for example his familiarity with the financing of business development, and the intricacies of corporate balance sheets. Equally, however, his degree provided an impetus for learning new skills – without the luxury of his own secretary he found himself learning to use a computer for the first time.

In this respect, Coventry has been at the forefront in the use of technology and computers in learning and teaching. Professor David Morris, the Director of the E-Learning Unit at the University, remembers the initial pilots in Virtual Learning Environments (VLE) in the Business School at this time. Indeed the University was the first in the UK to roll out this technology, under the name of WebCT, across the whole campus. It enabled staff to upload lectures and students to find course information.

The acquisition of practical and transferable skills remains a hallmark of a Coventry University degree.

Above: *Lively Interaction is a key characteristic of the Coventry learning experience*

Placement and mentoring programmes remain integral to the experience of many students, affording tremendous opportunities to learn within a real working environment as well as in the classroom, lecture hall, and library.

Students like Doreen Wildenauer (European Engineering Business Management, 2006) continue to reflect on the benefits of work-related learning in ways remarkably in tune with the comments of their predecessors of 70 years earlier.

Wildenauer feels that the combination of technical and business modules in her EEBM course have helped her greatly in her subsequent career as a Communications Operative for Airbus CIMPA in Bristol. Her degree programme, which included a placement with German company KRONES, gave her a strong appreciation of both sides, making it easier to understand engineering requirements, and to react to them in her business field.

Similar developments have taken place across the University. In healthcare, for example, where partnerships are with NHS organizations and service users, the Faculty has trialled inter-professional learning, outreach courses – such as occupational health with Staffordshire – and assessments of working practices in the NHS. One particular example has been assisting Accident and Emergency departments in dealing with children with serious injuries, the learning from which is not only transferred onto paramedic and child nursing courses but is shared with all relevant professional end users.

In all these ways, Coventry seeks not just to be up with current trends and practices in business and the community, but to shape them with the research that it does – as illustrated by Professor Ian Marshall in the following pages.

Below: *The Department of Nursing, Midwifery and Healthcare, within the Faculty of Health and Life Sciences, offers graduates the skills and qualifications needed to enter the workplace.*

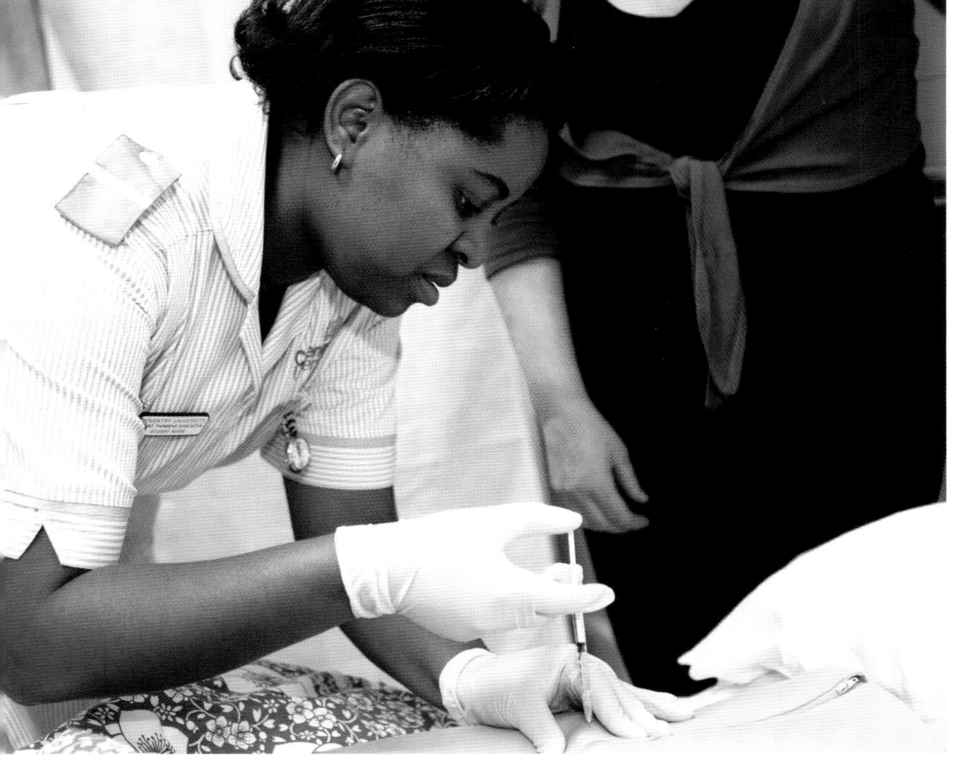

'I became familiar with many cultures and nationalities while studying at Coventry. It is a good place where everybody, including students, tutors, and neighbours meet and discuss peace and reconciliation. What I really liked about Coventry was the student-centred approach. The class size is relatively small so it is very easy to get to know other fellow students. Tutors know you as an individual not just a student. They were very friendly people and always available to talk to you when you needed help. All tutors seemed to really care about your success, both in their class and in your future. I could have never imagined being away from home for one year, and this stay has made me a more mature person. Coventry is the perfect place for a student to succeed.'

Ea Meng-Try, Peace and Reconciliation Studies, 2002
went on to study a PhD at Rutgers University, US, and to undertake senior responsibilities in the Cambodian Truth and Reconciliation process.

Applied Research for the Wider Community

IAN MARSHALL, PRO-VICE-CHANCELLOR (RESEARCH)

Coventry University's definition of applied research encompasses traditional research through to knowledge transfer partnerships, consultancy, and continuing professional development. As explained in the section 'The Atkins Years', it is both a key ingredient of the Coventry offer and an exemplar of the type of university that Coventry seeks to be.

Founded as an industrial university, Coventry's research originally focused on the needs of major multinational automotive companies such as Jaguar, Rolls-Royce, Land Rover, Ferrari and Ford. Since then the University's capacity has grown, and today applied research activity is undertaken in practically every subject area. From art to design, health to sports, regeneration to human security, mathematics to engineering, and computing to communications, staff are encouraged to apply their knowledge and skills in the external world.

Above: *Students at work in the 3D modelling Laboratory within the Bugatti Building.*

Left: *Vehicle aerodynamic testing in the smoke chamber.*

Right: *Automotive Design student presenting his work to Anna Maria Palmagiano, Alfa Romeo designer from Italy, and Frank Stephenson, Design Director for the FIAT Group.*

Bottom right: *HeliSafe – helicopter crash simulation.*

Rather than undertaking research for research's sake (although this is done as well), the University looks to staff to apply their expertise to solve problems for the wider community. The objective is to bring our intellectual thought and expertise to bear on issues of local, national, and international importance. Hence Coventry has developed expertise in peace and reconciliation alongside the efforts of Coventry Cathedral, and then evolved into related sectors such as global security and community cohesion, with the successful launch of iCoCo (the Institute of Community Cohesion) in 2006, led by the highly influential Professor Ted Cantle. This institute has quickly established itself as the authority in this field, and carries out major studies both for national government and for various local authorities.

Such activity is disseminated through publications for national and international conferences, journals, reports, designs, works of art, patents, and products. In 2007–8 the University's external research funding was in excess of £17m, rising from around £7m over two years. This funding comes from a variety of sources including industry, government agencies and departments, the European Union, charities, and research councils. It is forecast to reach £30m by 2010.

The following are examples of recent projects from Departments, Applied Research Groups, Centres, Institutes, or Coventry University Enterprises (CUE) Ltd.

ENGINEERING AND DESIGN

Automotive Design Excellence

Coventry University's Department of Industrial Design has won the Queen's Anniversary Prize for Higher & Further Education for its work in automotive design. Building on its reputation of more than 30 years, the department is continuing to pioneer new developments in the field. It is

Above: *One of three flight simulators in the Aerospace lab which support the Aerospace Systems Engineering BEng Honours degree course.*

regarded as a Centre of Excellence by the higher education sector internationally, and by the automotive industry itself for its contribution to the education of tomorrow's world-class designers. Key to this success are its innovative industry-focused courses and applied research, which have been highly influential in helping to maintain the UK's position as a leader in automotive design. Its capabilities are explored more on pages 112–5 in 'Designs which work and designers who go to work'.

Helicopter Safety

Flying fatalities are ten times more likely in civil helicopters than in aeroplanes, statistically speaking. Many accidents are survivable however, because helicopters often fly at lower altitudes; the impact with which they hit the ground is usually less than that involved in a motorway car collision. Coventry University is the sole UK representative on a €4.8m project 'HeliSafe TA' (Helicopter Safety Technology Application), designed to boost the survival chances of pilots and passengers involved in crashes. Working with 11 partners across Europe, HeliSafe TA will identify and evaluate a range of advanced crash protection systems based on interacting safety features such as seats, harness restraints, and air bags. Facilities at the Italian Aerospace Research Centre in Capua have been used to carry out a full-scale crash test with a civil helicopter, to assess the efficiency of existing safety features using crash test dummies. Taking these results as a benchmark for future protection systems, computer-aided engineering models were built to simulate the effectiveness of new features.

Engineering Measurement

In safety-critical applications, risks of product failure arising from any measurement inaccuracies can have costly

Above: *The NP Aerospace bomb disposal suit, the 'Mark VI explosives ordnance disposal (EOD) suit', is the most advanced of its kind in the world today. The company is presently working with two teams at Coventry University to investigate new advanced sensing technologies, as well as looking at ways to minimize the thermal strain of such protective clothing on the wearer.*

Above right: *Occupational Therapy students. Coventry University offers a wide range of specialisms in this field, with extensive research possibilities.*

implications. In the aerospace industry for example, even the smallest deviation from the exact dimensions specified can seriously impact a product's ability to operate as designed. To avoid potential safety risks for end users, the rigorous requirements of aircraft manufacturers mean that whole production lines can come to a halt if flaws are identified – a fact equally true in many other industries. The West Midlands Manufacturing Measurement Centre (WMMMC), based at Coventry University's Technology Park, is responsible for increasing the awareness and take-up of measurement as a key underpinning technology to boost competitiveness. Funded by Advantage West Midlands, the regional development agency, the Centre evolved from research which showed a noticeable gap in the general understanding and appreciation of measurement issues in manufacturing business advisors across the region.

Bomb Disposal Protection

The NP Aerospace bomb disposal suit, the 'Mark VI explosives ordnance disposal (EOD) suit', is the most advanced of its kind in the world today. Developed in close conjunction with the British Army, never has a piece of equipment of this nature been so extensively tested throughout all stages of its development. The suit is designed to protect the bomb disposal operative while any explosive devices are rendered safe. However, it is vital that the suit does not impede an operative's ability to undertake such a demanding task. The company is working with the University's Human Performance Applied Research Group and Cogent Computing to investigate new, advanced sensing technologies and to find ways of minimizing the thermal strain of such protective clothing on the wearer.

PUBLIC HEALTH

Hospital Safety

Around 900,000 incidents where NHS patients are either 'harmed' or 'nearly harmed' are estimated to occur in UK hospitals every year. Serious and largely preventable errors affect ten per cent of patients in general hospitals. However, concerted efforts to respond, by analysing reports and by targeting training, have been hampered by concerns about under-reporting and the quality of information recorded. Research has looked into the causes of under-reporting of

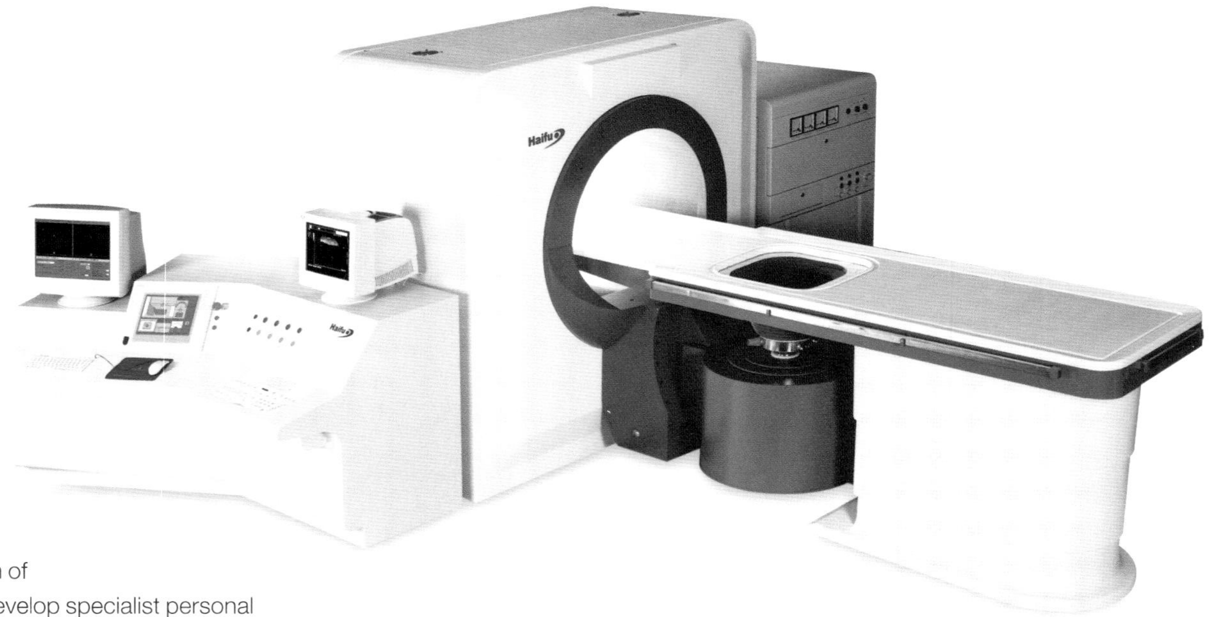

critical incidents and suggested ways to drive improvement, including the use of ward rounds, staff reminders, and the use of technology such as handheld mobile computers. In 2006, a team of experts was brought together to develop specialist personal digital assistants: this involved the Applied Research Centres in Health and Lifestyle Interventions and eWorking. With personal digital assistants, staff can collect data on the job, and the information is forwarded immediately on a wireless network to the risk management team for analysis. Carefully designed systems can provide an easier method of reporting, greater control and flexibility, and, potentially, increase the volume of reports and the quality of the information contained in them.

Killing Cancer

Ultrasound has been employed in a variety of medical ways for many years: in diagnosis, to look inside the body and observe a growing foetus; in physiotherapy, as a tool to aid the rejuvenation of muscles and help pain control. Now it is finding a use in the treatment of tumours. High-intensity focused ultrasound (HIFU) employs equipment which emits high-frequency sound waves. Patients lie over a small bath of water containing two concentric ultrasound transducers. One transmits a low-power diagnostic beam, allowing the doctor to visualize the tumour and guide the treatment; the other produces a high-power focus which targets and kills the cancerous cells by heating them to temperatures of up to 90ºC. The present work at the University's Sonochemistry Applied Research Centre grew from a meeting with a group of Chinese researchers who developed the HIFU system. Trials and tests on the effectiveness of HIFU on kidney and liver cancers have been completed. Feedback from UK patients who have been successfully treated using the new technology has been extremely positive, with no reports of pain, side-effects, or marking on the body. Patients are also often able to return home the next day. Follow-up MRI scans have shown the tumours to be dead and even beginning to shrink.

Above: *Ultrasound (HIFU) equipment used to locate cancers and is also used in physiotherapy as a tool to promote the rejuvenation of muscles and aid pain control.*

Sex Education

The UK has the highest rate of teenage pregnancy in Europe, and instances of sexually transmitted infections are also rising alarmingly quickly. Research by Coventry University's Applied Research Centre in Health and Lifestyle Interventions examines the sexual activity of over 3,800 school pupils in England aged 13–16 years. The results suggest that in order to be effective, sex education needs to be tailored to these very varied levels of experience, and that a more personalized approach, carefully timed and relevant to the individual, would improve engagement. There is a need for parents, who can make a vital contribution, to put aside embarrassment and start talking to their children.

Sustainable Drainage

Flooding suffered in parts of the UK during the summer of 2007 highlighted the need to revisit the way in which drainage is managed in the UK. For the last 100 years we have increasingly covered our urban areas with layers of concrete and tarmac, which prevent rain penetrating the ground and slowly soaking away. Research in the area of sustainable drainage looks at ways of addressing issues which are not just a UK problem: they have relevance internationally. It is not a new problem; the University's

Right: *Flooding, a widespread natural hazard that the University seeks to overcome with sustainable drainage.*

'The University has been active in the provision of short courses and consultancy in response to the needs of those involved with emergency planning and management, disaster relief, and development. We are increasingly exploiting cutting-edge and innovative technology in the delivery of our courses, such as the use of serious games programming to enable emergency practioners to train for dangerous, real-world situations within a safe, virtual "online" environment which can be manipulated to create infinite scenarios, and where responses can be reviewed and assessed.'

El Parker, Principal Lecturer in Natural Disasters

research in this area stretches back over 20 years. Most of this work has involved collaboration with industry on the practical solutions to this pressing problem.

Disaster Management

The ability of hospitals to respond to major incidents is increasingly under the spotlight. Working with researchers from Coventry University's Disaster Centre Emergo Team, the Health Protection Agency (HPA) is providing hospitals with the opportunity to assess their policies and protocols in managing all aspects of a large-scale emergency. An assessment and training tool for decision making, the system is used to aid personnel involved in planning and managing the response to a complex incident. The simulation exercises are run over a period of two days, and include a five- or six-hour, real-time exercise. Over 140 hospitals have taken part, involving up to 60 staff each time, including senior consultants, accident & emergency, radiography and theatre staff, as well as non-clinical hospital management. Feedback from the exercises is being used by the Department of Health to make comparisons with an earlier report published by the National Audit Office in 2004.

BUSINESS

Employer Engagement

Another initiative which puts weight behind business is the Employer Engagement Programme, an exemplar of University and employer partnership supported by the Higher Education Funding Council for England (HEFCE). This is designed to improve higher-level skills and capabilities in the workplace. The pilot study is changing the way higher education is provided. Employers are helped to identify their development needs, and then the University works with their employees in the workplace to deliver

Coventry
University
Serious Games Institute

'The Serious Games Institute (SGI) aspires to be the global thought leader in the application of electronic games and virtual world technologies to real-world social and economic issues such as environmental sustainability, education, health, e-commerce, and corporate development. It is a unique model that brings together applied research, business incubation and technology showcasing, and attracts potential clients and partners from all over the world. It is the most innovative and entrepreneurial environment to work in, and attracts talented and passionate researchers and developers to work with those leading-edge and emerging technologies which will shape the way we live, work, and play in the new millennium.'

David Wortley, Director, The Serious Games Institute

Opposite: *The Serious Games Institute building was opened in 2007. Since then the £3m Institute has become a showcase for the latest serious gaming technology which advances the traditional use of electronic games beyond entertainment. Now home to over eight fledging enterprises the SGI also boasts an international body of knowledge on gaming methodology underpinned by its own state-of-the-art applied research centre.*

relevant higher education. This project provides an opportunity to investigate the effectiveness of educational and business development activities.

The University has now further developed its interests in this area by placing this initiative within a new subsidiary, ACUA, and by bringing in specialist staff to run the business.

Serious Games

At the groundbreaking Serious Games Institute (SGI), developments in the latest computer gaming technology – designed to drive innovation and training – are underway. Serious games make use of interactive electronic game technologies for non-entertainment purposes, such as business simulation, corporate training, and emergency and disaster management, and is particularly effective in situations where it is too costly or risky to train people in live situations. The SGI is intended to be a national and international Centre of Excellence, and a regional hub for the emerging serious games industry. This exciting project is a new model for industrial/higher education partnerships, combining advanced research with business incubation, digital media clustering, and sophisticated networking and demonstration facilities. Jointly funded by Advantage West Midlands and Coventry University Enterprises, the concept for the institute originates from the West Midlands' strength in the global electronic games market. Pioneering work in the adaptation of electronic games technology to serious business applications, such as e-learning and simulation, make Coventry the ideal location for the SGI.

Above: *PIXELearning, one of the tenants based in the Serious Games Institute.*

GLOBAL

International Development

Our second Queen's Anniversary Prize for Higher and Further Education in 2008 honours the achievements of Tabeisa, a pioneering project to help reduce poverty in Africa, and in which the University is one of the main partners. The Tabeisa project represents a consortium of six higher education institutions, including Coventry University, the University of Greenwich, and four partner organizations in South Africa. Working with poor communities in sub-Saharan Africa, it is tackling poverty by supporting small business and social enterprise projects. Since 1994 Tabeisa has supported over 1,000 commercial start-up enterprises, developed over 200 social enterprises, created over 2,000

Tabeisa

Coventry University is committed to enterprise development and entrepreneurship. Since 1994, the University has played a leading role in Tabeisa, which seeks to reduce poverty in Africa by supporting people in poor communities to start their own enterprises. These photographs demonstrate Tabeisa at work.

Left: *The designer jeans were recently featured in a London fashion shoot for the Exclusive Roots catalogue, Exclusive Roots being the fair trade trading arm of Tabeisa.*

Above: *Privaling is a women's cooperative which Tabeisa helped to establish. They operate from an old shipping container in Khayelitsha, which is one of the oldest townships in South Africa. Through support from a Tabeisa designer, the women were trained to manufacture designer jeans.*

new jobs, and distributed 150,000 AIDS awareness packs. Its successes include a tie-up with a leading high-street fashion store to sell ethically-produced clothing made by women's collectives in Ghana and five Tabeisa Enterprise Centres in South Africa and Ghana.

Soft Landing Zones

A particularly good example of practical work in the commercial community is the unique Soft Landing Zone programme, launched in partnership with UK Trade and Investment, the government's trade promotion arm. This provides access to international markets through a network of offices based in science parks across the globe. Any business interested in starting up in that country is provided with dedicated office space, access to IT and meeting rooms, and 'hands on' support in developing their proposition, contacts, and sales – including access to finance. The first offices of the University's commercial initiatives opened in Malaysia, Romania, and Singapore as a precursor to operations in countries as diverse as China, India, Brazil, Mexico, Turkey, and Hong Kong. This project draws not only on the expertise of staff within the commercial arm, Coventry University Enterprises Ltd (CUE), but also provides an ideal opportunity to make use of the experience of academics involved in international trade and business development research. There are now more than 20 such offices in operation.

COMMUNITY

Digital Dance Archive

In a unique collaboration, researchers at Coventry University are working together with Siobhan Davies Dance, one of Britain's leading independent dance companies, to create an online archive of the company's extensive body of work. Including material in a wide variety of formats, this unique resource will be fully accessible to dance researchers, students, and art enthusiasts of all ages. The archive will comprise an assortment of filmed and recorded performances, photographs, posters, memorabilia,

Right: *The Futures Institute, opened in 2005, provides a home for programmes around the related themes of regeneration, human security and community cohesion.*

scholarly accounts, and new, original, analytic commentaries. Siobhan Davies Dance currently holds a collection of more than 2,500 resources, but lack of access has been a serious limitation in the development of academic and artistic discourse around contemporary dance. The process of collation and digitalization represents an opportunity not only to open up access in a way not possible before but also to preserve valuable, and sometimes vulnerable, materials.

The Importance of Faith

According to the Countryside Agency (now Commission for Rural Communities), the church is one of five local facilities of particular importance to rural people (along with the pub, village hall, shop and primary school). Research carried out by Coventry University's Applied Research Centre in Sustainable Regeneration (SURGE) shows that both church ministers and church buildings help people bond, building bridges between diverse groups within communities. They are a vital resource in villages, and add to the community by providing links with business and voluntary activity that influence village life. Responses to rural issues concerning quality of life, care in the community, affordable housing, schools, community meeting spaces, and community empowerment, must not ignore the contribution of the church. The challenge is to learn more about faith and to work more cooperatively, developing initiatives to prevent exclusion. There also needs to be more dialogue across different faith communities.

CONCLUSION

Applied research often draws on expertise from across more than one academic area, enabling the university to tackle complex problems outside the scope of any one individual consultant or researcher. The University has established 12 Applied Research Centres and 24 Applied Research Groups to undertake specialist or interdisciplinary research and consultancy. In 2008, new research institutes at the University's Technology Park were coming on stream: the Futures Institute, the Serious Games Institute and the Health Design & Technology Institute. The University raised in excess of £6m of external funding to establish these institutes, and more are planned. The University is well on the way to achieving its first Five-Year Plan targets, and is now looking to further growth in the future.

Jobs:
Search and Find

Each autumn about 10,000 hopeful students descend on Coventry University. Young and old, from the city, region, nation, and world, they share a desire for improvement, the same desire which primed the Mechanics Institute in 1829. The younger ones want the University to offer a springboard into employment; those already employed want their expertise burnished by new skills.

The University's ability to meet their hopes is one measure of its prowess in the academic and commercial marketplaces. The hopes of its students are its own hopes. Its courses are designed so that students will become, as the corporate plan describes them, 'enterprising and entrepreneurial graduates, contributing to innovation, creativity, and productivity in their organization or community of practice'. The University wants its students to 'develop rewarding and interesting careers'.

The extent to which the University is realizing the ambition is calculated by a survey, Destination of Leavers from Higher Education, carried out at the request of the national Higher Education Statistics Agency. In June 2007,

Left: *thefutureworks – the University's own commercial recruitment agency. Based on campus, in the Students' Union building, thefutureworks is run by staff from Coventry University Enterprises.*

Above: *Classroom-based teaching for nurses.*

it followed up the 3,465 students who had left the University at the end of the 2005–6 academic year and had responses to its questions from 1,878 of them.

More than 75 per cent of the leavers had found employment. Just over 15 per cent had either resumed study or had combined study with employment. So less than ten per cent of the leavers were left looking for a job or were not bothered about obtaining one. The Coventry graduates, in short, found a demand for them and their new-found skills.

In fact, those general figures do not give a complete picture because they do not cover students coming from overseas. It is likely that more than 75 per cent found their way into employment at home: many of them would have been sent on courses by their companies, others would be returning to markets where the employment prospects for foreign-trained graduates would be better than for those educated domestically. At any rate, evidence on the movement of Coventry's foreign graduates is anecdotal, but the anecdotes stretch back for years.

When Michael Goldstein, as Vice-Chancellor, attended a Malaysian reunion in 2003, he was told by Arzmi Yaacob, who had been through the Business School: 'Almost all Coventry graduates have found jobs almost immediately upon returning home. The success of many in competing with graduates from other universities to win entry into highly regarded institutions such as Colgate and Palmolive, Unilever, Shell, Esso, Petronas, Proton, and Bank Negara Malaysia speaks volumes of our alma mater … we cherish the time we were at Coventry.'

But so too do UK graduates, also spread across industry, services, and the professions at home and abroad. Professor Donald Pennington, Coventry University's Pro-Vice-Chancellor with responsibility for teaching, assessment and learning, said: 'There's a Coventry graduate in every car design studio in the world'. Paul Ivey, the University's Dean of Engineering and Computing, observed that Marshall Aerospace Cambridge, the leading independent aerospace contractor, 'is predominantly staffed from Coventry and from Hertfordshire University – there are hardly any graduates from Cambridge'.

The demand for Coventry graduates stretches beyond engineering and design. The 2007 survey, Destination of Leavers, showed that 86 per cent of graduates from the Faculty of Health and Life Sciences had moved into employment, or were continuing to study while working. In the case of the Faculty's Nursing, Midwifery and Healthcare, that percentage jumped to 95 per cent.

The graduates are like threads, linking the University and its predecessors to the wider community. Goldstein, as the first Vice-Chancellor, calculated that in his 17 years at Coventry, 80,000 graduates went out into the world. As a testimony to the variety and practicality of the Coventry offering, the graduates surface in dispersed places. At random: Graham Selden, once in the Business School, now

'The course was excellent and I liked the fact that I was continuously challenged to think critically. I believe that the course provided me with numerous transferable skills, such as a well-developed analytical and critical thinking style, sound reviewing and research skills, and a strong proficiency in report writing and presentations. Most of the staff were consistently available to offer advice and support if it was needed. I'd like to give a mention to Dr Laura Taylor because I don't think I'd have got this far if it wasn't for the support she gave me. Without this high level of support I wouldn't have had the confidence to apply for the scholarship at Harvard.'

Carly Charalambou, Psychology and Criminology BSc, 2007

Left: *Graduate Kevin De La Noy on the set of Blood Diamond.*

Below left: *Coventry University branding campaign celebrating the success of Mike Short, alumnus and Vice-President of O_2.*

a supplier manager for Boeing; Kevin De La Noy, a Hollywood film producer whose film credits include *Titantic, Mission: Impossible,* and *Saving Private Ryan,* who graduated in communication studies; Mike Short, Vice-President of O_2, studied economics and mathematics; Graham Henderson also studied mathematics but at Lanchester Polytechnic, and he became Vice-Chancellor of the University of Teesside; Kevin Corti, a graduate in disaster management, set up his own company, PIXELearning, on the University's Technology Park, at the Serious Games Institute.

In terms of Coventry University's role in the wider economic picture, Corti's experience is one which both University and regional authorities would like to see repeated. 'The West Midlands has a skills gap at graduate level', Professor Pennington explained. 'Coventry University has a good record here. Just under two-thirds of our graduates go to employment in the West Midlands.' Corporate plans commit the University to further that level of regional retention.

This commitment puts the University in the centre of plans for the regeneration of the region, 'raising the profile of

'In my second year of university, we were required to go on a placement and I secured myself a place with 3form, a Birmingham-based design and online technology agency. This gave me valuable experience in a real-world agency and led to further opportunities later in my career. In my final university year I began taking on freelance work in order to make the transition into work easier. I was taken on as a freelancer by another Birmingham-based agency and was doing work for them while finishing my last year.'

Cassie Leedham, BA Hons Graphic Design, 2005

'During my third year I spent six months on a placement at Opel in Germany. They kept in touch with me and offered me a job when I had finished my degree. The placement was essential; it not only got me my first job but also gave me confidence, because I could put what I had been learning into practice. Coventry is still, by far, one of the best universities training up future graduates in this industry. As a Chief Designer I am now responsible for the creation of future vehicle concepts, show cars, and the development of future design visions and strategies. I have also worked and lived in Italy and North America. I like living in a different country. I think people change in a positive way when they have worked and lived abroad.'

Richard Shaw, Transport Design, 1988, is a Chief Designer at GM Europe in Germany

the city, bringing business/employment to the city and its citizens.' Professor Pennington noted that around £9.4bn (and rising) is being invested in Coventry during the first two decades of the century. To make investment work involves, for the University, the provision of its panoply of business supports, which are discussed in later chapters. At the same time it places a premium on equipping students, young and mature alike, with the qualities required in both the private and public sectors.

Coventry has always been a practical university. As its ties with business have strengthened, so it has become easier for it to understand what the outside world requires from graduates entering employment, and what it might do to help that process. Three strands of initiative stand out as techniques of student support. If they are taken together they offer a warning to potential entrants to the most rewarding sections of the employment marketplace: in the 21st century, learning is not enough.

The first strand deals with the frequent and longstanding complaint of employers that recruits often lack communication skills; they have lamented shortcomings in analytical ability and mathematical competence. Two innovative centres have been established to address these problems.

The Centre for Academic Writing – recognized in an award from the *Times Higher Education Supplement* – provides intensive and personal tutoring in the techniques of writing. Conceived originally as an aid for students from environments without a tradition of higher education, it is available for any student who wants it. The Centre for Excellence in Mathematics and Statistics Support, called SIGMA, seeks to do for numeracy what the Centre for Academic Writing does for literacy. SIGMA is a joint venture with Loughborough University, recognized by the HEFCE as a Centre of Excellence and funded by it with £2.35m. It too provides help for any student who wants it.

The second strand is the Add+vantage Scheme, introduced in 2006–7 and described by Professor Pennington as 'unique in the sector'. Students choose one module a year as part of their degree.

Add+vantage modules add up to what the University calls an 'employability learning programme', and range from Mandarin to project management to arts funding to climate change. They have one thing in common, and that is 'they have been selected to meet the requirements of employers'. Students work to obtain the modules in parallel with their normal course work.

The third strand involves work placements. Across the UK and in other parts of the European Union, the University has a network of companies and organizations which are prepared to offer Coventry students a taste of the workplace for periods of up to a year. A third of the time taken to acquire a degree could be spent in the workplace. Students taking work placements can use credits granted by the University as part of their degree, allowing practical experience to merge with academic endeavour.

'If a student does a work placement he or she has a better chance of a graduate job', noted Professor Pennington. Often the company which offered the internship will later offer a post. Citing Manchester University research, Professor Pennington added that the work placement could give a student 70 per cent security of a post later.

Once in a graduate job, the former student, with initial hopes realized, will need to keep finely honed the skills acquired at the University. They may embark on part-time study. They may rely on company training. If the latter, they could find Coventry University coming to them. The University is spreading its wings to take its expertise into the workplace, with courses designed to meet company needs, as it has done for the AA (the Automobile Association), and Caterpillar.

Enterprise On-Campus, Off-Campus and Out to the World

The ambitious student, the putative business leader and nascent entrepreneur wanting his or her own business, could arrive at Coventry University and start commercial life almost immediately. There would be access to market research, help in devising the business plan, a mentor to help put it into effect, office facilities in the Technology Park, and advice on penetrating export markets. All on the campus.

Coventry University, through its trading arm, Coventry University Enterprises (CUE), sees itself as an economic development agency, like many other universities. But it differs from most, both in the width and depth of its operations, and in the way it has made commerce feed off the University and the University feed off commerce.

'The role of the operation', said John Latham, Pro-Vice-Chancellor Business Development, 'is to support economic development and regeneration as a means for the University to engage with its own environment'. Its focus is productivity and innovation, 'the high-performance end of new product innovation'.

This is a journey with no final destination. There will be new projects, new schemes, which knit the University into a more powerful academic-commercial nexus. It was always thus. The journey so far has not been accidental but the speed of it has increased markedly in the 21st century.

From the days of Alan Richmond onwards, staff at College, Polytechnic, and University have been involved with the business community in ways which have gone beyond the mere training of employees and apprentices for local industry. Norman Bellamy, the long-serving engineer and eventual Pro-Vice-Chancellor, recalled that for 20 years from 1973, half his salary came from industry; he had a research team of up to 18 people which, during one year, contributed 20 per cent of the institution's budget.

Since the late 1980s, there have been two phenomena, one widespread and the other more specific, which have led Coventry to its position as a university for enterprise.

The first was the growing official acceptance in the UK that higher education institutions could be both a hub of, and a stimulus for, economic growth. This had already happened in the US and Germany. That acceptance coincided with the

Left: *John Latham, Pro-Vice-Chancellor, Business Development.*

ACT UK A
Conference Centre 1
Design Hub 2
Enterprise Centre 3
Health Design & Technology Institute 4
Innovation Village B
Institute for Creative Enterprise 5
Serious Games Institute C
TechnoCentre 6

necessity to recalibrate the Coventry and West Midlands economy, to foster its redevelopment: the future would not centre on large, mass-manufacturing plants controlled from outside the region, but in a multitude of smaller enterprises of local origin, using new skills and reliant on constant innovation. More recently, the 2003 Lambert report, sponsored by the government, urged a much higher level of collaboration between universities and business.

The place of Coventry University in the collaborative movement was obvious: here was a concentration of expertise to push out into the wider and more diverse economy. That in turn meant that the University could expect access to public funding to aid the push.

The sources were varied: European Union, central government, the regional development organization called Advantage West Midlands, Coventry City Council, Warwickshire County Council, and HEFCE. The University could anticipate that once the push from the public purse could be seen as serious and sustained, interest from the private sector would grow. Success would beget success.

The second and more specific phenomenon sprang out of the first and more general phenomenon. This was the establishment in 1997 of the Coventry University

Above: *An aerial view of the Technology Park.*

Simulation Construction Centre

A ground-breaking centre for the construction industry, located in the Coventry University Technology Park, opens in Autumn 2009.

Called ACT-UK, it is funded by the regional development agency, Advantage West Midlands, who have contributed £6.6m, in partnership with Coventry University and the construction industry, with agency funding providing a further £2.1m to the project.

It introduces a pioneering form of simulation training for the building and construction industry using skilled actors and a virtual reality auditorium which comprises a 16 metre, curved widescreen. A 4-D simulation projected onto the screen enables trainees and management from the industry to navigate through every aspect of a building project recorded from real life. Details are such that every nut and bolt in every part of the building can be accessed. Industry leaders are working with the University and ACT-UK to develop courses and scenarios to exploit this technology.

Right: *The historic wrought-iron panel that formed part of the gate for the Armstrong Siddeley Motor Works, and subsequently the Rolls-Royce factory, that stood on this site before the TechnoCentre was constructed.*

Technology Park. The concept drew on the experience in collaboration of universities in Finland, the Netherlands, Sweden, and the US, and fitted it to local application.

From the first, the Technology Park grasped the symbolism of change, because it started on the site of a disused Rolls-Royce plant. It became, as Latham described it, 'a centre for business support with property, rather than a property venture with some business support'. It has never been, nor will it become, an office park masquerading as a science park.

How the Technology Park works is discussed on page 100. However, in general terms, Latham noted:

> *'The Technology Park is the physical embodiment of our activity. It provides us with our own test bed. For example, it can offer support for companies at the regional and national levels; it can provide services wherever they are demanded. Thirty or forty years ago, companies would cluster around an original equipment manufacturer but now they cluster around a science park – that is the economic driver. Companies using the Technology Park aren't doing blue sky research; at the most, the work they're doing is five years from the market.'*

The attitude of the University in general and CUE in particular is resolutely global. Latham, indeed, spends 90 per cent of his time outside Coventry. This is recognition of the past, the long history of Coventry industries succumbing to outside competition, and acknowledgement that even small businesses cannot count on success without an international dimension.

It is at this point that the width and depth of the University's business support becomes evident. CUE can nurture entrepreneurs from the first spark of a business idea, through the creation of a business plan and the design of product or service, to marketing, eventual sales, and a presence in the international marketplace. Equally, it can provide specific services and undertake projects from training to testing, from design to debt management. As a support agency, Latham said, CUE is helping 6,000 companies a year and has a staff across the world of 200.

CUE is the link between the academic activities of the University and the outside world. It offers a means through which graduates can develop a business. It can take applied research from the University's research centres and institutes, and help to work it into a commercial shape. At the same time it is the avenue along which outside individuals and companies can approach the University and tap into its centres of expertise through, for example, consultancy contracts.

When these two strands come together, they feed into the academic process. The presence of companies on the Technology Park, the Institutes located there, and the breadth of the contacts between the University and the commercial

'The Park's facilities are enough to support any business which needs to get a head start, including larger units in the Enterprise Centre, as well as invaluable support for the fledgling business that doesn't require office space yet. Budding businesses can have a virtual base offering a range of services such as mail and telephone, corporate identity, and conference services. Everyone here is in the same boat with their small business, and it's a fantastic networking opportunity for everyone. It's like being at work without really being at work! They're flexible and there are lots of places to meet people – like at the Bistro (the on-site café). The friends and contacts are what the TechnoCentre provides you with, and this is the sort of thing you miss when working in a big organization.'

Jo Cameron, Engineering 1994, Entrepreneur, TechnoCentre tenant and previously a contender on *The Apprentice* (BBC)

world combine to offer students and staff work opportunities which not only foster collaboration in the wider sense but also provide experience which can translate into degree modules.

The habit of collaboration has a compound effect. The readier the University is to engage, the more skilful it becomes in using its expertise and helping companies to use theirs, the more it is likely to grow. Already, Latham observed, it is attracting overseas companies 'that contribute to the University profile'. Increasingly it is apparent that what Coventry offers differentiates the University from its competitors. The exclusive relationship with government for the Soft Landing Zones (as described on page 64) is evidence of this. And strengthening outside enterprise strengthens the University's enterprise.

Given the University's aim of playing a wide and stimulating economic role, its own growth has been steady but continuous. Parallel with the University's aim of tripling applied research income during the first decade of the 21st century, CUE is expanding its facilities. 'We plan to double the size of the Technology Park and that is part of the University's investment programme', said Latham.

Investment is not speculative. 'We do nearly everything in partnerships, so there has to be a demand and a need, and from that springs a partnership.' The nature of the partnerships changes the more the University becomes involved with the wider community. The Technology Park is unlikely to have started without help from the public sector at international, national, and local level. But the balance of financing support has been tilting, so that private sector finance has been assuming a gradually more important role and that, Latham thought, would continue. The trend is an indication of the University's success as an agent of enterprise.

The effect of that on the University's own fortunes is significant. CUE is a source of independent income for the University. While it is paid by national agencies for the teaching of students, those budgets are tight and leave only marginal leeway. To meet the costs of the investment programme involves both the assumption of debt, which has to be serviced, and the use of funds it generates itself. The more the University's corporate activities are successful, the more funds are available for its academic work which ultimately feeds back into the commercial world. Academia and commerce run hand-in-hand.

Idea to Product:
The Sprue Aegis Story

Supporting enterprise, venturing University capital to help small business, is the risky task of trying to pick winners. Sprue Aegis is a winner, quoted on the PLUS market, the successor to OFEX and a favoured London exchange for small companies.

Nick Rutter and Sam Tate conceived a rechargeable battery smoke alarm during spring 1998. Over the next three years the idea transformed into a marketable product.

First Rutter and Tate enrolled in the Start Your Own Business course of the University's Graduate Enterprise Scheme. They used the forerunner of the University's Product Development Technology Support Unit to help with the design and prototypes and used the facilities of the Centre for Advanced Joining. They had help with the initial marketing. They were able to use the patent collection in the

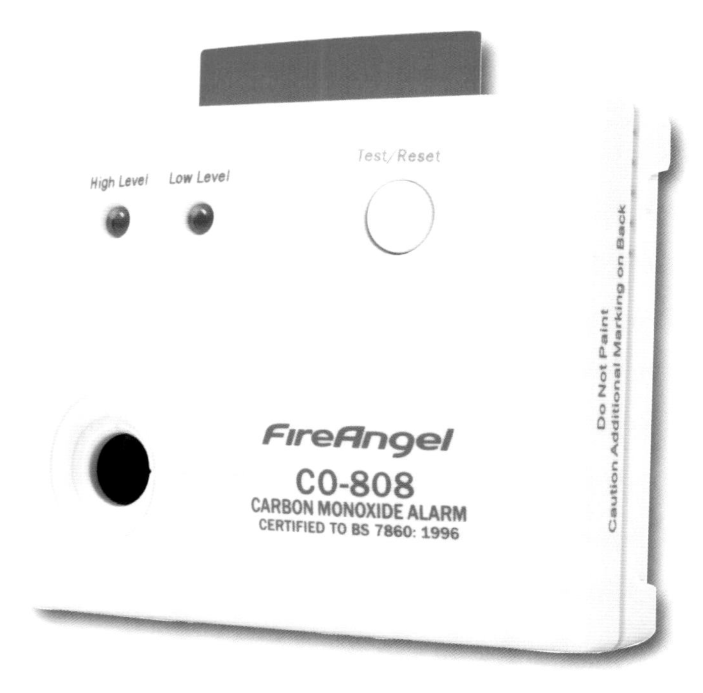

Above: *Coventry University alumnus and co-founder of the Sprue Aegis company, Nick Rutter, with Chairman Graham Whitworth, surrounded by a selection of the life-saving products they are responsible for.*

Opposite: *FireAngel smoke detector (left) and Carbon Monoxide Alarm (right).*

University Library to conduct searches, and the Intellectual Property Committee to file a patent. As well as being able to use the University's facilities, thus reducing development costs, Rutter and Tate negotiated funding for Sprue Aegis. The University's Graduate Enterprise Scheme invested £55,000 in exchange for 20 per cent of Sprue Aegis equity. Later Coventry University Enterprises (CUE) granted a further £10,000.

Resident in the TechnoCentre on the Technology Park, Sprue Aegis has access to the University's facilities. This is not just the rent of space, but the opportunity – encouraged by the University – to engage with the technical experts among the academic staff.

Coventry**TechnoCentre**

Bellamy Sees the Future

During 1996, when the University's Technology Park was in the early stages of construction, Norman Bellamy, the Pro-Vice-Chancellor responsible for campus development, reminisced about the Park's conception. He explained, for the University's annual review, how the idea had first come to him in the late 1970s.

At that time the conditions were not sympathetic to such developments. But more than 10 years on he was driving along Rolls-Royce Parkside and saw the demolition of its training centre.

'When I realized that Rolls-Royce was planning on moving out completely, I began to understand the potential that the site offered for a Technology Park for the University. It was the perfect distance from the University, I knew we would never get a chance like this again.'

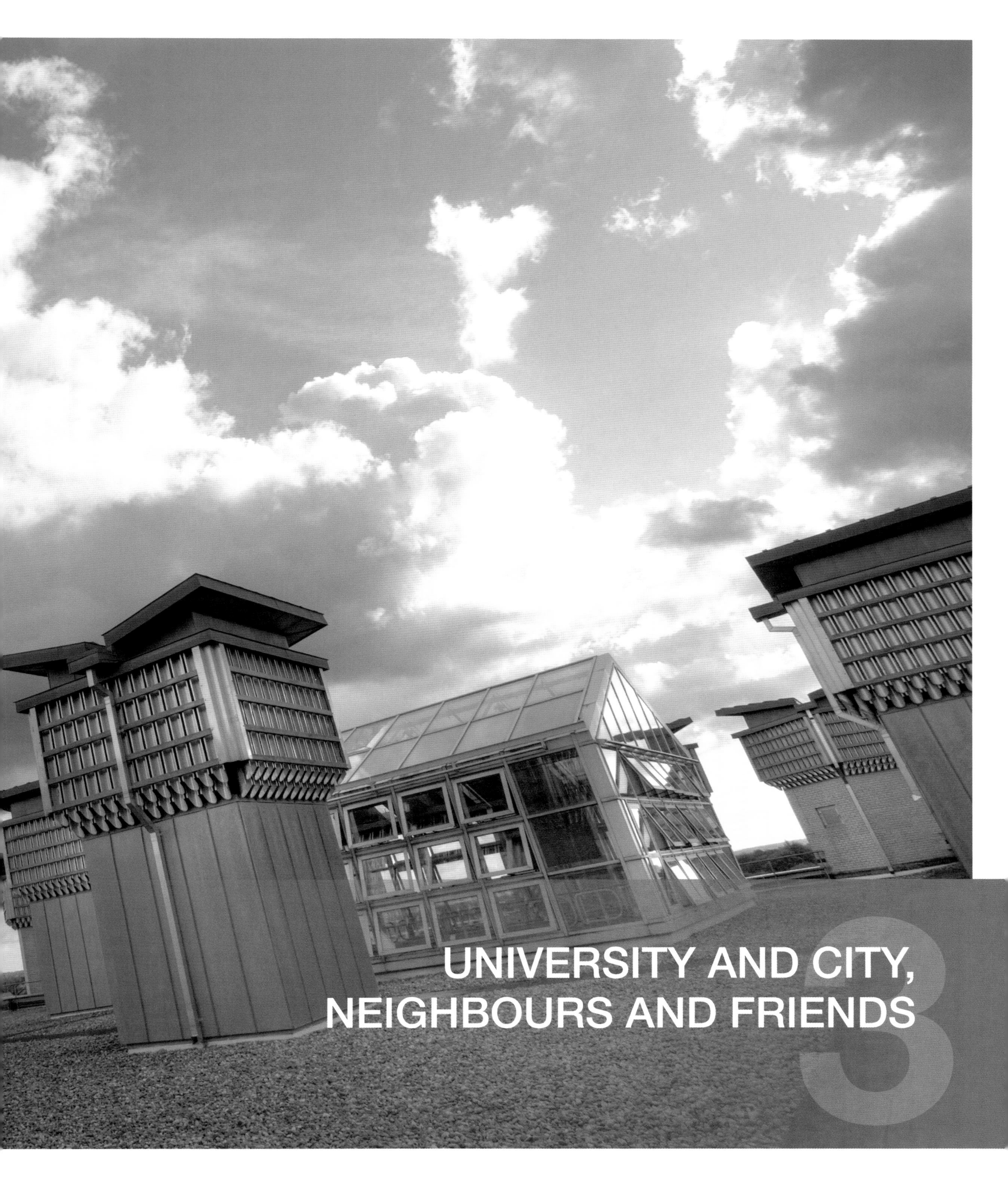

3 UNIVERSITY AND CITY, NEIGHBOURS AND FRIENDS

Campus:
Fifty Years of Expansion

PROFESSOR CLIVE RICHARDS, ASSOCIATE DEAN,
COVENTRY SCHOOL OF ART AND DESIGN

Coventry University's extensive estate has a very substantial physical presence in the city, with more than 40 buildings. This presence, from small beginnings, has been beneficial to Coventry by making a positive contribution to the urban landscape.

The estate is largely made up of buildings commissioned by, and constructed especially for, the University or its predecessors, dating from the 1950s to the present day, many of significant architectural interest. It also comprises a few older buildings of historical importance. These older buildings are part of the architectural heritage of the city and have been revived through acquisition and use by the University. While adapting them for their new educational and research functions, care has been taken to maintain the architectural integrity of each of these sites, whether their original purpose was industrial or recreational, and from whichever period they originally dated.

City Heritage Buildings

The Gaumont Palace cinema on the corner of Jordan Well and Whitefriars Street, or Odeon, as it was known in more recent years, is now the Ellen Terry Arts and Media Centre, named after the famous Victorian actress from Coventry. The frontage of this famous Coventry landmark is in two styles. There is the majestic, white stone frontage of the earlier Coliseum Ballroom with its domed pinnacle, and then there is the adjoining classic Art Deco cinema façade of 1931. Acquired by the University in 2000, the building now provides radio, TV, photographic, dance and theatre studios

Left and below: *The Gaumont and Coliseum Ballroom, then and now.*

Opposite: *Pathway between the Herbert Art Gallery extension and the Alan Berry Building (F Block).*

Previous pages: *The distinctive roofline of the award-winning Frederick W. Lanchester Library.*

for performing arts and media work. Alumnus Ron Hill (Electric and Electronic Engineering 1939), on his return to campus in 2006, recounted the tale of attending the opening night at the Gaumont and watching the screening of *The Professionals*, a black and white film, in 1931. He even recalled the names of the leading actors.

The University's William Morris Building, named for the industrialist, on Far Gosford Street was an engine plant and a munitions factory, constructed in 1910, and came into the estate in 1993. The building has been renovated, now combining harmoniously the original red brickwork with additional new features, including two extra floors on top, and the distinctive curved roof. The building contains classrooms, seminar spaces, and lecture theatres for various programmes including those of the Business, Environment and Society Faculty.

It is interesting, from a design point of view, that its sloping site and footprint are similar to the famous Art Nouveau-style Glasgow School of Art building designed by Charles Rennie Mackintosh. The Alma Building in Alma Street is another example of Coventry's industrial heritage, a former factory building of the 1920s, fitted out for the new purpose of administrative offices for the University, and now used also for teaching in the Engineering

Above: *The William Morris Building (W Block), with the Lanchester Library on the right.*

Below: *Charles Ward.*

Below left: *The George Eliot building (B Block), named in honour of the pseudonym of Coventry's most famous novelist, Marian Evans (1819–90), who spent her school years in the city. In her longest and most complex novel, Coventry appears as Middlemarch.*

Below right: *The old Art School in Forge Street, 1960s, prior to its removal to make way for the ring road.*

Far right: *James Starley (inset) and the building (D Block) named in his honour.*

and Computing Faculty. This building now contains the motor sport and aerospace departments – with simulators, racing cars and a Harrier jumpjet – and proves a great attraction on Open Days.

The 1950s and 1960s

Most of the University campus started as part of the post-World War II development of the city with buildings which were originally to be the new College of Art, Technology and General Education. The first of these buildings was in Cope Street and is now called the Charles Ward Building, and houses part of the Health and Life Sciences Faculty. Ward was a city councillor closely associated with the University. Ron Hill recalled Charles Ward as a very good goalkeeper while they played together in the same football team in the 1930s!

Opened in 1952, it was built in the then fashionable modernist mode of the period, exhibiting stylistic influences of the 1951 Festival of Britain. Older citizens of Coventry may remember the highly decorative chapel-like Victorian building which was the old municipal art school in Ford Street, just around the corner from the Old Fire Station, now the Myo

restaurant. The Ford Street building was sadly demolished in the 1960s to make way for the new Coventry ring road.

The 1956 Government White Paper on technical education set up colleges of Advanced Technology. This led to the construction of the buildings now called James Starley (1958) and George Eliot (1960) currently housing the faculties of Health and Life Sciences, and Business, Environment and Society. Starley was the famous Coventry cycle designer and Eliot the local novelist.

These buildings are in Cope Street and Cox Street respectively. At the time of its construction the James Starley Building boasted the longest continuous corridors in the country. Also built in 1960, and commemorating the jet engine designer, was the adjacent Frank Whittle Building, which contained the Faculty of Engineering and Computing workshops and classrooms. This was demolished in 2009 to make way for a new Student Enterprise Building, housing the Students' Union, retail outlets, and catering and entertainment facilities.

These buildings and the College of Art building were to accommodate the then new Lanchester College of Technology which led to the separate development of the College of Art. While premises were shared for a time on the Cope Street site, a new College of Art building was commissioned and opened in 1968. This building makes a substantial visual statement from its commanding position on the corner of Cox Street and Gosford Street – it has many characteristics of buildings of the period with its unashamed and confident use of slab concrete.

It is an imposing building and is now a well-known and highly regarded city landmark. Called the Graham Sutherland Building, to commemorate the artist who designed the Christ in Glory tapestry hanging in the new Coventry Cathedral, it contains numerous art and design

Left: *The statue of Sir Frank Whittle was unveiled on June 1, 2007 – it would have been the 100th birthday of the inventor from Earlsdon.*

Far left: *Lanchester Library cataloguing system provides access for students to 350,000 books and 20,000 electronic publications.*

Above: *The Graham Sutherland Building (M Block).*

Right: *The Alan Berry Building (F Block).*

studios and workshops. It additionally contains the University's own exhibition space, under the name of The Lanchester Gallery.

Another development in the 1960s, opposite the Cathedral in the recently landscaped University Square, is what is now the University's 'front door', the Alan Berry Building, in memory of a former chairman of governors. It was erected in 1963 and houses the institution's biggest lecture theatre, administrative offices, and the Vice-Chancellory. Very typical of its period, this building features exterior vertical steel 'I' beams in homage to the modernist

Far left: *Richard Crossman (right) was a key member of the post-World War II Labour Party, serving as MP for Coventry East from 1945 to 1974, and in government as Secretary of State for Health and Social Security from 1968 to 1970.*

Left: *Slade, the support act for Chuck Berry, performed alongside Billy Preston (below left) in February 1972 at Tiffany's in Coventry to the delight of the audience, which consisted largely of Coventry students.*

architect, Mies Van Der Rohe, who used this architectural device on his famous Seagram Tower block in Manhattan.

The monumental rectangular grey slate front arch entrance to the building, with its gilded carved phoenix, was a later addition to the Alan Berry Building. The exterior 'I' beam motif also features on the James Starley Building running along Cox Street.

Priory Hall student accommodation came in 1964–6. These buildings bridge Priory Street, and the 19-storey tower provides one of the taller city landmarks. The nearby Students' Union building was also added in 1964 and its basement has provided the venue for several famous gigs over the years.

The Polytechnic Period

The next phase of development followed the creation in 1970 of the Lanchester Polytechnic, initiated by the 1966 White Paper, A Plan for Polytechnics.

The building, named after the Coventry politician, the late Richard Crossman, now houses the Health and Life Sciences Faculty. Constructed in 1971 it stands directly opposite the Herbert Art Gallery and Museum in Jordan Well, and was originally the Lanchester College of Technology Library. Its tall dark brick façade and concrete TV-shaped window frames speak of architectural fashions of the period.

The 1978 building in Far Gosford Street, directly opposite the William Morris Building, is named after one of Coventry's most famous car marques, the Jaguar. It is now the home of the University's Graduate Centre. Directly behind this is another building celebrating a famous

'There was a "no good will come of it" attitude to the ring road which turned into an "I told you so" attitude when the lamp post fell (see below). The Polytechnic was still fairly new the year it happened. Regrettably, I never even bothered to go to look at the accident site. We were offended that it had fallen on part of our campus at the time, but I think I must have had my mind on exams. At that time we were more concerned about D block (now called James Starley) – the longest academic building in Europe – where the upper floors were cantilevered out over the ground floor and were beginning to sag like a large, alarming letter W.'

Chris Hutchinson, Applied Social Science, 1973

Above: *The new Herbert Art Gallery extension was opened in 2008. It offers space for temporary and permanent art collections, as well as housing archives for over 800 years of Coventry's history.*

Coventry car maker, Armstrong Siddeley. This building was opened in 1973, and houses part of the Faculty of Engineering and Computing. Next to this is the University's Computer Services building with its unusual curved footprint. Built in 1980 it again has Jaguar associations, named after the founder of that company, Sir William Lyons.

In 1983 a major building was completed in Cox Street opposite the James Starley Building. This was named after Maurice Foss, a former deputy director of Lanchester Polytechnic, and it was built to accommodate growing provision for automotive and engineering programmes.

'The whole campus was very much smaller in the 70s and indeed, for the first few weeks of life there, the Halls of Residence were not completed and people were being bussed in from the Rugby campus. The view from the third floor of D Block over the central admin block to the Cathedral was magnificent, and still lives very much in my memory. I am now working in Mergers and Acquisitions for a division of Associated British Foods, so clearly the grounding that I got at the Lanch was a superb one. I still visit Coventry on a fairly regular basis and have kept contact with one of the students that I lodged with over the last two years of my degree. Among my other colleages was John Kettley, the weather man, who was on the same course as me. It is clear from conversation with other graduates that we loved and still treasure the time we spent in Coventry.'

Trevor Theobald, Chemistry/Zoology, 1975

Independence

On 1 April 1989, under the terms of the 1988 Education Reform Act, Coventry Polytechnic (as it was then called, having dropped the title 'Lanchester' in 1987) ceased to be part of the Local Education Authority. This heralded a new phase in the development of the institution, but one in which the name Lanchester would live on.

The Frederick Lanchester Building, called after the entrepreneur and inventor, is the current University library and is directly behind the William Morris Building. This magnificent edifice is a true landmark building, both visually, with its distinctive convection ventilating towers, and ecologically, being a very 'green' low-energy building. Costing £16m, it opened in 2001. The winner of various design awards, it was designed for the University by the Alan Short Partnership.

Above and opposite top right: *Cox Street then and now – the Gaumont, seen in the background, is now the only recognisable building.*

Above left: *Maurice Foss (left) and Geoffrey Holroyde (right), with city officials, at the opening of the Foss Building, 1983.*

Coventry's New University

In June 1992, the Further and Higher Education Act enabled Coventry Polytechnic to become Coventry University, and further estate developments followed.

Since 1965 the student accommodation has been greatly enhanced and extended, including the addition of the Singer Hall complex in Canterbury Street, completed in 1994 and named after the nearby former Singer factory.

Behind the Graham Sutherland Building in Cox Street is the Bugatti Building, erected in 2002. This houses full-size automotive styling laboratories and associated digital design equipment, including motion capture and virtual reality projection facilities.

Other developments include the University Sports Centre (2004) in Whitefriars Street and, near the Whitefriars Monastery off Gulson Road, the new Student Centre (2006). Between 1998 and 2007 various new buildings have been erected on the University Technology Park, the former site of the Rolls-Royce factory. With their distinctive blue curved roofs, they include the TechnoCentre, Design Hub, and Enterprise Centre. Opposite the Technology Park in Parkside is the University Institute for Creative Enterprise, opened in 2008 – another former commercial building rehabilitated for university use.

Under construction during the late 2000s, at the Technology Park, the Health Design and Technology Institute building will embody much of what the Institute is promoting. As well as being a low-energy building it has been designed using ergonomic and inclusive design principles promising to be a major point of reference for buildings of this type. A unique simulation laboratory for the buildings construction industry, to be operated by ACT-UK, in partnership with the University, is also being added to the Technology Park.

The Future

The University is committed to high-quality buildings which contribute to their civic setting. It is working with the city to improve the estate and adjoining public spaces. Consultants have been engaged to scope various joint developments to improve the experience of the city centre. The University will also be a key player in the development of the educational quarter planned for the Swanswell area.

Bottom right: *Gym facilities within the University's Sports Centre.*

Below: *Singer Halls of Residence.*

A £160m University estate development programme has been approved by governors as the first phase through to 2011. In addition to the new Student Enterprise Building discussed earlier, the former Gulson Road hospital site is the location for a major new scheme – purpose-designed accommodation for the Faculty of Engineering and Computing. The new spaces this development provides will equip the University to offer innovative educational programmes, and to deliver the applied research needed for Coventry as a forward-looking, business-facing University. These developments are referred to in more detail in the final chapter of the book.

The goal is to continue to enhance the built environment of the University for its students, staff, visitors, and citizens of Coventry, now and in the future.

The Cathedral and its Commitment to Reconciliation

THE VERY REVEREND JOHN IRVINE, DEAN OF COVENTRY

From early times, Coventry has had a strong Christian witness. A large Benedictine monastery flourished until the dissolution of the monasteries carried out by Henry VIII. The medieval Cathedral of St Michael's had stood for hundreds of years until it was bombed along with the rest of the city on the night of 14 November 1940.

The raid was codenamed 'Operation Moonlight Sonata' and introduced a new verb into the German language – 'to coventrate', meaning 'to destroy utterly'. That night, 568 people lost their lives. Many more would die in subsequent air raids on UK cities. Of course, thousands more were killed in Allied bombing raids during the rest of the war, including Dresden, where Coventry now has particular links. Nonetheless, Coventry was the first British city to suffer in this way and the only one to lose its Cathedral as a result of aerial bombardment.

Opposite: *The famous 'Charred cross' at the Cathedral. In the January after the Blitz, Reverend Howard asked the cathedral's stonemason, 'Jock' Forbes to make an altar from the rubble and place behind it a cross made from two charred oak beams that had fallen from the roof. Forbes obliged with a sublime piece of craftsmanship and this has become the focal point of the ruins ever since.*

Right: *Sir Basil Spence, architect. Spence's radical vision of a new, modern cathedral rising from the ruins of the old won him the commission in 1950. He was subsequently knighted for his work at Coventry.*

The leader of the then Christian community at the Cathedral, Provost Dick Howard, committed the Cathedral to 'Reconciliation' rather than revenge. This was a prophetic but unpopular idea at the time.

Two of the charred medieval roof beams had fallen across each other in the shape of a cross. They were bound together and raised behind the former high altar in the ruins of the Cathedral. Three of the medieval nails from the roof were formed together in the shape of the Cross. This has become the symbol for the Cathedral and its ministry.

The ruins of the old Cathedral have been left as a stark reminder of the capacity of humankind to destroy. The decision to build a new Cathedral was taken on the morning after its destruction in 1940. Designed by Basil Spence (1907–76), who was later knighted for his achievement, the new Cathedral houses some magnificent works of art including statues by Jacob Epstein, tapestry designed by Graham Sutherland, and some fine stained glass by John Piper and John Hutton. In a recent poll, it was voted Britain's most popular 20th-century building.

Immediately after the war, the Cathedral began to reach out to the country's former enemies, Germany and then Japan, with an olive branch of reconciliation. From those beginnings, a network of 'Cross of Nails' centres has been established. There are now some 180 active centres all over the world involved in different aspects of reconciliation. As well as Germany and Japan, the reconciliation ministry now flourishes particularly in the Middle East, in Nigeria, South Africa, and the US.

More recently, the Cathedral has felt challenged to re-invigorate its own reconciliation ministry both in the UK and locally in Coventry. It is not much use proclaiming reconciliation on the other side of the world if it is not practised at home. Today we are therefore very much involved with other local groups in promoting reconciliation among the diverse ethnic groups within the city.

The new Cathedral houses a vibrant and growing Christian community with a fresh vision to reach out to a new, yet just as needy generation, with the message of reconciliation. In 2008, it appointed a new Director of Reconciliation Ministry: David Porter from Northern Ireland who has 25 years experience of reconciliation on the front line of that province.

The Cathedral's aim is to be a world centre of reconciliation, with new buildings to match the ambition by the time of its golden jubilee.

A further aim is to work together with Coventry University whenever possible, and gain the enormous benefits from the expertise and experience in peace and reconciliation studies there. Both the Cathedral and the University gain from their status as close neighbours. The Cathedral hosts special lectures, many student events, University social events, and welcomes overseas students. The highlight of the relationship is the annual graduation ceremonies. It is a great delight to welcome and honour those who have worked so hard for their achievements.

The 21st century has seen yet more fighting, killing, and conflict. The need for reconciliation is more obvious today than ever before. Along with the University, we are committed, as diverse bodies and neighbours, to living in harmony with all those round about us. We wish the University every blessing in their exciting and ambitious plans, and look forward to many more years of working together.

City at the Crossroads

JOHN McGUIGAN, DIRECTOR OF CITY DEVELOPMENT

No city stands still. They change, evolve, and respond to the environment and circumstances that they face. The world doesn't owe Coventry a future. Coventry, the 'Phoenix City', is perhaps the most demonstrable example of why we have to respond to change. Coventry University plays a key role in that change.

Coventry is at the crossroads. Fifty years ago it was Britain's boom town. A city of 380,000 people with more jobs than the city could handle. Only 523 people were unemployed – and it was hard to be unemployed in the early 1950s.

But the city was too focused on too few industries (notably automotive and machine tools) and couldn't see, or didn't want to see, the need for change as the challenges of global competition gathered strength and pace.

Of all those employed, 57 per cent were in manufacturing. The radical changes which Coventry has seen brought manufacturing employment down to 13 per cent in 2008.

Coventry was the first place in the UK where the working man earned £5 per week in wages. But from the peak of our boom times, the city, over the 20 years from the late 1970s to the early 1990s, was devastated by the huge downturn in manufacturing.

No unemployment became huge unemployment – at one point hitting over 20 per cent. It has taken Coventry over 25 years to turn itself round – recognizing that it needed to diversify its economy and then plan for and respond to the ever-increasing pace of change. What Coventry has learned, many other cities have witnessed. Standing still is going backwards.

But deeply rooted, below the energy – and later agony – of manufacturing, lay the real strengths of Coventry; in invention and innovation. At the turn of the 20th century more than 50 per cent of all the patents in the UK came out of Coventry. This was the time when Coventry and its people were inventing the things that we now all take for granted. This process was much wider than the automotive industry.

Below: *A Coventry landmark: Tower Court business centre, in the heart of the city-generated Foleshill Enterprise Park, was formerly Courtaulds spinning factory.*

Above: *The city at night.*

Right: *Electric Wharf, once Sandy Lane power station in the formerly industrial Radford ward, has been regenerated as a mixed-use residential site.*

The people of Coventry apply their strengths in innovation and invention on a very broad canvas.

What became an almost submerged strength during our successful manufacturing period is now re-emerging as our new selling point for today and tomorrow. And Coventry University is playing its role now, as it and its predecessors played in the past.

The city's shift to a diversified and sustainable economy may have taken 25 years but by 2008 the scale of investment and regeneration had become enormous. The city was five years into a £9.4bn (and ever-rising) programme of regeneration. Private sector investors provided 90 per cent of this sum, making it obvious that they see Coventry as a place worthy of their investment.

In addition – and for the first time in a generation – Coventry is now planning for transformational growth, not just in its population, economic basis, and housing stock, but in the overall size of the city, its crucial city centre, and its role in the wider region of the West Midlands.

As Coventry changes from a city dependent upon manufacturing to a city that must focus on quality of life, we increasingly look to Coventry University to be a bigger and bigger player in our future.

Coventry performs well in economic terms in comparison with the rest of the West Midlands. The region in 2008 had a £10bn gross value-added gap against the average of UK regions. Only the Coventry, Solihull and Warwickshire Sub-Region makes a positive contribution to that gap, but Coventry's economy is more and more attuned to a southeast economy rather than an historic West Midlands economy.

So what's the University's role in Coventry – today and tomorrow?

Cities are where people want to be – not just where factories operate or grand civic buildings stand in testimony to the past. More and more in the global economy, any city can be successful if it can offer desirable quality of life to all the people who want to be there. People – like ideas and money – can now travel the globe. Universities, like the environment, housing, and employment, are key players in offering a high quality of life.

The University's role has been critical in the successful efforts to bring new industry, new people and new thinking to the city, promoting its benefits and attractions. With the University of Warwick, it is seen to be one of the most important 'factories' for the future.

So the University is a key part of the city. It helps define what makes the city tick. It draws together people who have the intellectual capacity or entrepreneurial skills to create a positive future. What it offers is an important ingredient for both attracting inward investment and helping the growth of indigenous employment. It helps the city to raise its global profile. Students, publications,

Above: *The Herbert Art Gallery in the middle of Coventry University Campus, 2009, demonstrating the regeneration of the same area as shown in the image on its left, featuring post-blitz Coventry.*

Left: *West Orchards Shopping Centre.*

Coventry Transport Museum

Located in the birthplace of Britain's car and cycle industry the museum houses the world's largest display of British transport and is one of the UK's most popular transport attractions. The majority of the collection is Coventry-built or has a strong connection with Coventry, which over the years has had over 300 cycle makers, 120 motorcycle makers, and 130 manufacturers of cars, commercial vehicles and components. The city's contribution to transport continues today in the work of students and alumni from Coventry University and the museum is proud to work closely with individual students and academic departments. Like both the city and the University the museum is constantly reinventing itself as it fulfills its objective of enriching the minds of a diverse audience and inspiring students and visitors to turn an understanding of culture and history into a positive contribution to the world of today and tomorrow.

research, conferences, internet working, all give the city our window on the world.

Coventry University is a stimulus to change through its imagination, invention and innovation. Because it faces business, it helps strengthen and diversify our economy.

This is not new. The University has always had a key role in the city. In the 21st century it is playing to the strengths which have evolved over time, responding to the changing city, where design, engineering innovation, medical technologies and hardware, ICT, and creative industries are the elements of future prosperity. The University and the city of Coventry are changing in tandem.

In short, the University is focusing on areas where it can provide world-class, cutting-edge thinking, and the necessary facilities to help enhance Coventry's profile through, for example, new institutes covering advanced construction, serious games, health technologies, and

Above: *The Whittle Arches seen from Priory Place, one of two new public squares, along with two new public gardens, developed from 1997–2008 as a result of the £50m Phoenix Initiative, jointly funded by the City Council and the Millennium Commission.*

creative industries. All of that helps the city recruit the graduates and retain the skills for the future.

Coventry is a city that works through true partnership. The partnership between the city and the University is strong and growing.

We are working together at the front end of an inward investment process in promoting the city and its attraction to inward investors. There is stronger and stronger engagement with the universities in this key role. What Coventry University offers, and how it can respond to the needs of inward investors, will be crucial to Coventry's future success. This is demonstrated with the move of Severn Trent's national headquarters to the city.

The University also has direct involvement with vital economic and regeneration projects. These include Ansty Research and Development Park; Medipark; the 'Made in Coventry' presentation as part of the opening of the Ricoh Arena; the proposals for the 'Coventry Crown' to enhance significantly the environmental attributes of the existing inner ring road; 3D modelling virtual reality, and Second Life initiatives to present and promote the City Centre.

Above: *The Ricoh Arena, the stadium complex that is home to Coventry City FC, was officially opened in 2007. Coventry University students from the Media Production degree course helped set up and continue to operate live multi-screen coverage of CCFC's home games.*

The University's own Development Plan is a major part of the wider regeneration plans for the enlarged City Centre. The City Council has been working closely with the University to roll out the £160m Development Plan's first stage to upgrade the University's facilities. The University is also actively involved in ensuring that its plans contribute to the much wider £5bn regeneration of the wider City Centre.

In addition the University has been and remains actively involved in the Image Working Group, where key players within the city help promote and develop a positive image of the city for the future. Its engagement with the wider economic life of the city, Sub-Region, and Region, through Coventry, Solihull and Warwickshire Partnership, and Advantage West Midlands, our regional development agency, allows it to lobby decision-makers in central government and international industry.

Right: *Peeping Tom and Lady Godiva at the Broadgate Clock. Largely destroyed in the Blitz, Broadgate was rebuilt in the 1950s.*

The University is the lead partner in the Institute of Community Cohesion (iCoCo), located in Coventry and built upon the city's commitment to peace and reconciliation. ICoCo, working with three other Midlands Universities, under the leadership of Professor Ted Cantle, has established a national and international profile in supporting initiatives designed to enhance inter-cultural and inter-faith understanding and cohesion. This is achieved through policy development, advocacy, and training programmes usually with local authorities and other key community-based organizations.

The University supports the city in developing its role in sports: in 2005 the city hosted the International Children's Games, best described as the Children's Olympics; in 2007 the British School Games came together; after that the city and University started work on maximizing the benefit of the London Olympics in 2012.

The University stretches out to the young. It promotes the vibrancy and innovation of students in design and creative industries. It works in schools to help raise aspirations. In a wider social role it hosts or supports events such as the Godiva Festival and Made in Coventry.

As a large business in its own right, it is a significant contributor to the city economy, providing, each year, about £150m gross value added.

The city and University can provide mutual benefits but also have a mutual dependency on each other. The city has a clear vision for its future and the university is a key contributor to this. A successful city needs a successful university. A successful university needs a successful city as its home.

A university building up its own profile needs a city with similar aspirations. Success breeds success. Failure breeds failure. Any successful city must be at peace with itself: a place where people want to be, where families want to put down roots; where the diversity of colour, creed, religion, and lifestyle can live in harmony. That is what makes Coventry special among UK cities, and Coventry University plays a major role in this – now and for the future.

ENTERPRISE ON CAMPUS

4

Services Out and Services In

Julian Ingleby runs the Coventry University Technology Park. He does not have an office. John Latham is in charge of Coventry University Enterprises (CUE), of which the Technology Park is part. He does not have an office either. Nor do 70 per cent of Ingleby's employees. They work with laptop computers, linked to the world at large through broadband wireless connections.

This is not only a modern working practice which allows people to perform wherever they are. It is also a way for CUE to cut its overheads and operational costs by saving space and liberating room which can be rented to those who need it. It is called Location Independent Working. It is an example of CUE practising what it preaches. The experience has enabled CUE to package a service which can be offered to companies, passing on to them a technique of working freedom.

Companies visiting the Technology Park's Conference Centre can have a taste of this freedom; one of the first broadband wireless zones in the West Midlands has been installed in a suite of rooms for use by mobile executives keeping in touch with their own offices while doing business in Coventry. It became the biggest centralized wireless system in the UK's higher education sector.

Previous pages: *Inside the Design Hub in the Technology Park.*

Left: *Conference Centre guests at the TechnoCentre.*

Above: *Artist's impression of the Health, Design and Technology Institute.*

Below right: *Technology in the Serious Games Institute.*

The Conference Centre, which can accommodate meetings of up to 200 people, was in the first building constructed in the Technology Park. This enabled the Technology Park at the outset to fill a gap in Coventry's facilities for business visits, and to provide an income stream. The main facilities in the eight hectares of the Technology Park are the physical testimony to the 2004 award by the UK Science Parks Association for 'the science park making the most significant contribution to the exploitation of the knowledge base'.

- The TechnoCentre/Innovation Centre provides business space. It is the home for up to 60 small and start-up companies.
- Nearby, the Enterprise Centre, the second building on the Technology Park, completed in 2001, is like a second stage for young companies. When they grow out of the space in the TechnoCentre, they can move to the Enterprise Centre on longer-term leases.
- More recently, CUE went into a joint venture with a private sector developer to complete the Innovation Village. The result is a series of self-contained units available for lease. Companies selected to occupy the units manage their own premises within guidelines set by the Technology Park's estate managers.

designhub

- The Technology Park needed accommodation for visitors, so it sold a neighbouring site for a hotel which sits on the place where James Starley manufactured the first bicycle.
- The Design Hub, which was opened by Sir George Cox, Chair of the Design Council in 2007, plays to the historic strength of the University. It offers space to developing commercial ventures, and acts as a rendezvous for collaboration between students, experts and companies, for the sharing of skills, for the pursuit of design ideas and their transformation to commercial possibility.
- The Serious Games Institute is a hub for an emerging industry, a centre for the expansion of the technology already available in electronic games to other uses. It is, CUE claims, a model for partnership between education and industry; it links advanced research to new business; it opens up potential new applications in e-learning and advanced communications.

ICE institute for creative enterprise

- The Health, Design and Technology Institute brings companies together with those who use health products and who provide health services. It is concerned with professional development in the health sector, advancing the technology of health products and services, and offering multidisciplinary courses.
- Next to the Technology Park, the Institute for Creative Enterprise (ICE) is a new facility for postgraduate teaching and research in media, digital design, and performance, with space for new businesses in the sector. ICE is unique because it brings together students and the University and local creative businesses, who have relocated into the building. Examples are Arts and Media, Imagineer, Theatre Absolute, and Talking Birds. In turn, this combination has also attracted additional funding, for example from the Higgs Charity.
- The Metrology Lab started in 2006 as a manufacturing measurement centre, offering a one-stop service for companies looking for precision.

The buildings express CUE's function which is, said Ingleby, 'to facilitate the University's interaction with business'. The Technology Park is the infrastructure to promote what it does best. It is also the perfect illustration of the nature and closeness of the relationship between business and the University. In 2008, it enabled the University to provide

Above: *The ICE café.*

Left: *Margaret Hodge, then Minister of State at the Department for Culture, Media and Sport (centre), surrounded by University staff watching a drumming demonstration, at the opening of the Institute of Creative Enterprise in 2008.*

assistance to more than 6,000 small and medium-sized enterprises, while also maintaining business partnerships with more than 100 larger companies. This level of involvement is thought to be exceptional among universities in the UK.

Ingleby splits the work into two product divisions, the first dealing with enterprise and innovation and the second dealing with international business and knowledge transfer.

'The University leads an impressive range of research initiatives and projects, many in conjunction with external partners and organizations, which means that the University boasts a vibrant research community. With practitioners in a range of disciplines who are themselves leaders in their field, research is frequently practice-led or practice-based, all of which makes a distinctive contribution to theoretical, conceptual and pedagogical developments. For example, current projects in dance and performing arts are leading new initiatives in emerging fields, particularly dance and digital technologies. With the UK's first digital dance archive launching in 2009 (Siobhan Davies Dance Digital Archive), the University is well placed to expand its range of collaborations with high-profile artists and cultural leaders, allowing it to inform and inflect public policy in the area of arts and humanities.'

Professor Sarah Whatley,
Professor of Dance and Director, Centre for Media,
Arts and Performance

The first is strongly, but not exclusively, focused on the University's knowledge base, where teaching and applied research fuse together and manifest themselves in the applied research centres outlined in Chapter Two, and in a multitude of applied research groups. These bodies provide the expertise, CUE provides the support to turn the expertise into business, and the Technology Park provides the physical facilities to make the business a reality.

The process starts with the applied research groups. Academic staff combine and bid for University funds, typically in 2008 around £15,000, to push a project idea off the ground. If the project shows promise, then the group may turn itself into an applied research centre, a larger undertaking with a director and up to 15 employees. For that to happen, the putative centre has to bid for University funds of £150,000. But that money is not forthcoming without a three-year business plan, which must meet the University's expectation of a return at the end of the period. No return, no more funding. Immediately the academic staff have been placed in a commercial situation.

The staff, though, are not isolated. Each centre has a business development manager who takes in hand the business aspects of the applied research. It is at this point that the facilities of the Technology Park may be called into play, and one of CUE's support schemes may prove relevant. Indeed, companies on the Technology Park are urged to foster relationships with the University's academic staff.

The hard-headed approach to applied research fits the University's corporate ethos and is a necessary precondition to meet the target of tripling applied research income. At the same time this approach runs in parallel with CUE's panorama of business support schemes, which are available to all within the scope of Ingleby's first product division: enterprise and innovation. There is nothing exclusive about the work on the Technology Park apart from CUE's insistence on advanced technological prospects.

This panorama reaches into every corner of business, but has a special role in nurturing regional commerce.

- The Vision Works is directed at those who want to establish a business in the region, and brings into play experts to help and the space in which to develop.
- Business Enterprise Works, which has already helped more than 300 new companies, puts individuals in touch with business mentors and workshops which can address topics like accounting and marketing.
- At the same time, CUE has an extensive database, covering sources of finance from direct grants to business angels, which it can put at the disposal of the young company.
- CUE is also involved in Innovation Networks, a scheme to assist companies prepared to work together in the pursuit of a new product by providing revenue and capital grants.

The new companies, whether coming out of the University's applied research network or from the wider public, provide employment opportunities. Importantly for the University, they are one means of moving towards the aim of retaining more graduates within the West Midlands region. A bridge between University graduates and the commercial world has been built under the title of thefutureworks. This is a recruitment agency, based in the Students' Union, but working under the CUE aegis, which places students in part-time work and graduates in full-time career posts.

Ingleby's second product division helps to take the University out of the regional and into the global arena. It is concerned with international business and knowledge transfer. 'We want to develop links on a global basis. We encourage companies to look at international opportunities.' This is urging the private sector to do what the University has done itself in its own sphere: activity which is discussed from page 140.

One focal point for the international business aspect of this product division is the UK Soft Landing Zone initiative that has previously been described on page 64. This is a sole partnership between CUE and the UK government's Trade and Investment arm. The aim is to take UK companies into world markets and give them the opportunity to sell individually, and to collaborate with companies in those markets.

To this end, CUE and Trade and Investment have been setting up a network of bases in university science parks in some 20 countries, where UK companies can receive support on all the practical issues – law, finance, culture and so on – which will ease their movement into the particular market. A key area for the Soft Landing Zones is Asia: China, Hong Kong, India, Malaysia, Singapore.

At home, another scheme developed by the University and supported by UK Trade and Investment, is IntaTrade. This provides support, adjusted to the needs of the individual company, in finding markets, putting companies in touch with customers and potential partners, while leavening the package with financial support.

Meanwhile, through its connection with the European Business and Innovation Centres Network, CUE is busy looking for opportunities to bring together companies, universities and research institutions in projects especially related to biotechnology and renewable energy. The projects are a practical way of extending general links between different sectors of education and the economy, and of creating new links between companies and universities.

Above: *(Left to right) David Wortley, Director of the Serious Games Institute, David Pender, Advisor, Public Establishment for Industrial Estates, and Tim Luft, Director of European Innovation Ltd, based at the Technology Park.*

Coventry University has long been active in making links with the major companies of the West Midlands region. BT, for example, is a partner in the Technology Park. In recent years, however, it has been spreading its net and sees itself as a potential partner across a range of technical areas with multinational corporations. To this end the University has a Corporate Partnership Unit, which has refined a model of how to create and sustain a relationship.

The model owes its origins to D.J. Rachman but has been developed by Joanne Dobson of the University's Corporate Partnership Unit to the point where, Latham observed, the University is a leader. In the broadest sense, there needs to be a vision of how the relationship might benefit both sides, but both sides have to develop an intimacy before the relationship has an impact.

Dobson starts by setting a target, from the University point of view. Contact with the company would lead to one contract, and that contract would lead to another until such time as the University and the company touched each other at a number of different points. Then there would be a strategic partnership or, put another way, a habit of cooperation, running through consultancy contracts, mutual employment opportunities, and joint research.

A case in point is the link between Cisco Systems, the US communications group, and the University. Cisco has provided equipment and technology for the mobile and virtual learning world of the Serious Games Institute. But this is not an isolated provision. Much of the equipment used to refresh the University's electronic network, the smart campus, has also come from Cisco.

In the future, as the University's applied research agenda accumulates force and respect, cooperation on this sort of scale is likely to become more widespread. As that happens, more wealth will be created for the University and its partners. CUE itself has been generating a surplus in recent years and, Ingleby wrote, 'this has been achieved with additional income generated by delivering short-term projects on behalf of funding partners regionally, nationally, and in Europe, while the property portfolio has been developed and filled'.

But in terms of the corporate plan and its targets stretching into the next decade, the flowers have only just started to bloom.

Engineers Who Solve Problems

Engineering has been, and is, a bedrock of higher education at Coventry. From the days of the College, through the period of the Polytechnic, to the University itself, engineering has been at the centre of both pedagogy and collaboration with industry. But the offering has evolved as the economy has shifted, and as techniques in the educational world have changed.

When Norman Bellamy arrived from an industrial post in the early 1960s, the teaching, he recalled, was 'chalk and blackboard,' designed to provide certificates for technicians. Forty years on, the duration of a working life, students have access to jet aircraft and simulators, and they build their own vehicles to compete in motorsport races such as Formula Student.

The first graduates emerged in 1965, after completing sandwich courses, signalling that Coventry would be an institution not simply for technicians, but also for executives. This move into a higher reach of education coincided with the drive of the Labour Government to encourage private and public sectors to exploit 'the white heat' of the scientific revolution. Since then governments have not stopped driving and Coventry has not stopped responding.

Below left: *Computer programming at Lanchester College of Technology, October 1965.*

Below: *Compositor operating Linotype machine.*

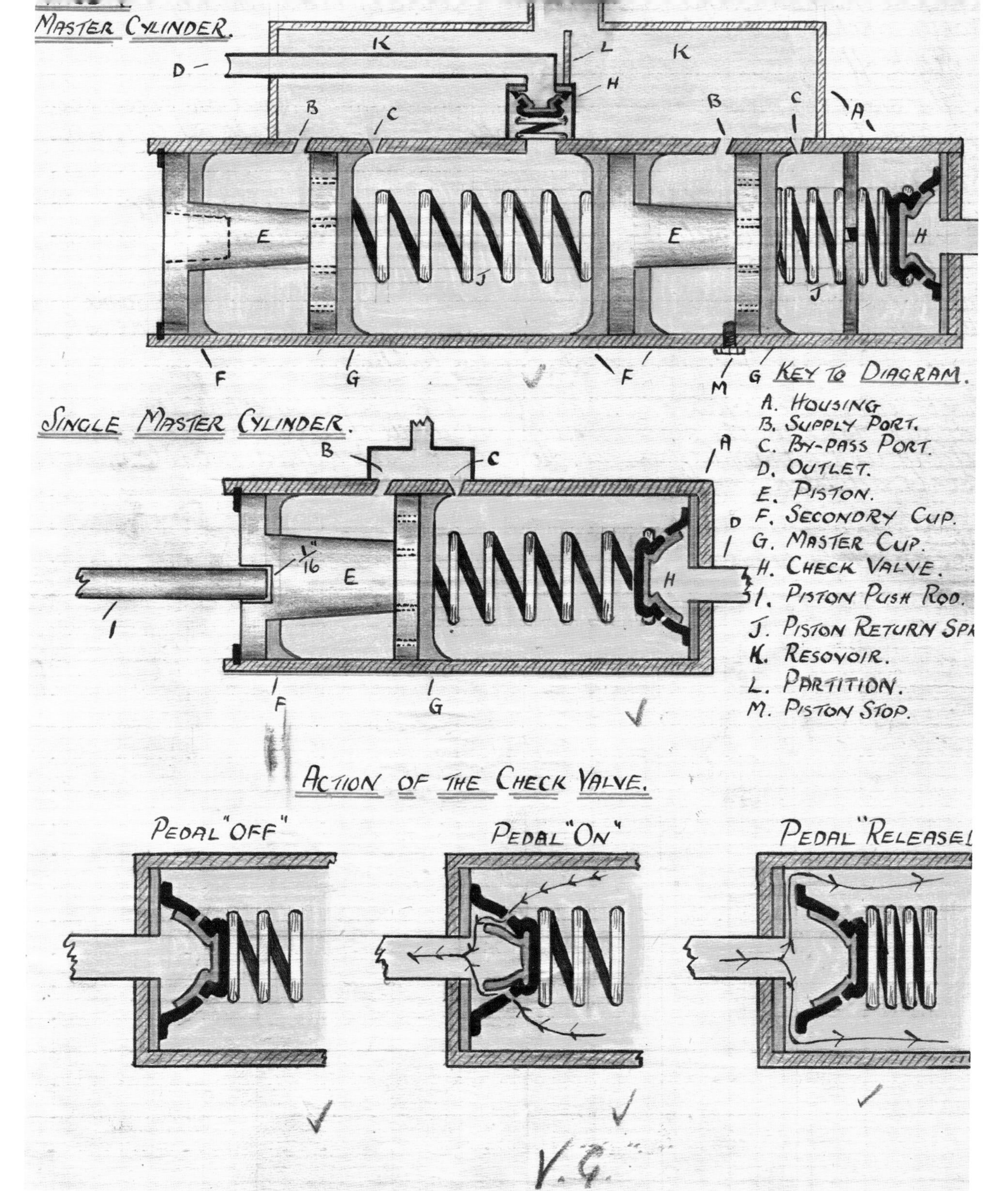

Right: *From wartime presentation coursework by Gunner EL Perkins, 419 Battery HAA, Royal Artillery, studying at Rugby College of Engineering. The work is dated 1943.*

Coventry's reputation during the 1960s was largely based on electrical and mechanical engineering. There had been a course of aeronautical engineering but that closed when the industry retracted as the Government, looking for economies, cut back its requirements for military aircraft. This was an early example of sensitivity to external demands.

Others came quickly. The arrival of electronics eclipsed electrical engineering: 'We had played that card', noted Bellamy. Mechanical engineering absorbed aeronautical, both staff and equipment such as wind tunnels. Opportunities began to emerge for a broader suite of courses, as Professor Peter White, Associate Dean in the Faculty of Engineering and Computing, explained:

'In the final-year of mechanical engineering, there were optional subjects, and those which ran were automotive-related. As we moved into the 1980s, we tried automotive engineering and that was very popular. From that we broke out another course, motor sport, and since then we have added two streams: powertrain and motorcycles. If we had offered only mechanical engineering, we wouldn't have the number of students we have now.'

Above: *Language laboratory lecturer's control panel, late 1960s.*

Above left: *Students with the car entered into the Formula Student national competition, 2007.*

Of course, the diversification of courses has not stopped there, but the evolution and diversification has taken place against a background of change in both industry and the expectations of students, both of which affect the position of Coventry in the educational marketplace.

The College of Technology by and large met the demands of the major companies in the area by offering training to their apprentices and younger employees through sandwich courses. Rolls-Royce and GEC, for example were strong supporters. In turn, they influenced the nature and content of the teaching. But two factors changed that, leading to the shape and style of the 21st-century institution.

The first was the reduction in scale, or elimination, of the big assembly operations which had given the city of Coventry 70 years of prosperity. The traditional apprentice disappeared and, with that, part of the demand for the courses of College and Polytechnic. The effect was marked, but not, as Professor White observed, fundamental. 'The industrial base shrank, but the loss was not high tech. Many of the companies involved would never have employed a graduate in a million years.'

The second was the coincidence of this shrinking with the strong expansion of the educational base, fostered by the policies of successive governments. This meant that the College, later the Polytechnic, shifted its ethos. Diversification of courses became more closely geared to individual demands, the number of students expanded, and Coventry started hooking business skills into its engineering courses. All of this led to the situation where, as Bellamy put it, 'we were meeting student needs rather than company needs'.

In the 21st century, the pendulum has swung back in the sense that the University is acutely aware of the needs of business, not least the perennial shortage of engineers. But the attitude differs from the 1960s. Instead of being a tool of business, the institution sees itself as a partner. For engineering and related sectors – computing, high-tech communications, management and so on – this opens up different styles of pedagogy and acknowledges different criteria in the way in which students approach the University.

For Professor Paul Ivey, Dean of the Faculty of Engineering and Computing, this involves dealing with what he sees as 'a mismatch between education and living

Right: *The Aerospace Lab contains a complete Harrier jump jet and a Scout helicopter. Two new flight simulators were unveiled in December 2007.*

afterwards'. The apex of the present system is the examination, but this is based on carefully calibrated questions, giving students just enough information to stimulate an answer within a discrete framework; it is tidy but unreal. Life is not so neat. It has jagged edges.

The response to this dilemma is to recast the way in which engineering skills are conveyed to, or discovered by, students. Coventry is staging a quiet revolution based on open-ended education: 'We are looking to blend education with employment', said Professor Ivey. This points to learning which is led by activity. 'We teach by the resolution of problems,' Professor White said. Education becomes problem-based, project-based.

There is a loose connection here with the pedagogic techniques, associated with the Harvard Business School, based on case studies. Imperial College, London, has been moving in the same direction, and there are other universities in Australia, Canada, and Denmark which have

'When we were there in '62 the site was only two or three acres with five buildings, and mostly concentrated on mechanical, production, electrical and aeronautical engineering. The course and facilities development is fantastic, and now seems to occupy most of the city to the west and south of the Cathedral. The architecture, both the new and the redevelopment of existing buildings, is excellent, and it felt like a great environment to study (and play) in. The library facilities are fantastic.'

John Robinson, Production Engineering, 1967

'I enrolled on Coventry University's MBA (Manufacturing) based in the School of Engineering. Studying part-time, the course took three years to complete. I really enjoyed it, and would say that the best experience was to be working together with colleagues who were also in the industry. We all faced similar problems. Because the MBA was based in the School of Engineering, there was a good emphasis on manufacturing technology and techniques that I was able to bring back to the company.'

Charles Morgan, MBA (Manufacturing) 1993

been following the same path. But there is no university in the Midlands with the same drive to activity-led education as Coventry, which is prepared to invest £60m on new engineering facilities to make it a reality.

Coventry University, in this regard, is becoming part of an elite group. Project-based learning is not exclusive to engineering. It has applications across a wide range of subjects and has the possibility of encouraging collaborative work across different disciplines and departments: construct a chassis for a car and it needs computerized equipment to control it, and a body designed to go on top of it. Each element requires thinking to resolve the difficulties of fitting it all together.

If students can demonstrate their ability to think their way through problems and understand how to overcome them, immediately they have a better chance of fruitful first employment. 'We are increasingly focused on first employment', Professor Ivey acknowledged. 'There is little choice.'

From World War II until the 1990s, higher education, its spread and its quality, was accepted as a public good. Potential students could rely on the public authorities for help in funding their education. To some extent they still can. But the introduction of student fees, and loan arrangements to meet them, shifted the balance. Higher education now is deemed a private need. Like all consumers, students accumulating debts expect to receive their money's worth.

'Students accept fees if the debt is surmountable by the first job. We must be focused on that', Professor Ivey noted. That focus on the first job has not passed unnoticed in continental Europe from where students are coming, precisely to take advantage of an education geared to employment in a way which is not generally followed in their own countries. The movement inwards is matched by work going outwards. Coventry actually has more engineering students, following its courses, outside the UK than it does inside.

An important element of meeting student needs is the direct link between the University and business. From the outset, engineers from the institution have worked with, and in, industry. A case in point is the work which has been done with Jaguar, the car group, and the companies in its supply chain, whose employees have frequented Coventry part-time courses.

More specifically, the University's energetic approach to student placements in industry has meant that students bring back specific company problems which can be addressed as projects in final-year assignments. Postgraduate students can earn their PhDs by doing projects specifically

Above: *Part of the Flight Simulation suite, the most advanced piece of aerospace technology to be found at any UK University.*

related to an industrial problem: the after-treatment of vehicle exhaust, for example. This is, on the one hand, industry outsourcing its research and, on the other, the University building up its portfolio of consultancies, both culminating in an academic achievement which can add to the corpus of the University's published research. For the student, the academic and business experience have merged to create the education-employment blend.

With new engineering facilities in a new building, for which planning was well advanced in 2009, the focus on projects will increase. Professor Ivey's aim is the growth of a community of learners, around whom there is a building. Teams of people can work together in their own dedicated space, working whatever hours they want, breaking the notion of nine-to-five working. The classroom becomes the workplace, the workplace becomes the classroom. 'Traditionally, you put laboratories in a building, but what if the building is a laboratory?' Professor Ivey asked.

The building may be part of the engineering faculty at the University, but it need not be exclusively for engineers. The teams working on projects at the student level almost inevitably include students from different disciplines and, indeed, from other countries. But this is also the case in areas of applied research, a longstanding facet of Coventry engineering.

One of the longest-running projects at the University has been wave energy and the equipment which goes with it, such as the development of the Wells air turbine for operating in fully reversing air flows. Bellamy started the work over 30 years ago, and it has been transformed into a European project involving civil engineers, mechanical engineers, electrical engineers, and experts in physics and mathematics.

A Coventry engineer should be able to cope with the complexities of international working. As Professor White commented:

> *'The engineer has a toolbox of transferable skills. He or she will always be asking the question – is this solution reasonable? – what if I changed this or that? They are always doing cost and benefit analysis.'*

All of which positions Coventry at the forefront of the evolution of engineering into the future. The Royal Academy of Engineering, in its report Educating Engineers for the 21st Century, emphasizes the need and desirability of industrial involvement, and practical experience in the education of future engineers. Because this has always been fundamental to the Coventry offer since Polytechnic days, it is in the strongest possible position to fulfil the Royal Academy's aspirations.

Designs Which Work and Designers Who Go to Work

Katie Bishop, in 2008 a final-year design student, has devised a new cast alloy road wheel. She turned her idea into a sketch and took that into a three-dimensional computer programme. She then talked with engineers on subjects like stress and thickness before settling on the materials needed for manufacture. She has been successful enough for Land Rover to decide it wants to use her design.

The wheel has been exposed to public gaze in an annual exhibition of Coventry University automotive designs, by final-year students, at the Coventry Transport Museum. This follows an internal exhibition at the University, where final-year students show their work; the best of that, judged by independent professional designers, is shown at the Transport Museum.

The way in which the independent judgments are made goes to the heart of the design ethos at Coventry. Half of the marks go to the design itself, a quarter to the practicality of manufacture, and a quarter to economies. Or to put that another way, the designed product must have a demonstrable use. The Coventry approach to designing is practical and vocational: 'We are trying to create intelligent designers ready to go to work', said David Browne, Course Director, Automotive Design, in the School of Art and Design.

For all that, Bishop's wheel is unusual in two ways. First, most of the exhibited designs are probably not commercial proposals as they stand. They reflect visions and possibilities. They are a showcase for designers rather than designs, as the students network to ensure that a company will see what they have done and encourage a job application.

Second, Bishop is in a minority. Very few women become transport design students, although the University would love it if more showed interest. Women are more

Below: *Katie Bishop shows off her integrated wheel design, now in production for Land Rover, at the 2008 Automotive Design exhibition at Coventry's Museum of Transport.*

Above: *Coventry fashion students' work shot on location in Venice.*

attracted to fashion design. To that extent the study and practice of design at the University conform to gender stereotypes.

Whatever the gender, by the time students have exhibited their work they will have had some experience of the commercial world they are being prepared to enter. The great majority of undergraduates are full-time students and, in the third year of a four-year course, their time will be spent on what the University calls professional enhancement. This is where the design courses are most obviously practical and vocational.

During the first term of that year, students will enter design competitions; they will have to produce designs to an external brief which offers no room for negotiation. Or a company could pose a test: Reebok did this with sports shoes, asking students to choose a sport and design an appropriate shoe for it. This is the first step into the outside design world. In 2005, for example, Coventry was one of four institutions across the world asked by Ferrari to design their concept car for 2010. Several Coventry designs were submitted from small teams of design students, of which one was progressed to further development at Ferrari, with the students spending time in Italy, and a second was the most popular design in a public vote and was strongly featured in the *Sunday Times*.

The focus in the second term is on collaborative projects, where, with a company or an agency, students will undertake an assignment, acting, as it were, as an external consultant. The students might work in small groups, to foster the idea of teamwork. The completed assignment will be presented to the company, which will then provide feedback.

In the third term of the year, students apply for work placements, where they would hope to be treated as a member of staff. One student ended his work placement at Reebok by having three types of shoe in production.

Cab of the Future

John Jostins and design colleagues at Coventry University designed and developed Microcab, a latterday rickshaw but powered by hydrogen fuel cells rather than human endeavour. It is a lightweight vehicle intended for cities, waiting for its time to come.

That will be when hydrogen charging facilities are widespread. Much of the design development work took place at the CU Advanced Modelling and Digitization Laboratory in the University's Bugatti Building, helped by financing from the UK's Department of Trade and Industry. By 2001, five Microcabs had been built.

The Bugatti Building is named after the great Italian engineer and designer both to recognize his skills and to acknowledge help given to the University by the Bugatti Trust.

The Microcab demonstrates the harmony of different disciplines, and the concern to design products for the future which not only have a use but are environmentally benign.

Right: *The Microcab is the product of innovative thinking by entrepreneur John Jostins, who first showed his design at Coventry University Design Institute open day in 2006. The result is a vehicle powered by a hydrogen fuel cell, pollution free and virtually silent in operation. The only emission is water vapour.*

This sort of approach, putting students at the academic-commercial nexus, is finely honed across the University. In the case of design, there is more than 150 years of experience. The first school of art in Victorian times started with designs for woven ribbons for local manufacturers hard pressed by French competition.

Ever since applied design at Coventry has been a key and highly regarded part of the University offering – except for one period, recalled by Professor Clive Richards, whose experience goes back to the 1960s and who is now Associate Dean in the School of Art and Design.

Fine Art was regarded as superior to design in the 1960s and 1970s. It wasn't vocational in the strict sense – there were no clients as such. But that attitude has fallen away and now that students pay fees there is a much stronger professional practice feel, and even Fine Art is interested in its role in a business context.

The University's design offering in its 21st-century shape has its origins in 1973 with the start of the UK's first 'industrial design (transportation)' course, now simply called Automotive Design. For 25 years, Browne said, the course retained its unique quality, although after that, rival courses emerged. Coventry was a niche supplier of designers to the transport sector and did not have the full range of courses of the metropolitan arts schools and universities.

It became rapidly clear that Coventry was very good at what it did and does. Polytechnic and University consistently gained awards, latterly culminating, in 2005, with its recognition by the Higher Education and Funding Council as the UK's only transport and product design 'centre of excellence in teaching and learning' and, in 2007, with the Queen's Anniversary Prize for Higher and Further Education, for 'educating tomorrow's leaders in automotive design'.

Equally important, Coventry's automotive designers have spread through the vehicle industry, responsible for parts of, or whole, vehicles everywhere from Aston Martin and Bentley through Jaguar and Land Rover to Toyota and Volvo. The collapse of the British-owned motor assemblers in the years following the start of the automotive design course has made no difference; the graduates have gone worldwide or into the smaller national consultancies and studios.

Automotive design has acted as a springboard for a movement into courses directed at other products and disciplines, so that the University is now much more than a niche supplier. This has been both a conscious programme of response to the needs of the marketplace and to the official concern, recently manifest in the review by Sir George Cox, chairman of the Design Council, that business had underplayed the significance of good design, and that the nation was not realizing the potential of its creative talent.

Car interior designs led into ergonomics, and ergonomics into fashion and fashion accessories. Automotive design led to the design of other forms of transport such as motor cycles, bicycles, and marine craft. 'We are always alert to new practice, and information technology had a huge impact', recalled Richards, not least for the first postgraduate course in Europe, during 1986, in electronic graphics. Design and digital media run together. This opened the way to new work in illustration, animation and photography.

Patience is a Virtue

Colin Slater studied painting in the Art Department of Lanchester Polytechnic from 1975 to 1978. During that time he acquired unexpected fame and an early boost to his career.

'I eventually spent my time working out of the studio, specializing in mural painting. This picture was painted in 1977 and became a landmark. It was painted on the building of the Polytechnic's Extension Studies building on Vine Street. I gave it the title "Patience is a Virtue" because it took so long to get the permission to paint it, not so much from the Poly but from the various departments of the City Council. Its projected life was three months but it stayed for 11 years.

'At the time, the mural received a lot of publicity in the local and regional papers. It also featured in a British Council exhibition of street murals that toured the world during the early 1980s, and appeared as a full-page colour illustration in *Street Murals* by Volker Barthelmeh (Penguin Books, 1982).'

The way in which one type of design can run into another, the way in which design can lead to other disciplines, emphasises that design cannot be cased in a silo. 'We are always looking for interdisciplinary activity, crucially where a lot of innovation and creativity occur', said Richards.

So it is that the Faculties of Art and Design on the one hand, and Engineering and Computing on the other, run courses jointly on industrial product and design. When Engineering produces a racing car for student racing, it builds the chassis and Design clothes it with a body. When the sports product design course becomes involved with sports shoes, it engages with the Faculty of Health and Life Sciences on foot biometrics. But sports products are frequently used as fashion items, so there is also a need for cross-pollination between sports products and fashion.

Below: *Jon Snow, TV newscaster and journalist, one of many speakers who come to Coventry University every year as part of the Coventry Conversation lecture series. Seen here surrounded by Coventry University media students in the Graham Sutherland Building (M Block).*

At the same time, the design teams are putting skills at the service of consumer industries through the Design and Ergonomics Applied Research Group, whose research work covers not only transport but also healthcare products, the search for the most favourable environment in which to teach, and computer-aided design.

A classic example of the use of computer-aided design is shown in fashion. The University's fashion courses specialise in the use of technology to develop new fashion approaches and ideas. This is proving both popular and successful; since the programme started in 2007, the students' work has been featured at fashion events such as the Clothes Show, and one current student, Kevin Geddes, won the 2008 Fashion Incubator Award to find the freshest new talent in British fashion, beating off stiff competition from 34 UK universities and colleges.

The University has also grown its profile and reputation in other creative areas. The media and journalism courses, for example, attract high profile visiting speakers to the weekly Coventry Conversations, which were set up by one of the lecturers, John Mair. In 2008–9, speakers included Jon Snow, Jeremy Paxman, the McCanns' spokesperson, Clarence Mitchell, and the Director of Corporate Affairs at Camelot, Richard Peel, who is also an alumnus of the University.

Widening the Horizons: Growing the Curriculum

'This is not just a technical institute', asserted John Gledhill, Executive Director to the Vice-Chancellor until his retirement in 2008. Nor indeed has it been since the college days of the 1960s.

Norman Bellamy, then at the start of his Coventry career remembered how, during a time of educational expansion, the Council for National Academic Awards (CNAA) thought that engineers needed also to absorb some alternative studies. The result was the creation, in 1967, of a department of liberal studies, which included marketing. 'It created a life of its own. It grew like a wild flower. It was the media studies of the day', said Bellamy.

The University has moved on a long way since that day. Old divisions which dispatch students and researchers to exclusive academic areas are outdated. An example is the management training given to executives of Emirates, the Dubai-based airline, who work both with the University's business departments and the Faculty of Engineering and Computing.

Similarly, with an institution whose modern life started with the attempted fusion of engineering and design, teaching these core subjects cannot happen in isolation. Over the years, therefore, academic skills have built up, and courses have followed, in economics, finance and international trade, business and human resource management, languages, politics, and history. There are two areas where this widening of the curriculum has been particularly noteworthy and successful in recent years.

Business, Environment and Society

The growth of the Business School over the last 20 years has already been referred to earlier in this book. This developed further in August 2005, when the new Faculty of Business, Environment and Society was formed, building upon the previous merger of the Business School with Law, International Studies and Social Sciences in 2002. The 2005 changes saw Geography, Disaster Management and Sociology/Social Policy added to the former Business School's portfolio. The Dean, Professor Dave Noon, summarized the objectives of the Faculty in his strategic plan in 2006:

BES comprises a broad range of disciplines and subject areas covering business and management, law, the social sciences, disaster management, and

Below: *Ground floor of the library.*

Above: *Stained glass in the Baptistry, Coventry Cathedral. Designed by the artist John Piper, there are 195 panes in a rich palette of colours. The Cathedral was re-consecrated in 1962, seven years after reconstruction began.*

International Studies

Coventry calls itself 'the city of peace and reconciliation'. Coventry Cathedral's temporal mission is also peace and reconciliation. The University has its own Centre for Peace and Reconciliation, set up in 1999 and inaugurated by Mary Robinson, the former President of Ireland and United Nations human rights commissioner. This works alongside and from time to time combines with the city and Cathedral in events around the common theme, such as the Coventry Peace Prize and Peace Month.

However the University, and the Faculty of Business, Environment and Society, has gone much further. Recognising that internationalization and globalization are increasingly having an impact in our lives, it has developed a suite of courses which utilise international partners in combining study with a period of either work or study overseas. These courses are concerned with examining worldwide issues such as the environment and global security, and with the conditions for people to live free from fear and free from want. This leads the University into partnerships with Governments and civil organizations pursuing the varied work of dealing with the tests of daily life, with economic development and climate change, corporate responsibility, humanitarian relief and response to disasters. It also prompts postgraduate programmes dealing with the manner in which organizations, public and private, react to, and cultivate, change. Hence the University now offers programmes on climate change, global sustainability, natural hazards and global security. It has developed a particular reputation in Disaster Management, as the agencies co-ordinating disaster and emergency management need professional staff with both practical experience and appropriate academic qualifications. The London Underground's emergency and risk management team at the time of the London bombings in 2005 was staffed by Coventry graduates. The University, moreover, is not just interested in responding to the disaster itself, but also offers specialist courses on Emergency Planning and Disaster Reconstruction and Development.

All these programmes are extremely popular with students from the UK and overseas, leading to an international culture and make-up within the student body at Coventry, with students from over 90 countries represented on campus. This is explored further in the next chapter. They also attract widespread support – such as from the Allan and Nesta Ferguson Trust for Peace and Reconciliation – and lead to further developments. Hence the University is the base for iCoCo (the Institute for Community Cohesion) which is discussed elsewhere, but is a natural bedfellow for these International Studies programmes.

Second Life

Second Life, the online virtual world, is not only a fun place to visit, with an entire Coventry University Campus to explore amidst its many lands, but also has a more serious research and teaching purpose. Staff at Coventry University are using it for real-time teaching activities. Maggi Savin-Baden, Professor of Higher Education Research and one of the UK's leading proponents of online innovations in education commented, 'We have been funded to develop online Problem Based Learning (PBL), where students in small project teams are set virtual problems to manage virtual life scenarios – we are some of the very few people in the world developing PBL in Second Life.'

aspects of the built and natural environment. It therefore provides opportunities to create courses relevant to the needs of modern society and to provide applied research and consulting services to meet a wide range of business and community needs. The juxtaposition of business and management, community and society, and environmental capabilities provides significant synergy to address some of the issues facing modern society, for example, global warming, community cohesion, corporate social responsibility, and international terrorism, while at the same time being relevant to the needs of a rapidly evolving international economic context. The Faculty also has a significant international profile across many aspects of its provision, and these are important in addressing the University's international aspirations.

This new structure has seen a 30 per cent growth in BES student numbers to a current level of 4,800 in 2008–9. This increase in the popularity of the courses, together with new income streams from research and consulting, has resulted in a 50 per cent increase in financial turnover since 2005.

The Faculty has developed new study programmes in both traditional subject areas, such as Finance, Accounting, and English, and in emerging and innovative areas, such as Global Security, Sport Marketing, and Events Management. Many of these newer programmes are informed by applied research activities, such as for International Studies as shown on the previous page. They are also proving particularly attractive to international students.

Performing Arts and Media

Media studies originally grew out of the design work in the School of Art and Design but are increasingly linked to what is going on elsewhere in the University. Automotive journalism, for example, links to the automotive engineers, illustration to computerized and graphic design. Its applied research agenda is also wide – from digital scanning of the new experimental space at the Belgrade Theatre to training actors for the new construction industry's simulation facility on the Technology Park, called ACT-UK.

It is with dance, music, and fashion that the University has particularly merged arts and science. In dance, analysis of movement and measurement, first practised in relation to vehicles, has now been adapted to help dancers reduce the physical damage they habitually suffer. A project with Birmingham Royal Ballet has dancers coming to the University, dancing on a specially sprung floor and having all their movements tracked to measure stresses and strains. In music, the University has developed an e-music course, one of the first in the UK, which examines the relationship between traditional forms of music and the new digital media. As an example, one student, Joseph Neal, has worked with the dance students to record and produce his own CD of original compositions, called 'Stolen Shadows'. In the same way, the fashion courses on offer from 2006 focus on fashion technology and computerized design rather than textiles or sewing.

Above: *The Ellen Terry Building. Formerly the Odeon Cinema, and before that the Gaumont Palace, it originally opened in 1935, when Coventry had no fewer than 22 cinemas. Today, it houses two University departments, Performing Arts and Media and Communication.*

And, of course, the University has also invested in these developments. The old Gaumont cinema building has been refurbished and named after Dame Ellen Terry, the Coventry-born Victorian actress and one of the great artistes of her generation. Here, the University has its facilities for rehearsal and performance, for television and photographic work. The fashion team has cutting-edge facilities in the Graham Sutherland Building, while the Institute for Creative Enterprise (ICE), where creative students and businesses come together, is in a print workshop close to the campus, refurbished with financial help from AWM and the Higgs Charity.

Underlying these developments, there is a solid economic base. The cultural industries are a sector of increasing importance in the international economy. It would be surprising if a university, which faces business in the manner Coventry does, had not introduced new programmes and research agendas to address it.

Above: *View from top of the library toward Gosford Street and the Graham Sutherland Building (M Block).*

Library and Lanchester

During summer 2008, the Lanchester Library at Coventry University opened for 24 hours a day. It was testimony to the importance of the resource and the accessibility of the material for students preparing for examinations. This would have been impossible for previous generations even to have contemplated.

When the library at Lanchester College opened in 1961, it had a total stock of 8,500 books and precisely 24 seats. Putting that in perspective, it would mean there would be seats for less than half the staff the Lanchester Library now employs. By 1966–7, the book stock had grown to 22,000. By the mid-1980s, the book stock had increased to more than 200,000 and a computer system was in place.

Now the Library has over 350,000 volumes and 2,000 periodicals. It has 1,200 spaces for study and 450 computerized work stations linked into the University's computer network.

The building opened in 2001, named after Frederick Lanchester, the pioneer of the British motor industry who made his business in Coventry and built, in 1896, the first petrol-driven passenger car. At a cost of £16m, the building was designed to exploit natural light and natural ventilation, hence the distinctive turrets which look out over the eastern City Centre.

The growth of the Library as a centre of historical record has been enhanced by its collection of Lanchester memorabilia. Lanchester was not only a pioneer of the motor industry but also was a noted polymath who, in his time, had 230 patents and a lengthy list of publications which have sold noticeably well in Japan. The University collection swelled in 2008 when Chris Clark, the historian and keeper of a large Lanchester archive, decided to donate documents which complemented and enriched the original Lanchester cache.

Healthcare and the Community

As outlined in Chapter 1, the University has been at the forefront of shaping health and social care for the community of Coventry since the 1960s. In recent years, under the leadership of Dr Linda Merriman, the Faculty of Health and Life Sciences has grown to provide education to over 4,000 students at any one time. Those students are studying courses as diverse as nursing, forensic science, physiotherapy and psychology. At the time of writing, the University provides education to registration in 14 different health and social care professions. Once awarded their qualification and registered, many of these graduates go on to practise their profession in the local community.

Below: *The Health and Life Sciences faculty attracts an increasing number of students.*

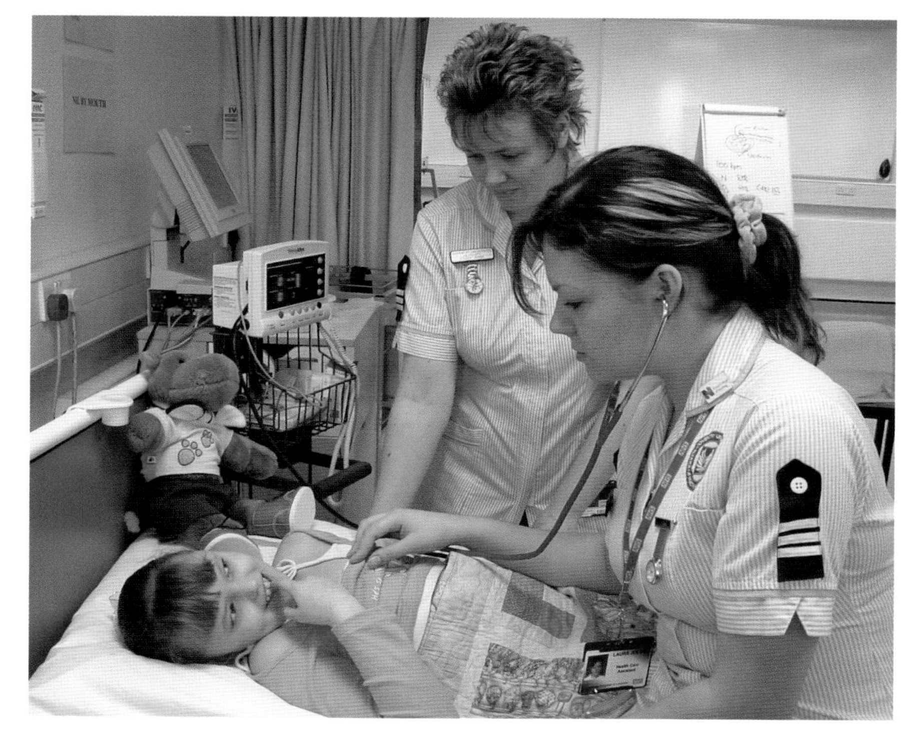

A cornerstone of the health and social care provision at Coventry is that the University works closely with its partner organizations in planning and developing its courses. Those partners naturally include local health trusts, strategic health authorities, and social care agencies. The University works with these organizations in the planning of local workforce need. It is then commissioned to educate the appropriate staff to fill that need. The relationship with these organizations and their staff doesn't, however, end with their initial education. Health professionals have a duty to maintain their skills through continuous professional development (CPD). This may be through discrete short courses, or full undergraduate and postgraduate qualifications. The University offers an extensive range of CPD opportunities to these individuals, and as with pre-registration training, works closely with their employing organization to provide post-qualification education that responds to the needs of the workforce. The postgraduate provision for health and social care professionals at Coventry is among the largest in the UK.

Another set of partners that are integral to the development of the University's educational provision are the service users themselves. Members of the local community who use the services provided by our students and graduates are actively consulted. They assist in

'Moving from Gulson hospital site into Richard Crossman, expectations were quite low due to the working conditions at Gulson Road and the look of the outside fabric of Richard Crossman, but the internal environment was excellent with new office furniture, well-equipped teaching rooms, and dedicated clinical skills labs. For example, we moved from working with BBC computers in the School of Nursing to a virtual learning environment at Coventry University. Looking back over the last 12 years since nursing and midwifery became part of higher education, we have all come a long way. Initially there were university systems and academic language to learn, and apprehensions as to whether they would meet all our professional regulations and ENB requirements, but today I feel we are truly integral to the University, and are part of a vibrant community on a campus in a city that is being regenerated. We are making a significant difference to the business and vision of the University.

We are working with different disciplines and sharing vision in terms of health and social care education. There are opportunities to learn and develop from and with students in the HEI and practice environments. The work of the applied research group for public health has received an outstanding social care award for partnership working in Improving Community Midwifery Practice to Reduce Infant Mortality in Coventry. The project group and the health visiting project findings were launched by NHS West Midlands across the West Midlands Primary Care Trusts.'

Natalie Mills, Head of CPD Health and Social Care

selecting, teaching, and assessing students and help guide the development of the University's curricula.

A strength of providing education in such a broad and diverse range of disciplines is that students gain experience of working alongside other professions. The inter-professional learning programme at Coventry has been commended, by the Health Professions Council and various professional bodies, as being an exemplar of good practice in health and social care education. Indeed the programme extends beyond the University to include trainee doctors from neighbouring Warwick University.

The strengths of the programme were recognized in 2005 when the Higher Education Funding Council for England established a Centre for Excellence in Teaching and Learning at Coventry, focused on inter-professional e-learning. This centre draws in another area of expertise in the University – that of electronic or e-learning. Many of the health and social care students spend a large amount of their time on placement in the workplace. E-learning allows them to access teaching materials and remain in contact with the University while working in a different location. The University has been innovative in the development of material and technology to facilitate this, and provide truly integrated courses.

Some of these technological innovations have allowed the Faculty of Health and Life Sciences to take the reputation of Coventry beyond the local to the national and global communities. Both Physiotherapy and Occupational Therapy have established outreach courses beyond the locality in Leicester and Staffordshire respectively. Further afield, Coventry health courses are being delivered in Southeast Asia and the Indian subcontinent. The latter development was undertaken in collaboration with the British Council. The expertise at Coventry in electronic learning has also facilitated the recruitment of students from across the globe. Specialist courses in areas such as Teenage Cancer Care are delivered to students from as far afield as Australia and New Zealand. Through the use of technology they can interact in real time with students in the UK and Europe, and lecturers back in Coventry.

As one would expect, the University is also driving innovation in health and social care through research and policy development. Academics such as Brian Toft, a leading expert on patient safety, and Louise Wallace, a pioneer in the application of psychology to health interventions have

Magnetic Bra

A Birmingham company has developed a new bra, for older and disabled women, which replaces traditional fastenings with magnets.

Adaptawear has worked with Coventry University's Health Design and Technology Institute (HDTI) to bring its front-fastening bra – the latest product in its range of adaptive clothing for men and women – to market. CoreBra has large finger loops to make dressing easier, and it is also proving extremely popular with carers.

HDTI Commercial Development Director, Guy Smallman, said this project was an example of how the Institute could make a real difference to an up-and-coming company in the assistive technologies sector.

'Our input has directly led to changes in the design of the bra, which in turn has helped Adaptawear to incorporate modifications in line with the needs of their target market,' Mr Smallman said. 'We are here to support small and medium-sized enterprises in designing products and services that will significantly improve community healthcare.'

Above and right: *Health and Life Science students are trained to fully professional levels.*

international reputations and are called upon as governmental advisors. Development of policy in areas such as work and pensions has also been taken up by national bodies and the government. The Health Design and Technology Institute (HDTI), headed by Simon Fielden, opens on the Technology Park in 2009. This brings together expertise in health with the University's other key areas of engineering, art and design, and business. The Institute will be exploring new ways of supporting people living in the community with long-term conditions, and those who wish to improve their health and lifestyle. An example of a product taken to the market by the HDTI is a bra with magnetic fastenings to assist elderly and disabled women (see above). Products such as this help to restore the dignity of those using them, and significantly improve their quality of life.

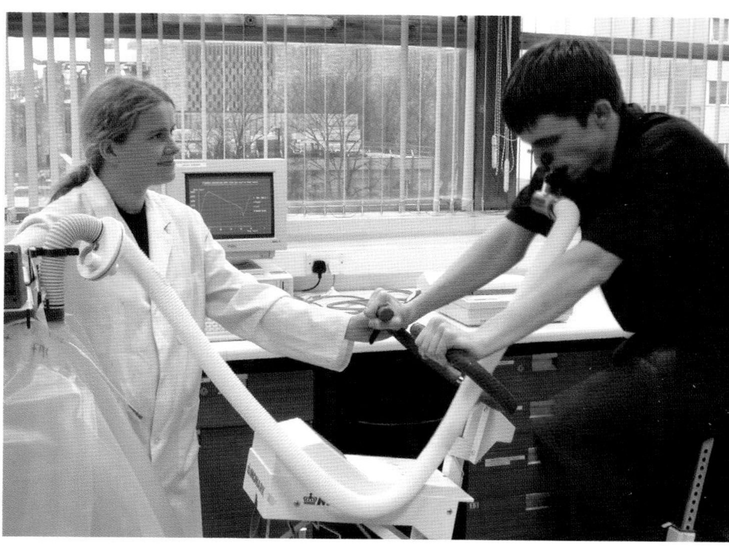

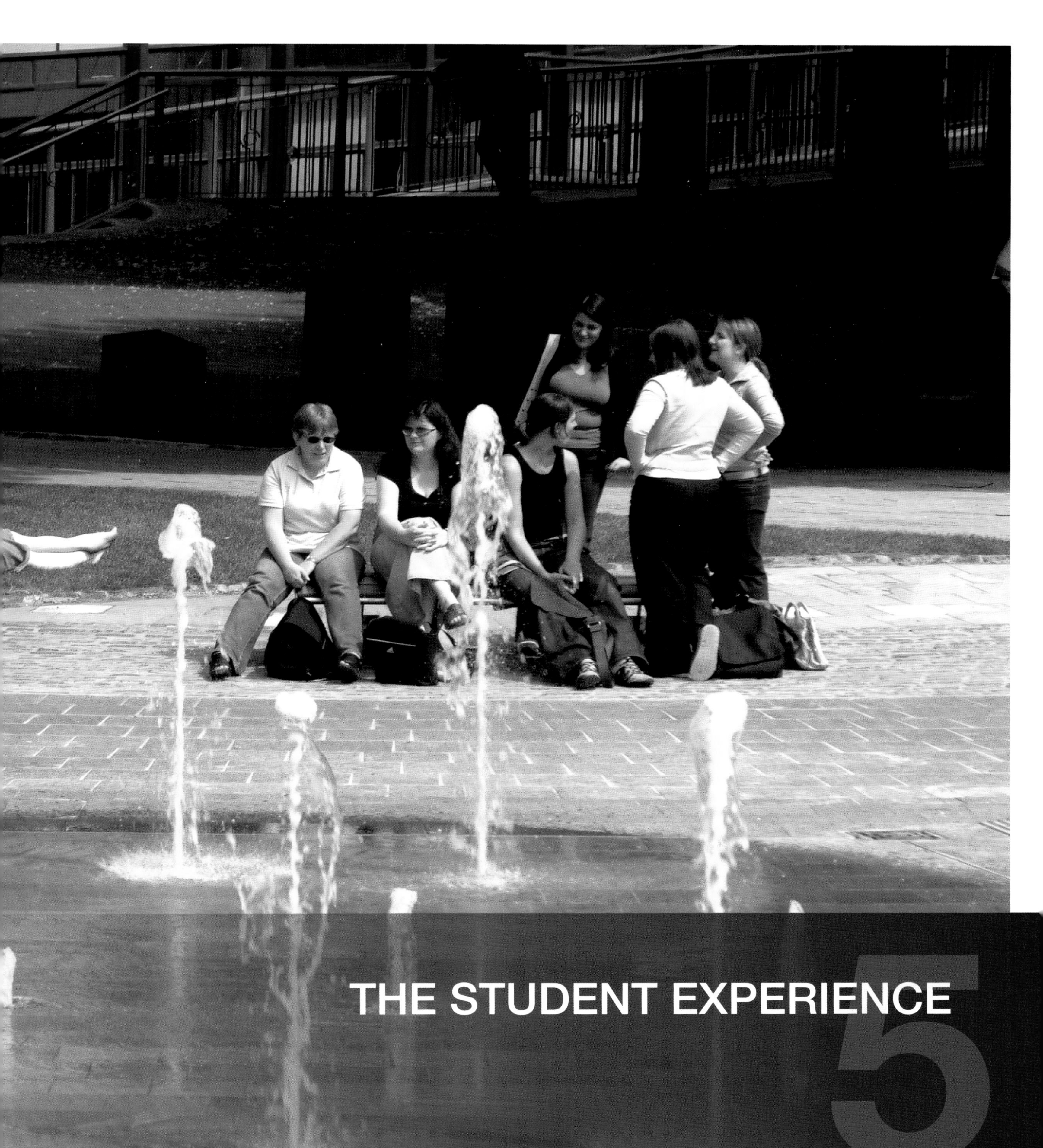

5 THE STUDENT EXPERIENCE

Diverse People, Diverse Needs, Diverse Activities

Headache pills, a National Union of Students discount card, camera, academic wall planner, bank account, bottle opener, condoms, and maps. These items, according to the Coventry University Students' Union guide for 2006–7, were the essential components of a student survival kit. Varied items for a varied student body.

The Coventry student is difficult to pin down. As Tom Wood, President of the Students' Union in 2007–9, noted, there is no such person as an average student:

> *'More and more of our members are studying while working full time and raising a family or returning to academia to enhance their career. There are still many 18–24 year old students who are living away from home for the first time but, increasingly, home is thousands, rather than hundreds, of miles away as Coventry attracts international students in greater numbers.'*

Over the last generation there has been a profound change in the profile of students attending university, and Coventry is no exception. Philip Pilkington, a long-time permanent official at the Students' Union, commented that 'an elite system has moved to a mass system of great diversity. Genders are in balance compared with the 1970s. Forty per cent of the students here come from ethnic minorities, against a national average of 19 per cent'. Numbers are edging up to 17,000 full-time equivalent students.

Above: *Students' Union Summer Ball, 2007.*

At the same time, the Students' Union has moved a long way from the militancy of the 1970s as experienced by Geoffrey Holdroyde.

Even as late as 1980, the Students' Union handbook listed a string of occupations, pickets and work-ins, campaigns against student costs, and a rent strike. Granted that student political activists have always been a minority, it is difficult to imagine such action at this point in the 21st century. When nationwide demonstrations took place during 2003 against the government's involvement in Iraq, there were no student protests on the Coventry campus. Rather than radicalism, social life, entertainment, and a place to meet became the priorities in the mid-1980s.

Left: *Graduating students, 2007.*

Below: *The Student Centre offers guidance and information on many aspects of student life including funding problems, careers, finance, course registration, and accommodation.*

'The Union and campus social life was anything but dreary 40 years ago. Life was buzzing – this was the time of the Arts Festivals when top 60s/70s bands like Aynsley Dunbar and Fairport Convention squashed into the Students' Union, and my friends who had gone to "posher" universities were very jealous of life in "Cov.", regularly coming to stay and joining in the fun. Every week there were discos, dances, and parties – some at the Union, some at the Art College, some at student houses or flats. There were Faculty-based dos, the best ones being the Law Socials and the Modern Studies. There was no shortage of dance partners or lifts home as the arrival of Year 1 of the Social Scientists seemed to have a significant social scientific effect on the campus itself, in that the demographic pattern was beginning to expand and include girls. Modern Studies was in its 2nd year, which was the only other one with significant numbers of female students. Looking back through the diary of that first term I am amazed that I even managed to complete Year 1!'

Chris Player (née Collins), Applied Social Sciences, 1972

In the late 1970s and early 1980s, Coventry, as described by Pete Chambers on page 137, became a centre for the UK music scene. The 'Lanch', and its Students' Union, became a byword for popular music. Students of the time look fondly back on the annual Music Festival and the major acts that were featured in the Students' Union gym of today, or in the Alan Berry Building, where the Goldstein Lecture Theatre is now. In 1985–6, more than 150 bands played at the Students' Union. Pilkington recalled that half of the Union's income went on underwriting the cost of gigs, but 60 per cent of the student population attended in a hall with a capacity of 1,600.

But now the Students' Union's position as a venue for pop music has eroded. The musical glory days have gone as larger venues in Birmingham and Coventry have become available and costs have spiralled. The big bands of today play at the Ricoh, not inside a university.

In turn, student life has evolved further. The fact that many students have outside commitments and interests means that the centre of student life is no longer the college

'Being the 1970s it was almost obligatory to be militant, and we had an all night sit-in in the facilities building – the reason for this escapes me now, but it must have been important at the time! I also remember my friend Marilyn and I supporting the workers at Triumph Meriden on their picket line to protest at the proposed closure and loss of jobs.'

Alison Holden, Applied Social Science 1974

'Are the students a less rebellious or anti-establishment lot than they were in the 70s and 80s, when I started here as a member of the mechanical set? In that time we were tasked to make clamps to fit to the outer doors from the inside when threatened with a takeover by students or a sit-in about grants or other social issues.'

John Collins, Technician, Estates Maintenance, joined 1965

bar, as it was 40 years ago. 'The Students' Union is no longer the focal point, in the way it used to be. It has had to adapt its role and purpose,' said Chris Smith, President of the Students' Union in 2006–7.

Social needs have changed in any case. Since student fees came into force, the young graduate is likely to leave with qualifications – and debt. This has meant a gradual change in the nature of the Students' Union. With students anxious to obtain their academic money's worth, often allied to obtaining experience which might be useful in the job market later on, loitering in the bar is less attractive. Tom Wood says 'while many student unions have declined over the last decade, Coventry has seen a significant increase in engagement from its members in other ways. More students are in societies, more students are getting involved in representation (for their halls and courses), and there is increased participation in student volunteering helping the local community. Interest in commercial enterprises may be less than it was back in the 1980s but our political, social, and cultural elements could not be stronger.'

Above: *Summer term in University Square.*

Far left: *Alison Holden's last day at 46 Kenilworth Road, 1974.*

'I just remember as soon as lectures finished, everyone would race out to have a cigarette. The lecturers would even smoke during the lesson back then.'

Kevin De La Noy, Communication Studies 1980–3,
Hollywood Film Producer

'The Tenpin Bowling Club represented the Lanch at a 12-hour marathon bowl over in Birmingham, where a number of other universities participated. I remember picking up a barrel of beer from the Student's Union in my Ford Anglia, getting to the bowling alley and setting it up behind our lane with a foot pump to pressurize it and a long spout out of which flowed the beer; you just wouldn't get away with that now! Needless to say, our performance did not place us in a position to gather an award!'

Trevor Theobald, Chemistry/Zoology, 1975

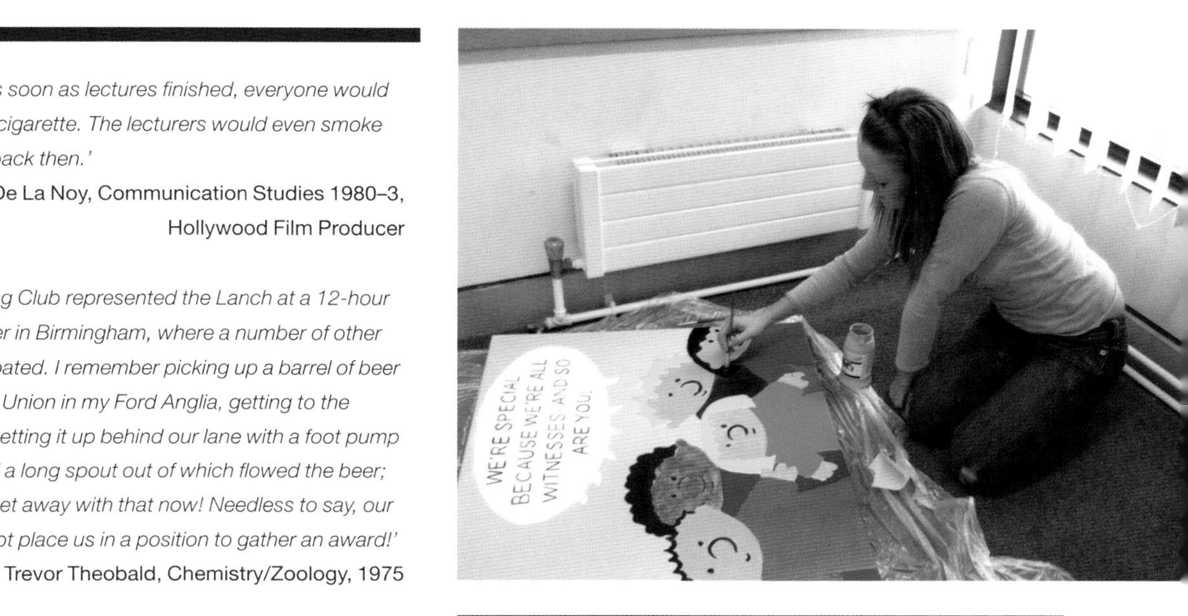

Above right: *HORIZON volunteering. The Horizon Personal Development Programme is offered by the Students' Union. It enables students to impact both the University and, through volunteering, the Coventry City community as a whole. Students gain new experiences, grow in confidence and take on leadership responsibilities.*

Representation now takes a number of different forms. For example, in a general sense, the Coventry Union has supported the National Union of Students in the campaign, which included a London march against education fees, and many of the SU representatives have gone on to become leading players in the NUS. For example, in 2006 alumnus Julian Nicholds was in his second term as NUS VP Welfare, Joe Rukin was NUS National Treasurer and Chair of NUS Services Ltd, and Georgina Toynbee and Laurice Harris were both NUS Regional Officers for the Midlands.

Yet, at the same time the Students' Union has run a scheme to help students avoid debt and, at a local level, has an advice centre to deal with individual problems. This centre handles some 50 enquiries a day, three-quarters of which are about accommodation, social security and academic concerns. Student problems with local landlords in 2006 led the Union to mount a campaign, supported by local newspapers, to make tenants aware of their rights. The advice centre is the only place on the campus licensed to give financial advice.

'One big difference that I noticed between the first time that I was there and the second was the lack of political activity on campus. The first time there was lots of activity. Moderate and extremist political groups seemed to be getting people to join. There were things like rent strikes going on. In 1985 some of us occupied B Block overnight in opposition to cuts in education. The security people were OK about it. Just asked us to clear up afterwards – which we did. This got a one-sentence mention in the Coventry Evening Telegraph. The second time though there was hardly anything. I was in one moderate political group. We had a couple of meetings. Then myself and the chairman decided to call it a day. We voted on it and wound it up. I did join the Anti Poll Tax Union. We were all meant to bring in our poll tax forms and ceremoniously burn them in a dustbin outside the Students' Union. I took mine along, fully intending to do that. However they were just quietly giving out photocopied forms for us to burn. So we just burned those instead. It got a brief mention on BBC Midlands Today.'

Gary Mark Stocker, Business and Finance 1985,
Engineering 1991

New Home: First Impressions

Sabine Kozdon arrived at Coventry University from Germany in October 1993. In an early assignment, she was asked to write, in English, her first impressions:

'When you arrive in a foreign country, you may have some preconceived ideas about what is good or bad. But when I arrived in Coventry, I soon realized that even those things you may consider to be ugly or unpleasant may have a certain attraction...

'I was quite happy to get a room in Priory Hall. You only had to get used to the frequent fire alarms at night. Of course this may be annoying, but on the other hand, you can be sure you are well-protected. In general the idiom "better to be safe than sorry" seems to hit the nail on the head: you are watched by video cameras and there are many security men everywhere. This may be due to the fact that the police are not armed so that you try to prevent crime in this more peaceful way.

'One of my next experiences was the English food, against which there are many prejudices. But the simple fact that the English are not starving proves that it cannot be that bad. Of course, English food has its particularities. The English breakfast, for example is well known, and chips, pies, and puddings (that resemble German cake) seem to be very common, while it is quite difficult to get some black bread, if you think you cannot live without it.

'Finally I would like to write about the notorious English weather. As far as I have experienced, it is no worse than in other European countries. And even the sun shines every day for 24 hours – only sometimes you cannot see it!'

Laura Haskins started at Coventry University in October 2007 and her poem 'One Room' led an edition of *Coventry Words*, which is used to make public the poems of BA English: Creative Writing students.

Quiet yet noisy
Scary, yet exciting
Clean yet messy
This is my room

Mine yet someone else's
Open yet closed
Spinning yet still
This is my room

Homely, yet far from home
Friendly yet lonely
Cosy yet cold
This is my room

So many feelings
So many noises
So many experiences
Trapped in one room

Above: *Coventry University is one of a select few in the UK to provide a dedicated facility for its postgraduate students. The Graduate and Continuing Professional Development (CPD) centre is designed specifically to meet the needs of postgraduate students, providing a pleasant environment in which to study.*

The Students' Union also plays a role within the community. It does this through Horizon Volunteering, which steers up to 500 students a year into community work ranging from tutoring in schools, to supporting asylum seekers, to charities active in helping people with mental health difficulties. This scheme has achieved national recognition – indeed one Coventry student, Chlöe Morton (Psychology 2008), received two major national awards in 2007 and was awarded the Cecil Angel Cup in 2008. These awards recognized her achievements as a University ambassador, student subject representative, and community volunteer. 'I have thoroughly enjoyed my time here; the University has given me all sorts of opportunities, which have led on to greater things', commented Chlöe. Her enthusiasm for the University's Horizon Volunteering programme led on to further voluntary work; as a listener for The Samaritans, as a mentor to young people for Workfirst, and as Head Supporter for a recovery-based self-harm support website, RecoverYourLife.com. 'The University always supported my volunteer work, and it gave me the confidence and encouragement to engage in other, very rewarding projects, where I was privileged to meet such a diverse range of good people.'

So, today the Students' Union is a complex operation, with its own officials and sabbatical officers elected by the student community. The 2008–9 President, Tom Wood, is in his second stint. He places great emphasis on trying to engage with students through clubs and societies – and through its own website, magazines (see opposite), and

Source Radio, broadcasting music and talk 24 hours a day. 'One of the largest ways we engage with our members is through our Societies, which have in total over 2,200 members getting involved in anything from International Disaster Concern to Snow Sports,' he said.

Lastly, and very significantly, there is the role of the Students' Union as a channel of communication between

Student Magazines

A magazine called *Elephant and Castle* was the student publication until 2000. The material in it might best be described as soft. This gave way to the new title, *Source*, which became a newspaper in 2002. The change brought with it a quantum leap in journalistic standards, with more news and more general information. The improvement might be expected to continue, given the range of media courses now available at the University.

'Whoever said school days are the best days of your life obviously didn't go to university! My university experience was and still is one that I will hold with me forever and always look back on with great pride and fond memories. I loved it and my time in Coventry was the best five years of my life. So much so, that upon graduating, completing my Sabbatical Officer experience and three years working in South London, I am now back in the city in my professional capacity, and witnessing another chapter in the remarkable story that is Coventry and Coventry University. Living and studying here was great. Not only did I gain my degree, I learned new skills that will last me a lifetime.

I first visited Coventry in March 1998 for an Open Day related to my chosen course of study. Living a two-hour drive away and having never been to the city before, the nature of a City Centre campus where you could walk to lectures and to the bars and shops from your first-year accommodation was instantly appealing. The Open Day was put together well, and being a keen sportsman and sports fan, I was attracted to the University by the course and the range of modules that covered sports policy, marketing, sports coaching, science, and finance. Priory Hall was the location of choice, and with a morning and evening meal provided Monday to Friday as part of the package, I was sold on coming to Coventry even though I was yet to experience standing out in the cold at 4am on numerous occasions, after the fire alarms had been set off following a good night out! Annoying as this was, it was all part of university life and only added to the incredible first year of my university experience.

During my time at Coventry University, the City Centre and the University itself underwent some massive changes. The Planet, our very own and much-loved Students' Union night club, was closed and subsequently reduced to rubble. It is now a car park! In its place a new Students' Union entertainment building was opened in addition to the main admin block on Priory Street.'

Tom Clift, Leisure Management 2001, Vice President Sports & Societies 2001–2, President CUSU, 2002–3

Above: *Graduation Day in University Square, July 2007.*

those attending the University and the University authorities. Student representatives are on all the major formal committees of the University. There is also a Pro-Vice-Chancellor, Donald Pennington, who has responsibility for the student experience.

Underneath the titular representation, there is for the University, an important point of policy. 'In an increasingly competitive higher education market, a vibrant Students' Union is a real asset to its university', Professor Madeleine Atkins, the Vice-Chancellor, wrote in the Union's 2005–6 annual report; 'The more active the Students' Union, the greater the level of student participation, the more rounded the student experience is likely to be.

'The Union's ability to give students a chance to try new things…is of enormous benefit. The Union's work in developing sports and societies means we can offer students more than just an academic experience at Coventry,' Professor Atkins added. There are, indeed, more than 80 societies in which students can participate.

University authorities and students can and do act as one on key practical and academic issues. A case in point is facilities. For the longer term, new accommodation for the Students' Union is integral to the University's campus development plan. While the University prioritized this itself, the proposals to bring the split facilities into one new building, tied in directly with what the Students' Union had been recommending. The planned building, the Student Enterprise Building, will bring under one roof all of the student services, some of which are mentioned above, together with faith and health centres, and extensive social space – 'soft space, bean bags, linked to café culture', as Chris Smith put it. Moreover, very deliberately, this building is set to be central to the campus, located on Jordan Well backing onto the Alan Berry and George Eliot Buildings, and next to the James Starley Building on Cox Street.

Another example of collaboration involves the academic regulations. Staff and students engaged in discussions which resulted in a reduction of the number of modules, from eight to six, which students would be expected to study each year. At the same time, the Coventry University Students' Union became the first union in the UK to offer part of an academic programme from its own services. Thus it is that volunteering in the community and working in the Union itself can contribute modules to a degree.

Obviously the level of influence that the Students' Union can exert within the University depends on the strength of its representatives. A self-elected cabal will be denied the

respect and attention afforded to genuine representatives, democratically elected. Further, students at grassroots need to know that they have a channel of communication to the officers of the Students' Union.

The Students' Union seeks to ensure grassroots engagement through a system of representatives elected by the students on each course, and in each of the halls of residence – 530 in 2005–6. Those elected receive training on how to handle queries and problems. The controlling body of the Students' Union is the Union Council – five students on sabbatical leave, working full-time, five part-time officers, and 13 elected officers.

The organization masks a fundamental and lasting truth, caught by Alan Richmond, Director of the Lanchester College of Technology, when he commented on the opening of the College Union building during 1965–6. It 'contributed more to the corporate life of the College than any other single happening over the five years of the College's existence'.

Performance and Participation

The biggest event in the Coventry University sporting calendar is Varsity Day. 'It is the one day of the year when all the teams compete on the same day, about 30 of them', explained Andy McMath, the Students' Union Vice-President for Sports and Societies during 2007–8. The event is classified as friendly, but it is the time when Coventry competes against its nearest rival, Warwick University.

Which university, in recent years, was the overall winner was never clear. Both claim victory, and the result depended on the weight given to one sport against another. Warwick was stronger in the traditional team games, Coventry in newer and more esoteric sports. This reflected the different student profiles of the respective universities.

Coventry, said McMath, an engineering student, has always been stronger in non-traditional sports, citing as an example the automotive engineers with driving aspirations who naturally veer towards go-karting or motor racing. Achievements in older sports on a national stage have been spasmodic: swimming, linked to the City of Coventry Swimming Club and the adjacency of a 50-metre pool in the early 2000s, boxing in the late 2000s.

Nevertheless, the University has had some real successes in recent years, both at an individual and team level, particularly since the arrival of Vince Mayne as Director of Sport. The successful sports scholarship scheme brings in around 30 sportsmen or women each year – all playing at an international representative level. The University provides funding towards their courses and sporting activities, and support from physiotherapists and trainers on fitness and

Above: *The new University Sports Centre, situated in the centre of the campus, is superbly equipped for a wide range of recreational and sporting activities.*

Left: *Westwood Heath astroturf pitch, opened in 2003.*

Left: *Neal Martin (holding stick) with staff and students. In 2004–5 he led Coventry Blaze to a domestic treble Grand Slam season. During each of his four seasons with the Blaze he was voted onto the Elite League all-star team.*

Below: *Returning alumni tackle students at the annual Alumni Sports Day held at Westwood Heath.*

'As a Sports Scholar the University's help allowed me to enter a large range of competitions across the country, and attend training camps that I couldn't otherwise have afforded. In my last year of University it allowed me access to strength and conditioning training with a qualified instructor and Sports Psychology support. I am currently using these techniques in my training towards the 2012 Olympics, and would like to thank the University for the difference their support has made.'

Colin Geenes, Sport and Exercise Science 2008,
Archery Sports Scholar 2005, 2007 and 2008

injuries. The sports that they come from are varied – from hockey and rugby to triathlon, road running, and rhythmic gymnastics. All will testify to the help that they received in their careers

The University also works closely with the major sports clubs in Coventry. For Coventry City FC, the University has provided the video and match footage on the big screen at the Ricoh Arena, with the filming being carried out by media and production students. Coventry Rugby Club has players at the University and uses the University's Westwood Heath sports complex for their training. The University supports the coaches at the City of Coventry Swimming Club, and has water time for swimmers of varying standards from international downwards.

In addition, the University has been a key partner for the highly successful Coventry Blaze ice hockey team since they moved to the city from Solihull in 2002. The relationship was established by David Morris, the then Dean of the Business School, when he was approached by two Canadian players in 2003 to see if they could supplement their playing commitments with study for undergraduate or Masters degrees. He set up a scheme whereby the School funded the cost of this study, thereby allowing the Blaze to offer a rather different package to overseas players. Since 2004, some 20 players have taken up this offer, benefiting both the Blaze and the University. The current squad has some eight players with close links to the University.

Hence the University has been able to contribute to three championships and four cups over the last four years, all of which has made ice hockey the second best supported sport in the city. The University has enjoyed the quality of the students who have come through – such as Neal Martin, a Canadian international, who was generally reckoned to be the best player in UK ice hockey. He did a three-year undergraduate degree and a one-year Masters – all of which enabled him to play for the Blaze for four successful years. And the partnership was illustrated by the awarding of an Honorary Degree in 2007 to Paul Thompson, the Blaze and UK team manager, for his work for ice hockey and the local community.

'I chose the sandwich degree programme at Coventry University because it gave me the opportunity to practise in the workplace what I had learned in the classroom. Setting up the Aspire Group was an opportunity to join with other like-minded people, and build on my experience in sport management. My career has always been about turnarounds and start-ups. At the University of Denver, I oversaw the transition of their athletic programme to Division One, which meant building $300m worth of facilities. With the Pittsburgh Pirates baseball team, I helped turn them round from losing $10m a year and drawing only 700,000 fans a year, to operating profits of $3m and a franchise record of 2.2m fans over their 81 home games.'

Bernie Mullin (Business Studies, 1972) is one of the Principals of the Aspire Group, a global marketing and management consultancy focusing on the sport, entertainment and media sectors in America.

In all these ways, the University has used sport and performance to raise student standards and to enrich the life of the University.

The players testify to the international diversity of Coventry students. In basketball, played worldwide, there were 10 different nationalities in the Coventry team. A substantial part of the cricket team was made up of Indians and Bangladeshis, not surprisingly, given the importance of the subcontinent in the international game.

For all that, sport as such is a minority pastime at Coventry. Student fees have forced a change over the last five years, McMath observed. 'Students come here to learn, and because they have paid so much money, they can't afford not to.' The sports clubs have about 1,000 members, but the University's Sports Centre has around 4,500, he noted.

Rob Wells, the Students' Union Sports and Societies Development Manager, made another point. 'Women don't take part in sport any more, but they do take part in exercise.' While some female students would challenge this assertion, it does lead to a debate about resources – what is needed where, and for what purpose.

Above: *Westwood Heath cricket facilities include nets purchased thanks to support from Awards for All, who distribute funds raised from the National Lottery.*

The argument is about performance, in sports, and participation, in exercise. It is a question of whether the resources should be made available so that everybody becomes involved, or whether they should be focused on sports performance and the provision, for example, of sports scholarships. The trend has been towards participation combined with scholarships for elite sportsmen and women.

The most obvious signal of this direction was the opening in 2004 of a new Sports Centre with full physiotherapy facilities. The Sports Centre had two extra benefits: its activities could be tied in with academic studies in health, and it is open to the public, thus adding another stitch to the fabric of the University's relations with the city.

It also acts as a base – albeit already requiring expansion – for all the sports, exercise and 'wellness' programmes offered by the University. Newest among these is the Centre for the International Business of Sport (CIBS) headed by the high-profile sports academic, Professor Simon Chadwick. Already Chadwick has greatly enhanced the University's reputation in this field, attracted a major international conference ('Play the Game') in 2009, and achieved extensive coverage on subjects as varied as the Olympics, sport in recession, David Beckham, and Lewis Hamilton.

A Sound Place to Learn:
A Musical Memoir

PETE CHAMBERS

Long before it was called Coventry University, it was the 'Lanch'. A magical place which had more than a little influence on my musical tastes. Every weekend it was the venue of choice for the teenager who liked his music heavy, and his dancing of the 'freak out' variety.

I came in the early 1970s, a decade famous for the Lanchester Festivals, a time when Coventry could command a plethora of top names, including Slade, Pink Floyd, Chuck Berry, Fairport Convention, the Move, Family, and even Elton John.

As a teenager the Lanch was my fountain of knowledge as far as rock music was concerned. Be it watching bands, talking about them, or even buying records from the cut-price vinyl stand in the Union bar. I can still recall many of the bands I witnessed down in the bowels of the Students' Union building: the blues-rock of the mighty Groundhogs, the mellow viola-sound of Caravan, not forgetting ELO's classical rock fusion, and the out and out rock of Thin Lizzy.

The Lanch Festival came to major prominence on the night of 3 February 1972 when Chuck Berry came on stage and recorded his only number one single, 'My Ding-A-Ling'. The concert was indeed part of The Lanch Music Festival, but the main acts that night, Pink Floyd and Berry, used the higher capacity Locarno for the shows, not the Students' Union hall (as often mooted).

By the mid-1970s, the backlash of progressive rock had begun, and the glitz of glam rock was transforming into something much more problematic. Punk rock was about to write the next anarchic chapter of popular music. Lanchester Poly played host to The Sex Pistols and The Clash on 26 November 1976. This was just 48 hours before Bill Grundy's infamous 'Say something outrageous' interview that ruined one career and helped to create another.

Below: *The Specials perform at the Lanch Festival, September 1980, and are joined by audience member Suggs (lead singer of Madness), shown here in the first picture.*

Punk rock had yet to reach critical mass, and it remained for at least a few hours or so just wacky column inches inside the pages of the dailies. Just 48 hours later though, on 2 December, 'The Filth and The Fury' headlines would kick in, and popular music would never be the same again. Musically, the night was brilliant; sadly the night

Top left: *The Specials, with Terry Hall on lead vocals, perform at height of their fame in 1980.*

Above: *Poster memorabilia from iconic Coventry music events.*

Left: *Established in 1998, the annual Godiva free summer festival attracts over 70,000 visitors to a 30-acre site in Coventry's War memorial Park for three days of music and family oriented events.*

Right: *Coventry music guru Pete Waterman is the proud recipient of an Honorary Degree from the University (2001).*

Bottom right: *Panjabi MC performs regularly at the University.*

would end in a stand-off, between the bands and a National Union of Students treasurer, who had refused to pay them, mistaking them for fascists, rather than misguided swastika-wearing pseudo-anarchists.

Coventry's finest, The Specials, owe their very creation to the Lanch. Had students Jerry Dammers and Horace Panter not met at Coventry University, we can only assume The Specials would have been a different band altogether, if they had happened at all. Happen of course they did, and the Specials-Coventry University relationship continued, be it through signing their record contract in the Lanch bar, or filming the video for 'Rat Race' in the Main Hall.

I also had the pleasure of seeing them play the Main Hall in September 1980. I witnessed a band at the very peak of its career, the ska-punk fusion never sounded so good, and the gig was a perfect homecoming from a band which had its finger on the musical pulse of a nation. Because of all this, 2008 saw the University becoming number one on The Two-Tone Trail.

Fast-forward a quarter of a century, and forward-thinking Coventry University awarded honorary degrees to Coventry music guru Pete Waterman and Two-Tone creator Jerry Dammers. I never had the pleasure of a conventional Coventry University education myself, but I guess I probably learnt more about music at Coventry University than anywhere else. I can't wait for next term!

'Music was a huge feature of student life. I remember happy days listening to Caravan "In the Land of Grey and Pink", and falling asleep to Mike Oldfield's "Tubular Bells" – LPs of course, no CDs then. We saw many great bands on site including ELO, Thin Lizzy, Chuck Berry, and Roxy Music. The latter dined in the same Chinese restaurant as my friends and I before the concert – seeing Bryan Ferry caused so much excitement we could hardly hold our chopsticks!'

Alison Holden, Applied Social Science 1974

The International Spread:
Defining the Dimensions

Throughout its history, particularly in the last 20 years, the city of Coventry has always been international in outlook. Coventry University has shared this appreciation of the value of international engagement. It was quick to identify the growing educational needs in many developing countries, and to offer a significant portfolio of activities including both recruitment to the campus, and in-country delivery. Coventry, indeed, has one of the most highly diverse student communities of any UK university, with significant numbers of students from all parts of Asia, Europe, and Africa. Students are increasingly drawn to study at the University, while, at the same time, the University is placing greater emphasis on ensuring that its outlook and academic programmes are global in nature. From the earliest days, the institution has seen itself as a community institution; in the 21st century the definition of community has changed from local to global.

In many senses, this positioning fits very comfortably with the multicultural community in which the University sits. Students from India or China find a substantial local population sharing their ethnic origins. The University itself reflects the diversity of the student base. While not a religious foundation, the University is committed to tolerance of all faiths, drawing on the humanist principles of the Cathedral to promote academic study on peace and reconciliation, social justice, and civil society. The University's Spirituality and Faith Centre, headed up by Reverend Jennifer Croft, seeks to serve and support all religions, including Islam.

So, towards the end of the century's first decade, the number of overseas students has more than doubled to around 2,000 from just over 900 in 1998–9, a rate of increase which substantially exceeded the targets laid down in the 2006 corporate plan. Indeed, David Gillingham, the Pro-Vice-Chancellor for Research, International and Commercial Affairs from 2000 to 2008, noted that the University had been one of the most successful recruiters of international students, in the top 25 per cent of British universities.

The number of students arriving in Coventry, however, gives only part of the international picture. As the map on page 142 shows, students are drawn from nearly 100 countries, and in engineering, for example, there are more students studying Coventry courses abroad than there are within the UK University.

Below and opposite: *One World Week – a week-long celebration of the unique nationalities, cultures, and interests that exist on campus.*

'The UK-India Education and Research Initiative (UKIERI) began in 2006, and has now committed all of its £24m funding on HE, FE and Schools. In the HE sector there are 102 research projects running, and 26 Collaborative Delivery projects. Our work provides the chance to benchmark approaches to learning and quality assurance with institutions in India, strengthening the international academic network and growing reputation in a new and vibrant market. UKIERI has accelerated the UK's educational links with India, and it has been great to see Coventry taking such a leading and supportive role in collaborative delivery through establishing three projects.'

Mike Thornton, UKIERI Operations Manager

This growth builds on a long history. During the mid-1980s, when Geoffrey Holroyde was still Director of the Polytechnic, formal academic links existed with colleges and universities in China, France, Germany, Poland, and the US. This was unusual for a university at that time. In one of the noteworthy foreign initiatives, during the early 1990s, under Michael Goldstein, the Polytechnic provided training for more than 550 managers from the Soviet Union. Professor Morris recalls that KGB permission had to be sought for clearance for these Soviet would-be students. This permission was received on the very same day that an agreement, to support a course on Women and Work, was confirmed by the Equal Opportunities Commission! And similar programmes exist today, with the initiatives led by Ian Dunn, Associate Dean in the Faculty of Engineering and Computing, bringing onto engineering programmes more than 500 students each year from France, Poland, and other parts of Eastern Europe.

The University has recently developed its vision for internationalization, aiming to move from being a university with many international students to becoming a truly international university. It follows from this that the international dimension of the University's work is expanding across faculties, departments, and research centres. It involves the specification of international criteria in the recruitment of academic staff. It takes in a programme of exchanges with foreign universities, not only for students but also for staff; the closer the partnership arrangements with other universities, the greater the opportunities for students from those institutions to come to study in Coventry. It also involves ample opportunity for the international students to gain practical experience through the University's close links with industry.

In a wider sense, embracing the global dimension means a commitment to internationalize the curriculum. Case studies involving interesting scenarios outside the UK, reading lists, materials used in teaching, and opportunities for students to learn in a global peer group with partner universities, all reflect this trend. A key part of this involves the use of modern communications technology – from dedicated video conferencing to more personalized desktop approaches – to support interactions.

Right: *International links continue after graduation for Coventry Alumni. Coventry representatives are pictured here with the Friends of Coventry University Malaysian Committee at the Kuala Lumpur dinner for over 130 ex students which was organised by the alumni themselves in 2006.*

The same dynamic is at work in applied research, where an already extensive portfolio of projects can be developed and diversified, enhancing the University's international reputation. The partnership between ZUMC in Hangzhou – one of China's leading media and production centres – and Coventry's School of Art and Design is just one such example; student numbers and staff exchanges have grown apace, and the University now has a Chinese office at ZUMC, staffed by Chinese alumni from Coventry. This was opened in October 2008 by Professor Atkins, at a ceremony that coincided with the 30th anniversary of ZUMC. In addition, the research agenda is developing rapidly, for example, through the use of split-site PhDs, and (from 2009) Coventry University Anniversary Scholarships, designed to support research involving key issues about, or relevant to, China.

Clearly, there are many benefits to be gained from this international engagement. It brings opportunities to learn from colleagues overseas; it enhances the student experience through an enriched curriculum and provides opportunities to travel and study in another country; it brings in revenue and it raises Coventry's profile, so that more people recognize the transformation that is underway in a university at the forefront of changes in UK higher education.

Below: *Coventry University's internationalism can be illustrated by highlighting the nationality of our students on a map and marking the locations of our overseas initiatives and partnerships.*

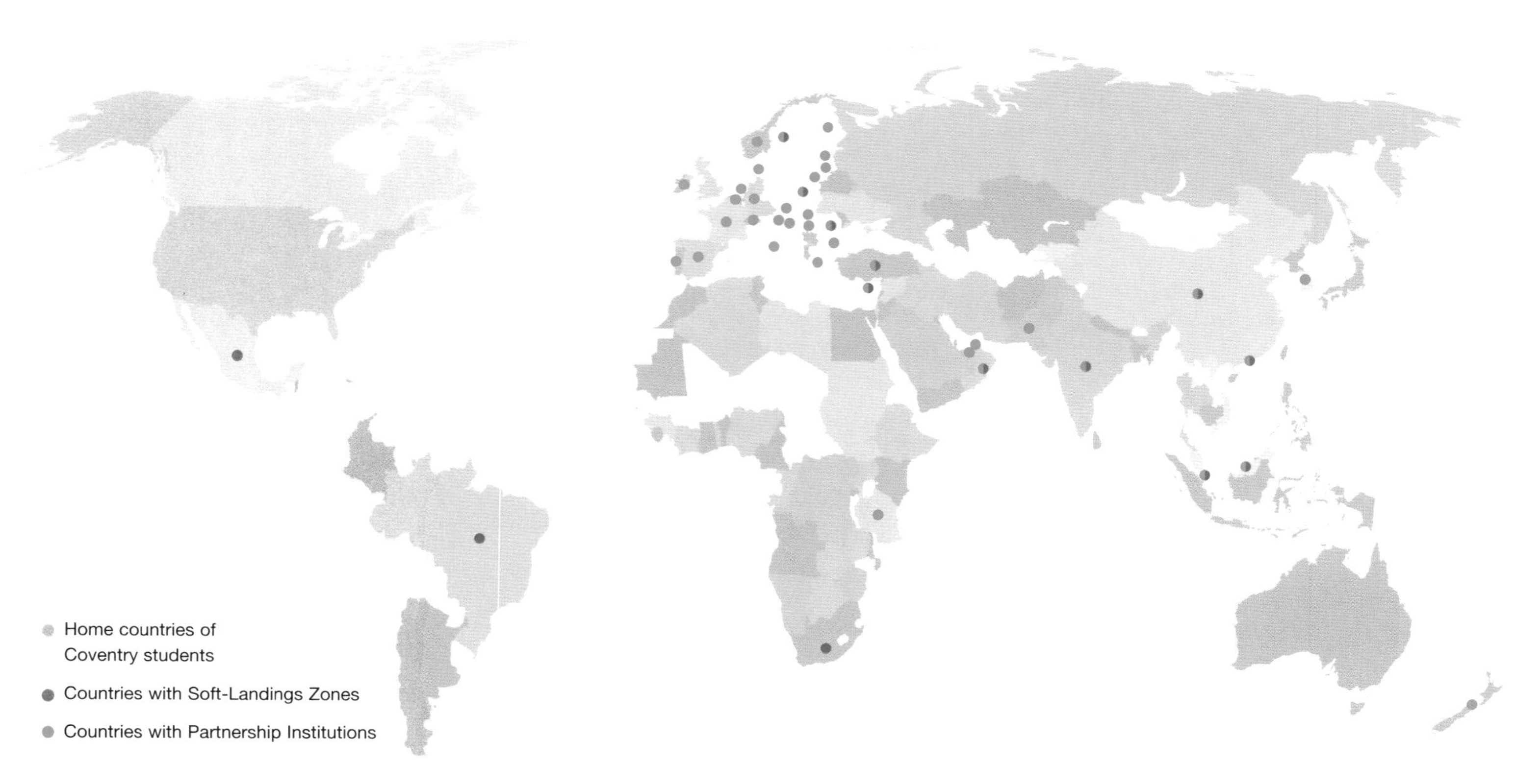

Students from Around the World

With rising numbers of overseas students on the campus, the University's aim is to foster the sense of a global community, ensuring that all students 'get a taste' of many parts of the world by coming to Coventry. The University seeks to support more interaction between students from different regions, in order to best prepare them for the global world of work, and for their role as global citizens. The University does not want cultural or linguistic barriers to interaction: it wants the domestic experience to enrich the international experience, and for the overseas students to bring a leavening of their culture to the home students. A recent Masters student, Craig Stokes (MSc Finance, 2008) is typical. He recalled that, out of 18, he was the only UK student on his course, but that he found the interaction of the nationalities immensely rewarding: 'I have been travelling in Australasia and the Far East since I graduated, and I found that my experiences at Coventry gave me the confidence to live and work in other communities, quite apart from the opportunity of meeting up with friends from my course across the world.'

Clubs and societies that make students feel at home also flourish – for example, the Chinese Society that organizes celebrations for the Chinese New Year. And, although the University conducts its business in English, for several years the University has been providing English programmes for these international students. Since September 2008, the University has provided students with the opportunity to enhance their English through a joint venture with Cambridge Education Group. This offers on-campus foundation courses with an emphasis on the English language, as well as pre- and on-course English tuition programmes for undergraduate and Masters students.

Coventry offers very good value to its international students and works hard to help them address the financial challenges they may face through scholarships and other financial support. For example:

- The University is linked to the EU's Erasmus and Leonardo programmes, which support a number of European students to study at Coventry each year.
- Funding is also supplied by external benefactors – international companies, local HE institutions, and individuals. The most prominent of these is an alumni of the Lanchester, Dr Majid Alsadi, an Iraqi businessman who is based in Jordan (see page 147).

Above: *Students' Union Summer Ball, 2007.*

But there are other factors that influence the choice of Coventry as a destination for international students. Christopher Gitsham, the manager of the University's International Office, listed four.

First is the level of fees, which can vary markedly from one university to another. Coventry tries to be competitive in its sector. That is to say, it does not compete with the older universities, but it does with other former polytechnics.

Second is the cost of living. Here, Coventry is at an advantage, especially when compared with institutions in southern England. Accommodation, for example, is considerably cheaper than in London. Third, students have a concern about safety. Once again, Coventry is well placed, being the UK's fourth safest city in 2007.

Last, students look at the profile of the courses offered by the University. Coventry's strong emphasis on the business world is attractive; the knowledge that former Coventry students have risen to senior positions in many industries is a telling advertisement.

From the University's point of view, diversity not only brings vitality to the student mix, but also financial stability. Reflecting on two previous downturns in the overseas market in Asia, Professor Gillingham observed that 'demand [from a particular country] can switch on and off in reaction to outside events. The Asian financial crisis of 1997–8 meant a drop in applications from that part of the world.' By taking students from many different parts of the globe, such risks are mitigated.

Coventry strengthens its position by its network of partnerships with universities overseas. This enables courses to be offered in partnering universities which spread the study across institutions: two years at the home university with one year at Coventry, or two years at Coventry and one year at an international institution, or another combination.

Coventry University courses provide sound grounding in mainline disciplines such as business and engineering and also have an international reputation in select areas. Automotive Design is arguably the best in the world, and this has fed into the respect obtained for more general product design. The Serious Games Institute is regarded as an innovative approach to a phenomenon of 21st century industry. The Centre for Peace and Reconciliation remains a world-class centre of excellence, and draws students from many countries, supported by the scholarship programme generously funded by the Ferguson Trust (see page 117). Again, it is clear how both students and the University have benefited. The Peace and Reconciliation groups contribute much – both to the success of the programme and, on graduation international students who take up important and influential roles in their home countries. Professor Hunter, the Director of the programme, explains:

> *'Every week we are made tragically aware of the consequences of violent conflict, which can so easily devastate individuals and communities. Peace is a bedrock of a fruitful human existence, as important as food or water. Coventry and its University rightly pride themselves on at least making the effort to understand peace and reconciliation, and to support those brave people who try to protect victims and transform conflicts. Many students and staff who pass through the institution contribute in important ways to the broad agenda of education, innovation, and social values which are embodied here.'*

Peace and Reconciliation Studies

'The course really was a fun and challenging adventure. It not only showed me the urgency to develop, but gave me a way as well. The course was more of a journey and experience than it was a course. It not only gave me knowledge, but skills and a better understanding of the world we live in. The rich experience of my fellow colleagues as well brought the world to me, and the extraordinary environment you put us in perhaps made it more beneficial than travelling to each of those countries. The fact that the course linked between information, tools, and skills relevant to our field, such as conflict resolution methods and project management for NGOs, has made a substantial difference in what I am now giving back to my country through the organization I work in, and in my struggle for peace. A big part of my work now is addressing audiences of the opposite side, and reflecting my position on very sensitive political issues. With the provocative reactions I often get, I would have had a destructive reaction myself had I not gone through the course and understood the meaning and feeling of inner and outer peace.'

Hitham Kayali, Peace and Reconciliation Studies, 2006,
Works in London and Jerusalem for an
Israeli-Palestinian peace movement

'Coming from Uganda, that has experienced violence and war, and having been one of the founders of Peace Studies at Makerere University, I needed to reflect more deeply about the content, skills, and methods our programme was following. The MA course in Peace and Reconciliation Studies at Coventry University has provided me with a broader picture of peace studies and peace education. The course has enabled me to understand the root causes of conflict, and provided me with the necessary skills of nonviolence, forgiveness, and reconciliation. I have sharpened my own attitudes by looking at history and life events more positively and constructively. The international and multicultural atmosphere at Coventry University and on the course has also helped to open up my horizons through interacting and learning from fellow students. I have made new friends and, in the process, discovered that peace building is about building human relationships. My qualification, experience, knowledge, and skills acquired are going to help me to develop a nonviolence, forgiveness and reconciliation programme in my country when I return. I will remain an active advocate and trainer in conflict resolution and peace education. I am also working with a team to set up the East African Institute of Governance and Conflict Management (EAIGCM), to provide a forum for further research and training in this field. I am therefore looking forward for further collaboration with the Centre for Peace and Reconciliation Studies and with Coventry University.'

Deusdedit Nkurunziza,
Peace and Reconciliation Studies, 2008

'My experience on the course was beyond expectation, and I am confident that the skills I have acquired will make a big difference in my contribution to peace building in Sub-Saharan Africa. A special feature of this year was the opportunity to meet people and make friends with colleagues from all over the world, especially those people who have some similar experiences and aspirations as myself. It would have been impossible for me to broaden my horizons in this way without attending this programme in the UK. I hope that more people will have this sort of opportunity, and will myself work to support talent in peace, reconciliation, and development in a similar way at every stage of my career. I now hope to promote better prospects for social justice in my country.'

James Kiven,
Peace and Reconciliation Studies, 2008

'I feel privileged to have spent my time in Coventry, where understanding the conflict and peace-building approaches are the most important aspect of the course. I have been encouraged to constantly rethink, question, and analyse my assumptions about conflict and peace issues more broadly. The course not only gave me new skills and knowledge but also delivered excellent practical understanding, and broader insights that equipped me to think creatively, work strategically, and correspond effectively. I feel full of energy and confident to contribute in conflict transformation and peace-building issues in the days to come at home in Nepal or elsewhere in the world.'

Netra Kaphle,
Peace and Reconciliation Studies 2008

Numerically, the two faculties at Coventry most favoured by international students have been Business, Environment and Society; and Engineering and Computing. Andy Nicol, the Director of the International Office, has noticed that Chinese students have a leaning towards business studies, while Indian students tend towards a mix of business and engineering. Students from North Africa and the Middle East have often gravitated to engineering and computing, with postgraduates steering towards management.

To support the international students, the University has set up a one-stop administrative and welfare facility in a dedicated Student Centre. This starts to work for the students as soon as they send in an application.

The applications come by any conceivable form of communication: email, fax, post, or a friend's rucksack. The first task is to respond quickly and appropriately, and to make direct contact with the applicant. The University aims to complete this preliminary work in two days, and, after contact with the relevant academic departments, produce a letter of acceptance or rejection in five days.

'Having the opportunity to study at Coventry taught me you can achieve anything in life if you have the determination. I wanted to further my studies so I could help other under privileged women set up in business. I have taught families at work and in church about starting their own income-generating projects and businesses, teaching them finance and management skills with a special emphasis on investing for the future. My MBA has given me confidence in myself and in the work I am doing. I have bought myself a house, built my mother a three-bedroom house, and also bought two new cars – all before I was married. I was empowered by my MBA – African society needs more empowered women so they can make a difference. Education is the key to success.'

Nonsikelelo Nkambule (MBA, 1998) is from Swaziland and is a Finance and Administration Manager for a children's charity

The University also has a team of skilled international officers who visit countries across the world to speak to, and counsel, students interested in coming to Coventry. These officers attend recruitment fairs; they work through embassies, schools, and colleges; they work with local, trained recruitment representatives.

Staff in the Student Centre also work hard to familiarize overseas students with life in the UK. The Centre stages a special 'welcome week' and, each weekend, organizes cost-price visits to social, cultural, and sporting events ranging from the London theatres and galleries to football matches at Manchester United.

In all these ways, the University seeks to attract international students from across the world, and to make their experience at Coventry happy and rewarding. This provides a solid base on which to build for David Pilsbury, who took over as Pro-Vice-Chancellor (International) in 2008. He has an ambitious growth programme. He

Above: *Students cutting patterns in the Fashion Studio within the Graham Sutherland Building (M Block).*

Making a Difference

Dr Majid Alsadi (Mechanical Engineering) is from Iraq and is a business entrepreneur who has developed a multi-million pound investment group called Eastern Holdings. He is a Patron of the new Engineering & Computing Faculty, has donated flight simulators to the Aerospace Laboratory, and also funds the Majid Alsadi Scholarship Foundation, which supports a dozen students every year. He lives in Jordan and is part of the Basra Development Commission helping to redevelop southern Iraq.

Dr Alsadi says, 'Everyone needs a start and Coventry was the place for me – it's where I discovered myself. I set up a market stall to fund my studies, and learnt a lot about business in the process. That's why I set up the Majid Alsadi Foundation to support gifted students from all over the world so they can enjoy MBA courses at Coventry that will change their lives. My business started when I used my engineering knowledge to develop a water pump that would not corrode. I made over $40m in the first two years of selling the product all over the Middle East. Since then my business has grown into Eastern Holdings and incorporates flight services, security services, and flight training centres, among other research and development projects.'

Right: *Dr Majid Alsadi with Professor Atkins opening the flight simulators in the Alma Building, December 2007.*

Below: *Students in the Aerospace Laboratory.*

explains: 'My vision is for Coventry to be the leading "internationalized" modern university in the UK, recognized by our commitment to international approaches to create value for individuals and for the University, and to have an international agenda that is embedded in all our operations.' Furthermore, Dr Pilsbury believes that 'While we are looking at a significant change overall, this is made up of a number of actions that are achievable, hence I am confident of success'. Dr Pilsbury concludes:

'Talking to today's international students, and our most committed Faculties clearly shows that the growth in international business that the University has achieved is not coincidental – there is a passion for this agenda that goes right back to the foundation of the University, and to the city's history and heritage.'

Marketing and Profile-Building

NICK STOKES, DIRECTOR OF MARKETING AND COMMUNICATIONS

Coventry University has always played a prominent role in the local community. As this book shows, in many ways this role has been a reflection of the success or otherwise of Coventry. As Coventry prospered, the University shared in the city's success. Indeed, at times, the University's profile became not just national but international.

The University has always been at the forefront of automotive design, for example, and in Coventry's heyday in automotive manufacturing in the second part of the 20th century, the Lanch was able to build on that reputation by becoming one of the leading polytechnics in the UK. Many Lanchester alumni will tell you that they chose the Lanch for that reason.

At the same time, the Lanch also became famous in other ways. As Pete Chambers has shown, it had a deserved reputation for popular music in the 1970s, through the Music Festivals, and as a showcase venue for the leading bands. This culminated in the Two-Tone phenomenon in the early 1980s, led by the Specials, when Coventry was truly the centre for popular music at the time.

However, as the city fell into decline in the 1990s, the University became, once again, much more of a local and regional University, priding itself on providing higher education opportunities to the local community. The University's profile and reputation, like the city's, fell back. Yet many of the factors that had made Coventry a successful polytechnic remained.

So, when Professor Madeleine Atkins took over as Vice-Chancellor in 2004, the building blocks to rebuild the University's national and international reputation were still in place. What was needed was a clear strategy and focus, which Professor Atkins provided, and a commitment to raise the University's profile through marketing, advertising, and PR, developing a consistent and common message across the University. The individual Faculties and Schools no longer had to stand on their own but could benefit from the University's growing reputation as an innovative, creative, and entrepreneurial University, with a particular focus on business.

The University takes pride in the changes and the progress that has resulted. Indeed, the publication of this book is just one example of that pride. The University, through buildings and directional signage, now has a distinct campus in the City Centre. People now know where Coventry University is. As the campus developments and new buildings programme gathers pace, the 'University Quarter' will become an increasingly distinct and lively part of the city, while remaining a place for communities in the

Below: *Profile-raising campaign 2006–7.*

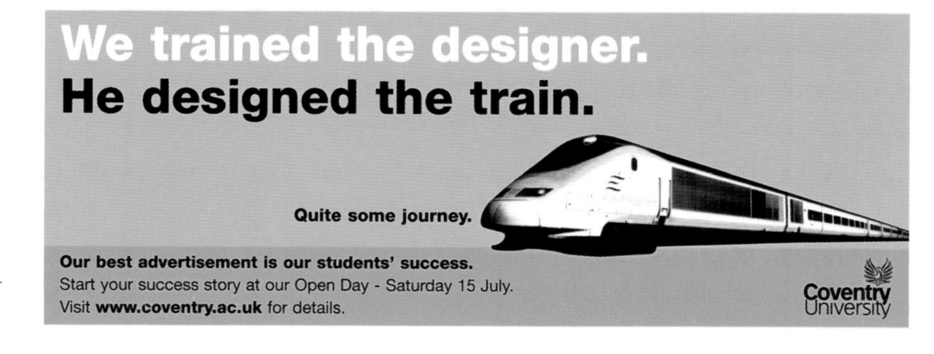

Above: *Cover of Undergraduate Prospectus, 2010.*

Bottom right: *Selection of clearing and recruitment advertisements, 2008–9.*

city and not just the students. Hence the new entertainment space in the Student Enterprise Building, on the corner of University Square, will not only add to the attraction of the University but be a venue for all the city.

More importantly, the University has gone out deliberately to tell its regional, national, and international audiences what sort of University it is, and why prospective students should choose Coventry. The highly successful 'Train the Trainer' campaign, that was developed in-house in the University's own design studio (largely staffed by Coventry alumni) provided evidence of the successes of Coventry graduates in an impactful and visually catching way, which served to change perceptions.

More recently, the innovative but controversial 'camper van' undergraduate campaign for 2008 entry played a significant role in the increase in student applications and enrolment, which occurred despite UCAS reducing the number of student choices from six to five universities per applicant. The International Office, likewise, has been successful in generating higher student numbers through profile-raising, and partnerships based upon the strengths that Coventry can offer.

Coventry University, today, takes pride in a deserved and growing reputation fuelled, in part, by this activity, and by a PR programme that now ensures that Coventry regularly achieves over 400 media cuttings per month across national and regional media. Indeed, in November 2008, Coventry was the only UK university shortlisted for three awards at the prestigious Times Higher HE awards ceremony in London. The University won the award for 'Outstanding Contribution to Leadership Development', and was 'Highly Commended' as 'Entrepreneurial University of the Year' from 34 submissions.

Such accolades demonstrate the growing reputation of the University. They also enable the University to play a key role in raising, in turn, the reputation of the city. As John McGuigan has explained (page 92), the University now participates in city developments and promotion through close working relationships with the City Council's Development and Planning teams, with CVOne (the City Centre's management company), and through active membership of the Image Working Group and other city organizations and businesses.

Coventry University is committed to developing these partnerships further. The University believes that Coventry has, again, been reborn in the 21st century and that it has played a key role in this rebirth. The University's development and building plans, and the profile they will generate, will help to sustain and grow this regeneration into 2010 and beyond.

transforminginventing**building** *futures*
expandingfashioning**changing** *futures*
nurturingdevelopingenhancing *futures*
designing**constructingshaping** *futures*
your *future*

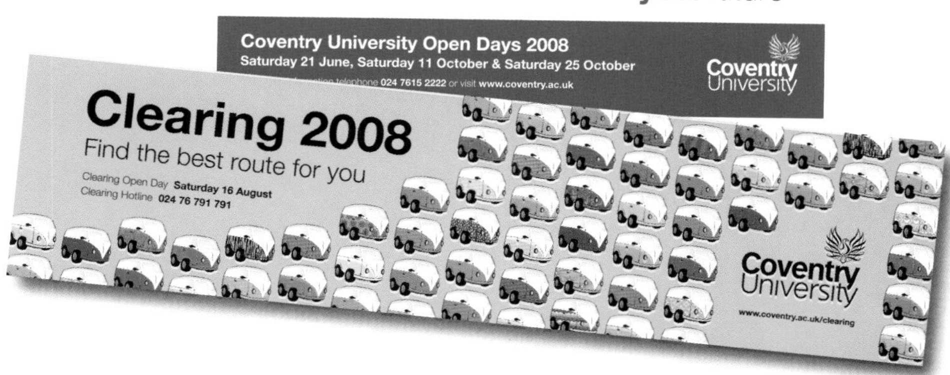

6 THE FUTURE

Innovation and Evolution:
Building the Future

Coventry University's commitment to innovation and evolution continues. In 2008 the University embarked on an ambitious redevelopment of its campus with a first phase costing £160m. The 'masterplan' was, from the outset, devised with a view to providing students with the very latest in teaching and learning facilities combined with open, communal spaces for relaxing, socializing, studying, and showcasing the University's talents in art and cultural enterprise.

The shape of the new campus emerged as a result of feedback from students, staff, and business partners; students clearly expressed a desire for a campus reflecting the innovative approach to teaching and learning firmly established at Coventry. Two iconic buildings set the tone for the development as a whole, which will span the next decade and beyond.

The first, to be built by Balfour Beatty and due to be opened in 2011 beside the University's library, is the new home for the Faculty of Engineering and Computing and has been designed by Arup Associates. The building, which features two 'arms' representing Science and Nature, will be highly sustainable, harnessing the latest in solar energy conversion technology in its skin. State-of-the-art lecture theatres, meeting rooms, labs, and a café maximize the use of natural daylight, providing an ideal environment for study. The Faculty has taken it as an opportunity and catalyst to reshape its approach to teaching and learning, incorporating conclusions from a study of best practice from across the world.

Previous pages and left: *The new Student Enterprise Building designed by architects Hawkins\Brown as seen from University Square (previous pages) and opposite the George Eliot Building (B Block) (left).*

Below left: *The pedestrain entrance to the proposed multi-storey car park, situated next to the Lanchester library.*

Opposite: *The new Engineering and Computing Faculty Building which is being constructed on the site of the old Gulson Road Hospital beside the Lanchester Library. Architects, Arup Associates, have created a building with two 'arms' one of which features a large roof garden.*

The second, the Student Enterprise Building designed by Hawkins\Brown and built by Laing O'Rourke opens in 2010. It has been conceived as the new heart of the University, providing first-class facilities for students and a new home for the Students' Union. Features designed into the building include all the main support services such as careers, medical facilities, faith centre, space for students to sit and work informally on their own or in groups, shops, bars, and cafés as well as an entertainments venue and creative space for students. A strikingly original aspect of the design is a roof garden – offering a haven of tranquillity in the heart of the city. Green roofs are very much a feature of the city's plans for its new landscape, so it seems fitting that the University reflects that theme.

As well as new builds, the coming years will see adaptation and refurbishment of most of the current estate to address both the 'green' agenda – measures to reduce carbon emissions – and to provide a 'smarter' environment for students, staff and visitors.

Integral to the plan from an early stage was the pedestrianization of much of the area inside the campus, creating a safer, more attractive site. Lighting, public artworks, seating, and landscaping are key elements in the masterplan, providing a first-class campus for our staff and students.

Hand-in-Hand with the City

The City of Coventry – like the University – embraces the themes of reinvention and innovation. The University's buildings are as much a part of the city landscape as the distinctive Cathedral spires. To complement the University's plans for a state-of-the-art new campus, the city responded by unveiling a £5bn blueprint for a new City Centre, including green parks and open spaces, a waterway following the path of the River Sherbourne through the middle of a new shopping quarter, with a new library at the heart of the groundbreaking design.

The new plans continue to embrace the city's rich history by showcasing its medieval heritage, tastefully combining the old with the new. A walk through Coventry's pedestrianized City Centre already offers over 1,000 years of England's history, ranging from the medieval charm of historic Spon Street to the architectural innovation of Millennium Place.

The Way Forward

The University is moving into a new era. As new surroundings come on stream, the University is also planning its objectives for 2015 and beyond. One element which will remain firmly on the agenda for the future is Professor Atkins' determination to strengthen applied research activity, solving real-world problems. Great emphasis is placed on the ability to transfer research expertise to external organizations to create innovative ways of working or to deliver economic, commercial, environmental, cultural, or social benefits.

The range of research activity undertaken continues to span every subject area. Ranging from art, health and sports, to human security, engineering, computing, and communications, University expertise is applied to tackle simple or complex problems for partners in the private, public, and voluntary sectors.

Many of these collaborations spring from the growing number of Applied Research Centres and Groups which undertake specialist or interdisciplinary research and consultancy.

In addition, a number of research institutes have been established, based at the University's Technology Park: the Futures Institute, the Serious Games Institute, the Health Design and Technology Institute, the Institute for Creative Enterprise along with the latest addition, the Institute of Applied Entrepreneurship. These Institutes provide a unique environment for applied research; normally they incorporate Applied Research Groups and Centres, research equipment and facilities for businesses to use, incubation and

Below: *A depiction of a classroom within the new Engineering and Computing Building as designed by architects Arup Associates. The projected faculty building is designed to offer new pedagogic opportunities with greater emphasis on practical based learning and will transform the experience of studying for future students.*

Left: *A courtyard view of the new Engineering and Computing Faculty Building, designed by Arup Associates.*

Below: *Successful graduates!*

commercial accommodation, communal social spaces, and training facilities. The aim of each Institute is to create an environment which supports a unique combination of business-facing activity and academic research. Coventry University's Institutes are often the subject of best-practice assessment by other universities. This reputation was a factor in Coventry being chosen as one of only four Government University Enterprise Networks, designed to develop skills among entrepreneurs and tomorrow's business leaders.

Foundation for Success

The University's success is dependent on its students, who flock to study there from all corners of the globe. Coventry's student population comprises a diverse mix of ages, backgrounds, and cultures studying a range of part-time, postgraduate, and undergraduate programmes. The University prides itself on the exciting and vibrant campus that this mix brings. Of the 17,000 students at Coventry University, over 4,000 come from more than 90 different countries.

Enriching the student experience is high on the agenda at Coventry University. This is borne out in campus developments, and in the range of the support services offered to students. Great emphasis is placed on student feedback, and this feedback is used to shape the future of the University. Even after students have completed their studies and moved on, the University maintains links through its alumni relations scheme, Friends of Coventry University (FOCUS), offering students the prospect of a lifelong relationship with the University, and encouraging them to network with their fellow Coventry graduates. In the words of Professor Atkins:

> *'The University acts like a proud parent in celebrating our students' success beyond graduation. We try to develop the skills of creativity, enterprise and innovation in all our students, and enjoy seeing the fruition of this as they progress in their careers. Our greatest success is, and always will be, our students.'*

> *'... we understand how strongly the University is connected to the business world, the professions, and the voluntary sector, and we need to keep going back to our roots in order to be innovative and creative and alive to emerging trends.'*
>
> Professor Madeleine Atkins, Vice-Chancellor

List of Subscribers

This book has been made possible through the generosity of the following:

James Alflatt
Alain Arnot
Helen Audsley
Philip John Badhams
Jeff Bakes
Guillaume Birglen
Raphael Andreas Bischoff
Oliver Philip Bowden
Rachel Califano BSc
Phil Carlson
Mrs J. Clements
Tom Clift
Delon Collins
Ben Cooke
Jackie Cowell
Philip Robert Crick BSc (Hons)
Dr Mark Cusiter
Jonathan David Davies MBA BA (Hons)
P.A.W. Deeley
Damien Derouene
Matthew Dethier
Paul G. Elliott
Nick Exton
Julian Fenn
Richard Forrester BSc (Hons) MBA MIET CEng
Tom Forster
Andrew J. Goldfinch BEng LL.B (Hons) LL.M
Stephen Hugh Grady
Glen Halley
Hatem Hanafi
Dr Achim Herrmann
Miss A. Holden
Geoffrey Holroyde
G.A. Johnson
Barbara D. Jones
James Eric Kavanagh BSc FCIOB
Reginald F. Kilby
Pauline Mary King
Stephen Kingswell
Rob Kirkbride
Dr Sabine Kozdon
John Mabey
Venthan J. Mailoo BSc (Hons) MCSP CertMgmt
Ramon Menendez-Manjon
Shashank Mimani
David and Sarah Morgan (née Cabell)
Sharon Morris
Cedric Mousin MSc
Georgios Mylonas
Barry E. New BSc (Hons) MCIOB FFB
Martin North
Colin Odell
Brian Parker MSc
Ian R. Parkin
Mingkwan Pattanawong
Euan Fraser Sim Pearson MRTPI MRICS
Hugh Pearson
Grant Perry
Sarah Jane Peters BA (Hons)
Professor Christopher Price
Richard Putley
Louise Rickwood
Christopher John Paul Ryan BA LL.B
Rosemary Sampson
Kunwar Vikrant Sandal
Lucy Smith
Mr Jeff Soulsby
Stavros Sourvinos
Roger Steele
Gary Stocker
David Sturges
Dr Trevor C. Theobald
Shaun Tyrrell
Sidney Tyrrell
Peter J. Udy
Hervé Venries
Derek Ward
Mark Wareing MSc
Kuncoro Wastuwibowo
Gareth Williams

'Facilities at Coventry University were excellent and I am still in contact with many of my fellow students that started with me in 1997 who are all now leading interesting and varied lives. I am now taking on a new job as a Critical Care Specialist, embarking on a self-build project in Brittany, managing a property portfolio and starting up a side business as a Wedding Photographer!

Coventry taught me that success doesn't come to you, you work hard and go and get it!'

Paul Willets, Pharmaceutical Chemistry 2001

Index of Names

Acknowledgements

The author and the publishers would like to thank the following for their invaluable assistance in producing this book:

Madeleine Atkins, Norman Bellamy, Andy Bridges, David Browne, Pete Chambers, Joanne Dobson, David Gillingham, Chris Gitsham, John Gledhill, Michael Goldstein, Graham Harwood, Rich Hayward, Geoffrey Holroyde, Julian Ingleby, John Irvine, Paul Ivey, George Lah-Anyane, John Latham, Ian Marshall, John McGuigan, Andy McMath, Kirti Mistry-McLaughlin, Ian Moore, David Morris, Donald Pennington, Phil Pilkington, David Pilsbury, Clive Richards, Andrew Rigby, Chris Smith, Karen Smith, Katie Southwell, Nick Stokes, Michael Tovey, Pete Walters, Rob Wells, Peter White, and the Coventry History Centre.

Picture Credits

Unless an acknowledgement appears below, the illustrations in this volume have been provided by Coventry University, with particular thanks to Graham Harwood. Every effort has been made to contact the copyright holders of all works reproduced in this book. However, if acknowledgements have been omitted, the publishers ask those concerned to contact Third Millennium Publishing.

Corbis: 48(Eliot), 48(Jones), 48(Whittle)

Coventry History Centre, Herbert Art Gallery & Museum: 14, 16(left), 16(right), 17(top), 17(l), 17(r), 18(t), 18(bottom), 19(t), 19(b), 20(t), 20(b), 48(Godiva), 48(Herbert), 48(Starley), 49(Crossman), 49(Hawthorne), 49(Mann), 49(Parkes), 80(b), 81(top right), 88

Getty Images: 48(Bardsley), 48(Mowlam), 48(Spence), 48(Waterman), 48(Wesker), 49(Duckham), 49(Hill), 49(Larkin), 49(Moorcroft)

Giles Halton, Marketing and Communications: Cover image

The Royal Hospital Haslar

A Pictorial History

Aerial view looking towards the south-west in 1984.

The Royal Hospital Haslar

A Pictorial History

Eric Birbeck, Ann Ryder and
Phillip Ward

PHILLIMORE

First published 2009 by Phillimore & Co Ltd
This edition 2013

The History Press
The Mill, Brimscombe Port
Stroud, Gloucestershire, GL5 2QG
www.thehistorypress.co.uk

British Library Cataloguing in Publication Data.
A catalogue record for this book is available from the British Library.

ISBN 978 0 7509 5607 9

Typesetting and origination by The History Press
Printed in Great Britain

Contents

Preface

The closure of the Royal Hospital Haslar after nearly 256 years of continuous service to the Royal Navy, to all three services at times, and more recently to the National Health Service, is a significant event in the history of healthcare in Gosport, Portsmouth and southern Hampshire.

This book is not a history of the hospital; that has been achieved by a number of historians over the years. The Haslar Heritage Group has put together a pictorial record of the hospital, attempting to cover as many periods of time and locations within the hospital as possible. Thus, the book cannot hope to be a complete record and there will inevitably be areas that are not included. It is intended to stir fond memories in those who have served, lived and received treatment at Haslar.

Eric Birbeck
Ann Ryder
Phillip Ward
2009

In memoriam

Surgeon Vice Admiral Ian L. Jenkins CB CVO QHS FRCS RN

1944 - 2009

List of Illustrations

Frontispiece: Aerial view looking towards the south-west in 1984

Acknowledgements

Illustration Acknowledgements

We would like to thank the following for permission to use their photographs:

The Scott Polar Research Institute, Cambridge for illustration 54.
The Imperial War Museum for illustrations 186 and 187.
The Late J.C. Lawrence, Photographer of Gosport, who donated illustrations 67 and 140 to Haslar.

The remaining illustrations are from organisations within and associated with the Defence Medical Services as follows:

The former Graphics, Media and Photography Department at Haslar, reproduced by kind permission of the Hospital Director Mrs Frances Allen.
Queen Alexandra's Royal Naval Nursing Service (QARNNS) and Voluntary Aid Detachment (VAD) archives held at the Institute of Naval Medicine, Alverstoke.
Members of the Haslar Heritage Group.

Other Acknowledgements

Quotations from 'A Visit to Haslar 1916' by Major General J. Richardson are reproduced by kind permission of the Medical Officer in Charge, The Institute of Naval Medicine, Alverstoke.
The 250th Anniversary Speech is reproduced by kind permission of Surgeon Captain R. Radford CBE, RN.
The Royal Hospital Haslar Closure Speech is reproduced by kind permission of Surgeon Captain J. Campbell FRCS(Ed), FRCS(En), RN.
The Haslar Heritage Group acknowledge, with grateful thanks, the assistance given by Captain Julia Massey RRC, QARNNS Archives, and Mrs Sylvia Bell, VAD Archives, in writing chapters and providing photographs.
Mr David Kirk's assistance in proof reading and helping the book reach publication.
The staff at Phillimore for their advice and patience.
Finally, the Haslar Heritage Group wish to acknowledge the support and encouragement given by friends and colleagues in the production of this book. Many of them are, like ourselves, serving or former members of the Defence Medical Services or civil servants associated with the recent history of the Royal Hospital Haslar. The responsibility for any errors or omissions, and for the views expressed in this book, is of course entirely our own.

Introduction

Before Haslar

Greenwich Hospital was established as a home for retired seamen, by charter of William and Mary in 1694, with pensioners accommodated there from 1705 until 1869. The serving sailor was less fortunate. Since 1660 ageing men-of-war, unfit for service, and hired merchant ships had been used as hospital ships. Overseas, sick-quarters were established in Jamaica in 1704, Lisbon in 1706 and Mahon, Minorca in 1708. Permanent purpose-built hospitals were constructed in Minorca in 1711, with construction at Port Royal, Jamaica and Gibraltar being authorised thirty years later in 1741.

At home, Admirals Drake and Hawkins had, in 1590, set up a medical fund for sick and injured sailors which became known as the Chatham Chest. During the Dutch Wars from 1652 to 1674, the number of injured resulted in four London hospitals being contracted to provide care for 'wounded and sick marryners'. The capacity to treat in London was inadequate. For the Portsmouth area, Portchester Castle was proposed as a site suitable for conversion to a hospital in1653, but the 'old ruinous castle' was not used. Instead, private contractors received a shilling a day to treat patients in a variety of accommodation, some described as 'lurid ale-houses'.

In Gosport, the Fortune Hospital owned by Nathaniel Jackson near the present Lees Lane opened in 1713. It grew to 700 beds but seems to have had more emphasis on profit than quality of treatment. 'Violent and malignant fever' (Gaol fever or typhus)

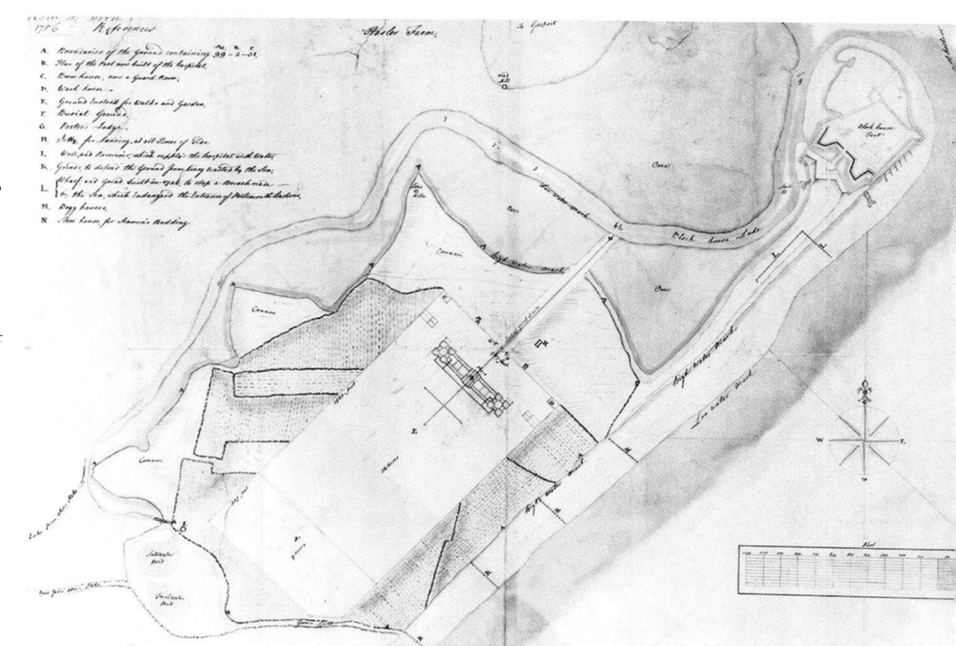

1 *The Haslar peninsula was selected for the new hospital in 1745 with 95 acres of land being purchased the same year. At the time it was an isolated place with the harbour entrance to the north, the sea, shingle and Gilkicker point to the south and east, and to the west Blockhouse and Alverstoke Lakes. The site would be convenient for patients brought ashore from Spithead or to the hospital's jetty from Portsmouth Harbour.*

from 1739 to 1741 stretched the facilities ashore. In Gosport there were 'two or three in a bed' and such a stench that 'may breed the Plague'. Hospital ships were used in Portsmouth Harbour, the Commissioners for Sick and Wounded Seamen noting the significant reduction in drunkenness, gambling and desertion. 'Water was the prison wall' noted the Commissioners, and Portchester Castle was again considered as a place of confinement for naval patients in 1740 but suitable terms could not be agreed with the owners.

King George II was petitioned in 1741 'relating to the matter of the building of Naval Hospitals'. Overseas hospitals were approved but not those at home. Further complaints relating to the Forton or Fortune Hospital followed. The Earl of Sandwich, First Lord of the Admiralty, submitted a further memorial to the King in Council on 15 September 1744. While there was felt to be a need for hospitals in Portsmouth, Plymouth and Chatham, the Admiralty reduced the overall cost by asking only for a hospital at Portsmouth for £38,000 to house 1,500 patients. An order in Council accepted the memorial and, surprisingly, approved all three hospitals. Building started first in Plymouth but Haslar was completed and accepted patients first. Chatham was not built for some time.

2 *The hospital seen across Haslar Creek; Haslar jetty is to the left. Ships are at anchor at Spithead.*

3 *Haslar from Old Portsmouth, 1864. In the foreground is a shipyard in the Camber. On the right, across the harbour entrance, is Fort Blockhouse. On the left, the hospital appears isolated with none of today's clutter around it.*

Planning and Building Haslar

The Admiralty had clear ideas of the way they wished to see the hospital built, instructing the Commissioners of the Sick and Hurt Board that 'they would have the hospital to be strong, durable, plain building consisting of three stories; the same to form a large quadrangle with a spacious piazza within, the out fronts to be decent but not expensive'.

Sir Jacob Ackworth, the Surveyor of the Navy, was asked to produce a plan but also to consult with Theodore Jacobsen, a merchant and amateur architect who had recently designed the Foundling Hospital at Bloomsbury. Jacobsen was 'not entirely approving' of Ackworth's plan and promised 'to make one of his own which he believes may be better for the purpose'.

Jacobsen's plan, when finally produced, met with approval and was later published in the *Gentleman's Magazine*. The plan was for a double row of buildings joined at intervals but separated by a distance of about 35 feet. The architectural style is described as Palatial without ornamentation and was the forerunner of the Pavilion system of hospital design.

5 *Theodore Jacobsen.*

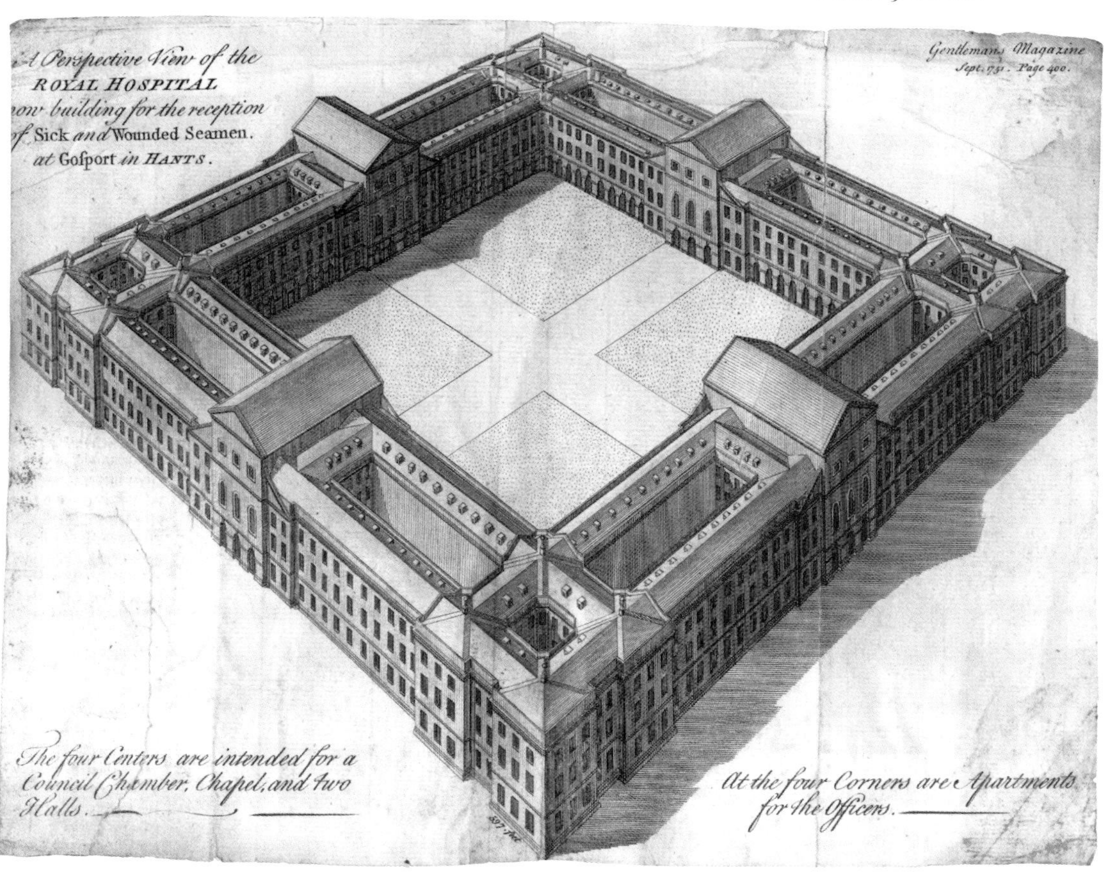

4 *Jacobsen's plan.*

Foundations were laid in 1746 and Jacobsen's plan was executed by James Horne, a surveyor who had worked on the Foundling Hospital, and John Turner, a master carpenter from Portsmouth Dockyard.

Delays were caused by Press Gangs targeting carpenters, bricklayers and labourers building the hospital and by a storm that breached the sea wall towards Fort Blockhouse.

In 1749 the Earl of Sandwich, First Sea Lord, visited and noted that the front block was already built. He observed that the intended Council Chamber covering two floors in the centre was magnificent and directed that it should instead have an additional floor inserted and be converted to wards.

By 1751 the front blocks were nearly finished. Particular trouble was taken over the sewers with a report noting that 'these sewers communicate with every ward in the building and are dug so deep that the sea flowing in every tide, carries off all the soil at each ebb so that nothing of this kind could be contrived more necessary for health and sweetness'.

The pressure of numbers of potential patients forced the hospital to admit the first patients in October 1753.

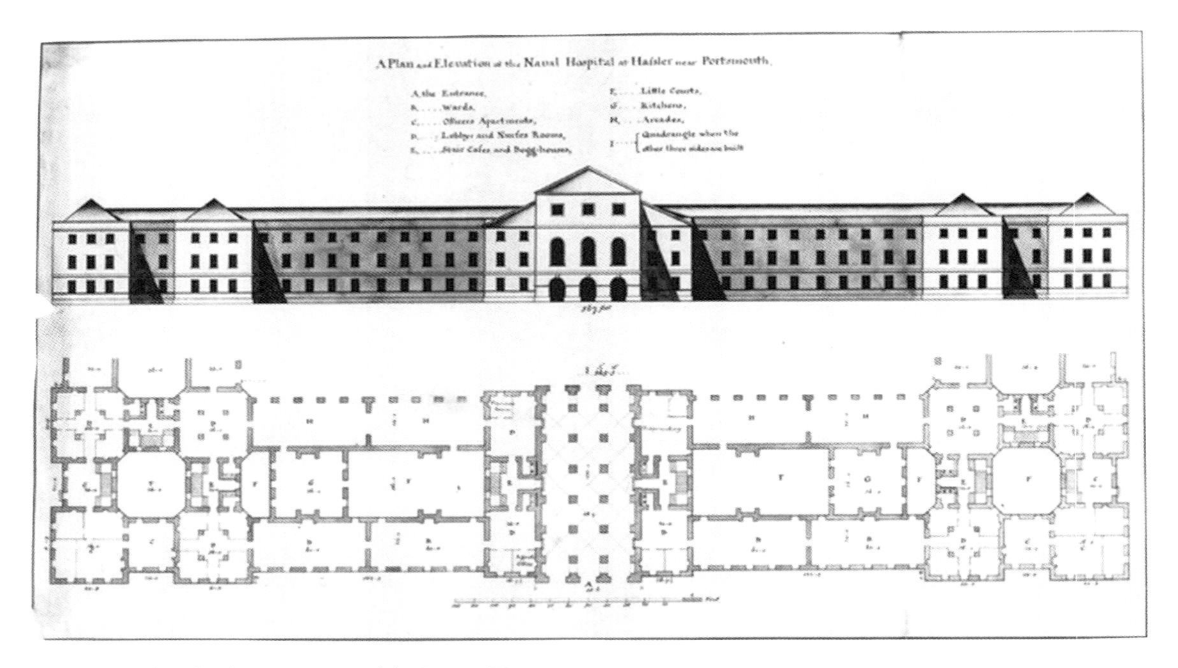

6 *Jacobsen's plan as executed by James Horne.*

The Largest Brick Building

The front of the hospital is 567 feet long and is the only side to resemble the original plan. In 1758, while construction continued, James Lind wrote, 'Haslar Hospital is an immense pile of buildings ... it will certainly be the largest hospital in Europe when finished.' He estimated the final cost to be £100,000, some two and half times the original estimate, even though the fourth side was not built.

The hospital building occupied about seven acres with walls of immense thickness, decreasing from four feet thick at ground level to 18 inches in the attics.

7 *This picture is probably from the 1880s and is one of the earliest views of the front of the hospital. In the foreground, and behind some trees, Haslar Cottages can be seen. Haslar Cottages were used as the hospital washhouse from 1756 to 1876 and were subsequently used to house senior estate workers and their families. Behind the Cottages stand houses 11 and 12.*

8 *A Victorian view of the hospital and the main gate. The tram and narrow gauge rails indicate that this photograph was taken after 1877. It would have been the first view of the hospital for patients and visitors.*

9 *An aerial view of Haslar taken in the early 1960s. St Luke's Church has no roof and awaits rebuilding. Entry to the hospital is by the main gate at the bottom of the picture. The Zymotic (Infectious Diseases) blocks can be seen top left. On the lower edge is open ground that would soon be occupied by a new galley and Senior Rates Mess.*

10 *An Edwardian view of the centre block of the main façade shows the entrance to the Arcade through which patients passed to the receiving room. In this view the siding for the ambulance tram can be seen, with the main line passing through into the Arcade.*

11 *From the Arcade, St Luke's Church is seen across the quadrangle. This view was lost with the building of the new Crosslink complex in 1980.*

12 *An 1880s view of the main hospital façade. Many of the staff lived within the hospital and the Medical Mess is on the left of the picture. In the centre of the picture, at ground level, can be seen an entrance to the hospital cellars.*

13 *The pediment at the centre of the main façade contains a sculpture carved in Portland stone by Mr Thomas Pearce in 1752. In the centre of this sculpture are the Royal Arms of George II. On the left a female figure represents 'Navigation': she leans on a rudder and pours oil on the wounds of a sailor. Above her head shines the North Star, and a compass rests at her feet. Further out, in the angle, the left face of the sculpture is completed by the stem of a ship, with shells, pearls and zephyrs. On the right, 'Commerce' is seated among bales and chests, distributing money, fruit and flowers. Further out, a sailor in distress is being succoured by the serpent of Aesculapius carried in the beak of a bird. At the extreme angle of the right face is a group composed of Boreas, shells and ornaments.*

14 *Taken in 1976, this view of the hospital shows how car parking has changed the grounds. Trolleys stand in wait outside the receiving room. Emergency patients now enter through the door on the right of the picture. At this time the main operating theatres were on the first floor to the right, with the first floor between the theatres and the central arcade being occupied by the earliest intensive care unit.*

15 *An early 20th-century view of the front of the hospital.*

16 *During the Second World War blast walls were built along the ground floor allowing shelter and access to the cellars. Attic windows are still present.*

17 *A Second World War sign is still visible in 2009.*

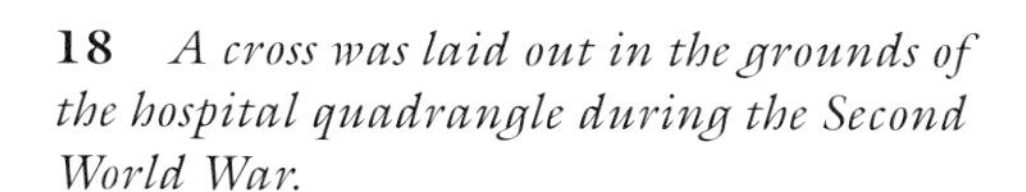

18 *A cross was laid out in the grounds of the hospital quadrangle during the Second World War.*

19 *A fine view of the quadrangle taken from the cupola of St Luke's Church. It shows the large number of chimneys across the roofline of the hospital. On the first floor over the Arcade can be seen the canopy added to increase natural light to the newly opened first operating theatre. On the ground floor is the open colonnaded area that afforded shelter for patients and a covered walkway between the wards for staff in bad weather. For many years the right-hand covered area was used for mustering staff for the fortnightly pay parades.*

20 *A Victorian view of the hospital quadrangle, referred to as a piazza in the original description of the hospital. Staff and patients pose for the photographer. The stone columns and chains still exist today and surround areas of the car park in the Crosslink.*

21 *This view of the quadrangle shows the centre blocks of the side range between the two ward blocks A and B (previously E and F) that were much reduced in size from the original design. The water tower dominates the skyline and at the top of the quadrangle can be seen a patients' pavilion surrounded by hedging.*

22 *Features can be seen in this 1956 view that have long disappeared. Top right are the tennis courts and the patients' airing ground. In the centre are houses 11 and 12. In between can be seen the remnants of the lunatics' airing ground. Far right is the bomb-damaged area where the hospital museum once stood. Work is underway to remove the chimneys and replace the roof of B (previously F) Block. The double block structure with courtyards between is clearly visible.*

23 *An aerial view from the south shows the size and extent of the hospital and grounds. At the top is Brunel's gunboat yard (left) and HMS* Hornet *(right). In the foreground is the Psychiatric block known as G Block (left) and Canada Block (right).*

24 *A view of the staff tennis courts in 1976 that was soon to disappear with the building of the new galley and mess complex.*

25 *E (previously C) Block and the original entrance to the Medical Officers Mess. The arched doorway and columns were retained when the block was refurbished in 1970. The Medical Officers Mess moved to a new building in 1899.*

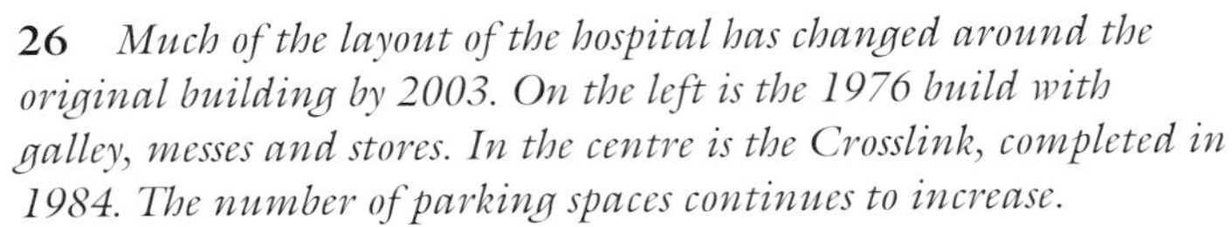

26 *Much of the layout of the hospital has changed around the original building by 2003. On the left is the 1976 build with galley, messes and stores. In the centre is the Crosslink, completed in 1984. The number of parking spaces continues to increase.*

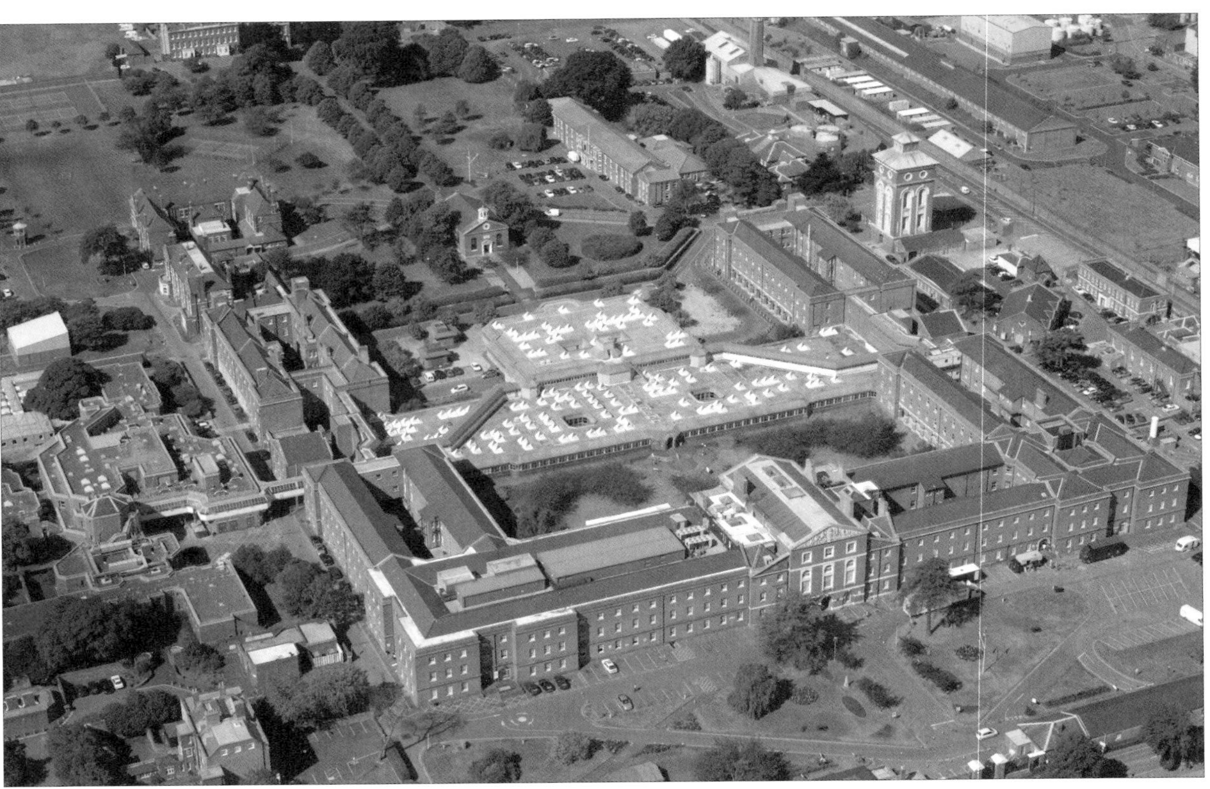

Hospital Interiors

When completed in 1762, Haslar had 114 wards, the majority having 19 or 20 beds, giving a capacity of a little over 2,000 beds. The maximum number a little later was probably nearer 2,500. Many of the original wards were in pairs, joined end on by a communicating door. Later these pairs were opened into single large wards, in use until the closure of the hospital.

In the early years the majority of patients were fever cases. The most contagious cases were, in 1787, confined to the upper wards and moved towards the ground floor for convalescence to give access to the open air. There were separate galleries for walking for patients recovering from measles, scabies, venereal disease and smallpox.

The arcade in the centre of the main façade was the entry point to the hospital with the receiving room and administrative offices opening onto the arcade.

In time, surgery became more common, initially performed amongst the other patients on the wards; the first operating theatres opened in 1897 above the arcade and overlooked the quadrangle. At this time, separation of the wards into Medical and Surgical became the norm.

The centre block over the arcade also contained the original X-ray department, opposite the theatres and, on the top floor, the first central galley.

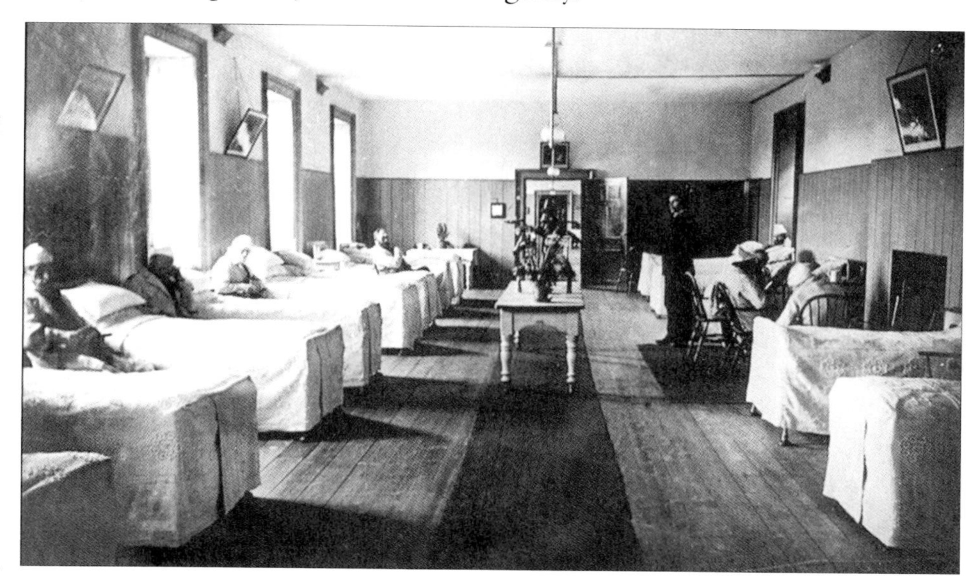

27 *This is one of the earliest photographs of a ward in Haslar. Patients are in hospital gowns, some sitting by their beds, others huddled around the ward stove. The centre ward door is open and we can look through into the next ward. In this picture the beds have day covers. The floor is of teak and patients would heat a poker and touch the knots in the wooden floor to make them sing.*

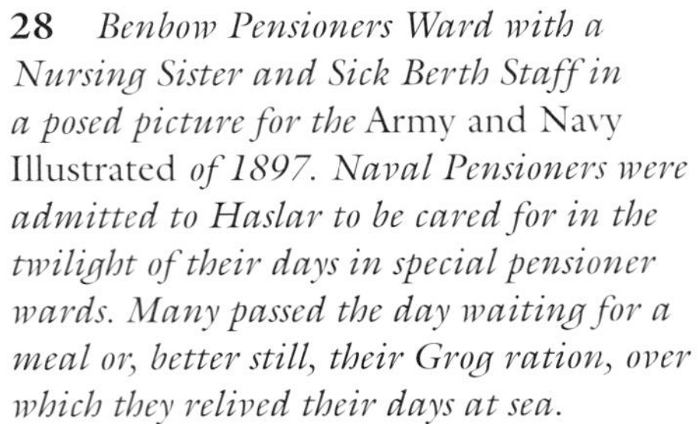

28 *Benbow Pensioners Ward with a Nursing Sister and Sick Berth Staff in a posed picture for the* Army and Navy Illustrated *of 1897. Naval Pensioners were admitted to Haslar to be cared for in the twilight of their days in special pensioner wards. Many passed the day waiting for a meal or, better still, their Grog ration, over which they relived their days at sea.*

29 *A ward stove, always glowing hot on winter days with patients huddled around them. It was the job of staff going on duty to carry scuttles of coal to the wards. This is a picture of the last remaining stove on A5 (until recently Day Surgery theatres) prior to its refurbishment in 1969.*

30 *On this ward the patients are of differing ages. Three Sick Berth Attendants stand to one side with another in the centre. The patients are in serge hospital uniform with hospital slippers and smocks. Some have head or arm injuries. Patients remained until completely recovered from their illness or injury and shorter hospital stays were uncommon before the 1970s.*

31 *With everything spick and span, this is a showpiece ward after 1905 and with electric light. The QARNNS Sister and Sick Berth Staff are wearing ward smocks and the patients wear hospital uniform and smocks. Two of the original wards have been joined, the connecting door replaced by an arch.*

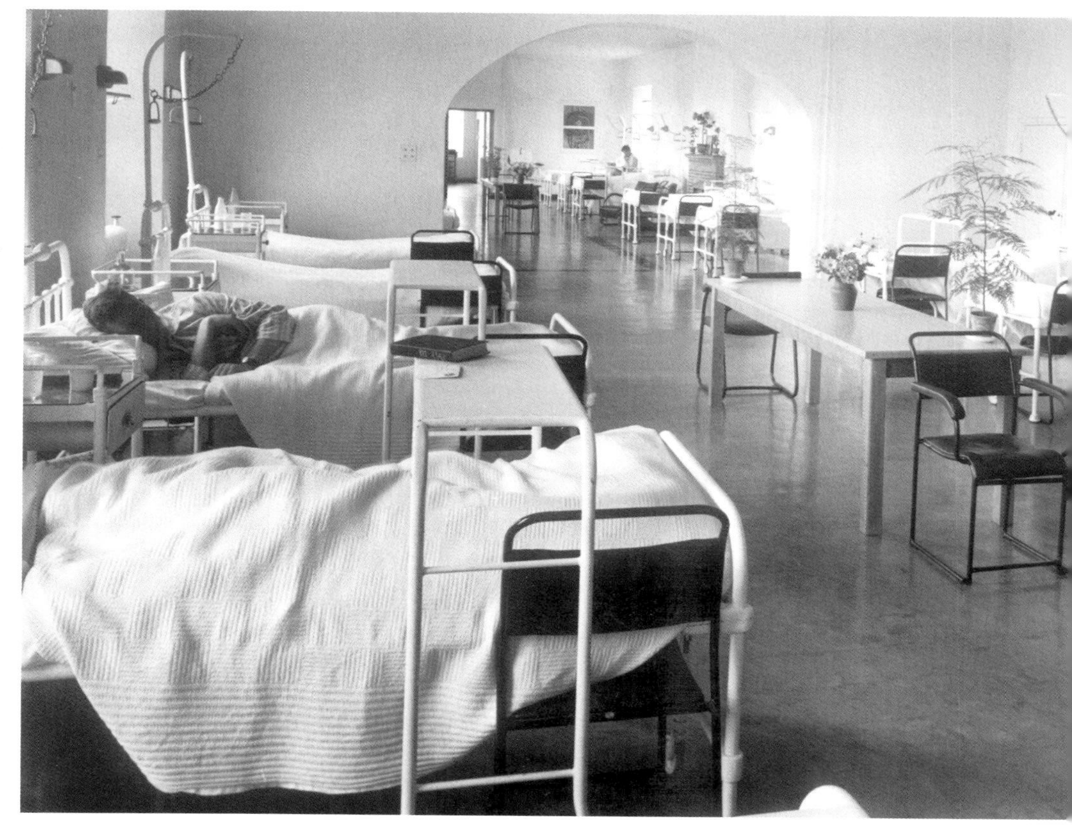

32 *A 1960s view of a ward with plants still permitted. In the distance a fireplace can be seen. The teak flooring is now covered with linoleum tiles which would be cleaned daily by the ward staff.*

33 *A 21st-century picture showing NHS staff on an orthopaedic ward.*

34 *NHS staff with a QARANC colleague on the Day Surgery Unit opened in 1998 on the first floor of D Block (previously A2 and 5).*

35 *RAMC and MOD civilian staff working together in the Clinical Measurements department.*

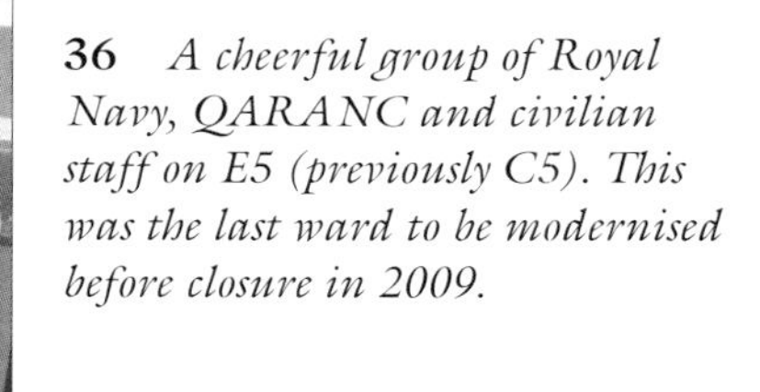

36 *A cheerful group of Royal Navy, QARANC and civilian staff on E5 (previously C5). This was the last ward to be modernised before closure in 2009.*

37 *Royal Navy, Royal Air Force and civilian Radiography staff pose in one of the X-Ray suites. The skeleton, rear centre, is understood not to be a member of staff.*

38 *The office of the Medical Officer in Charge in 1956, complete with name boards of previous Officers in Charge and the Queen Anne coat of arms that had been in the hospital since 1809. Through the window can be seen the quadrangle and ward Blocks E and F (previously C and D) in the distance.*

39 *In the cellars is the stout support for the hospital above. The bricks were hand-made from local clay.*

40 *The cellar under E (previously C) Block. This huge area below the original Medical Mess is thought to have been a storage space. The room in the distance through the doorway was used during the Second World War for underground operating theatres.*

41 *No Escape! The two Cellar corridors under C and D Blocks (previously B and A) run towards the Arcade underground and serve a series of vaulted rooms that were once used for anatomical dissection. The lower windows are barred to deter escape and can be bolted shut with original shutters. To the left and right are wooden piles in the brickwork. Many door lintels in the cellar are made from oak taken from hulks in the harbour.*

42 *In 1957 C (previously B) Block, where the hospital's second operating theatre complex was located, underwent a total refurbishment. Wooden stairs were replaced by a modern oval staircase with a ceiling light. This staircase has been admired by students of modern architecture but not by those who suffer from vertigo.*

43 *Haslar Museum was founded in 1827. It was situated in the block between E and F (previously C and D) Blocks. During the 19th century thousands of natural history specimens were sent back to Haslar by expeditions, including those of Sir John Richardson.*

44 *The first curator of the museum was Charles Barron. Despite having only two fingers on one hand and none on the other he was skilled in the preparation of specimens. Sadly the museum was destroyed in 1941 in a bombing raid. Staff who emerged from the shelters the next morning reported seeing many specimens hanging from trees in the quadrangle. A museum curiosity, the four-footed duck, was never seen again.*

45 *The hospital laundry, 1897.*

46 *The hospital galley in the 19th century.*

47 *Containers stand ready to hold the next meal for delivery to the wards.*

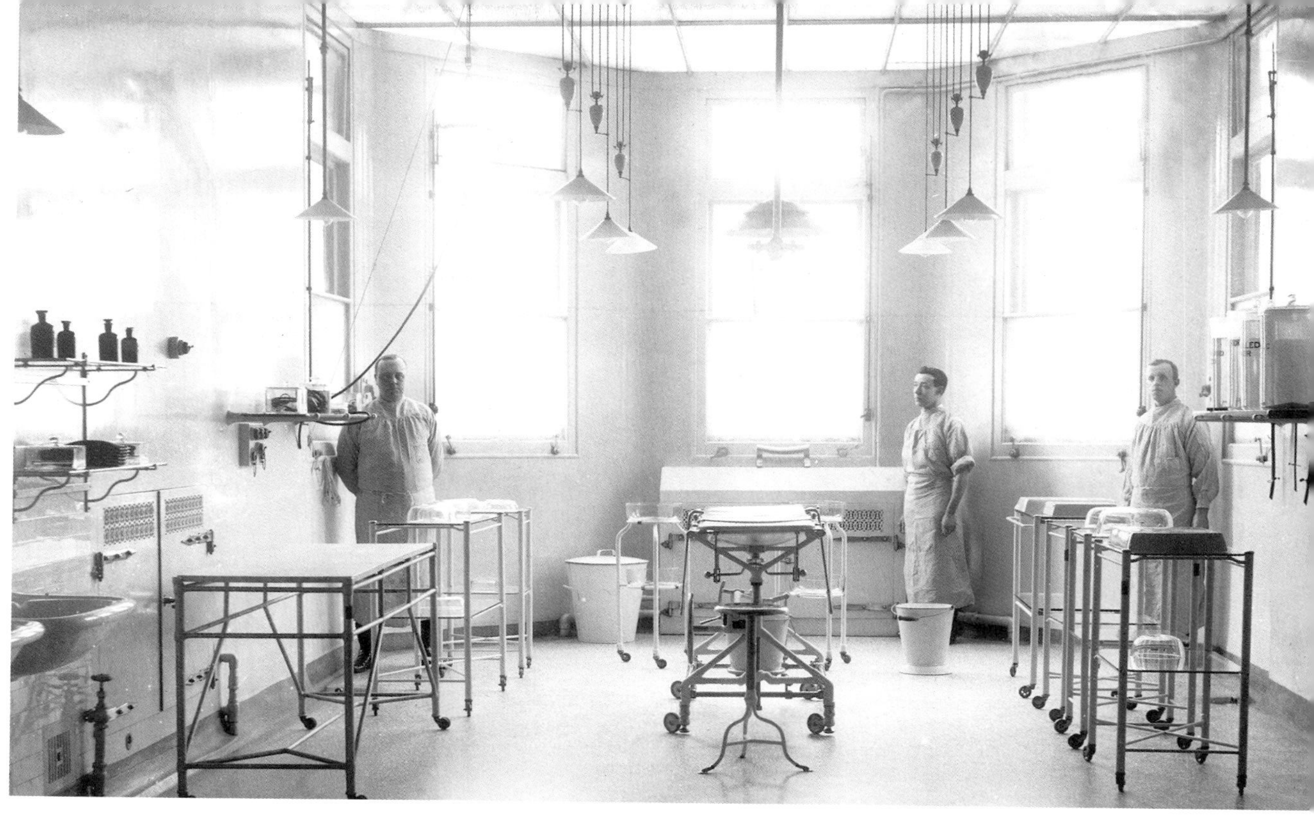

48 *The first operating theatre was above the Arcade and had a conservatory-style extension to admit more light. King George V visited the theatre in 1910. The brass stool, seen in the picture under the operating table, was still in use in the 1960s.*

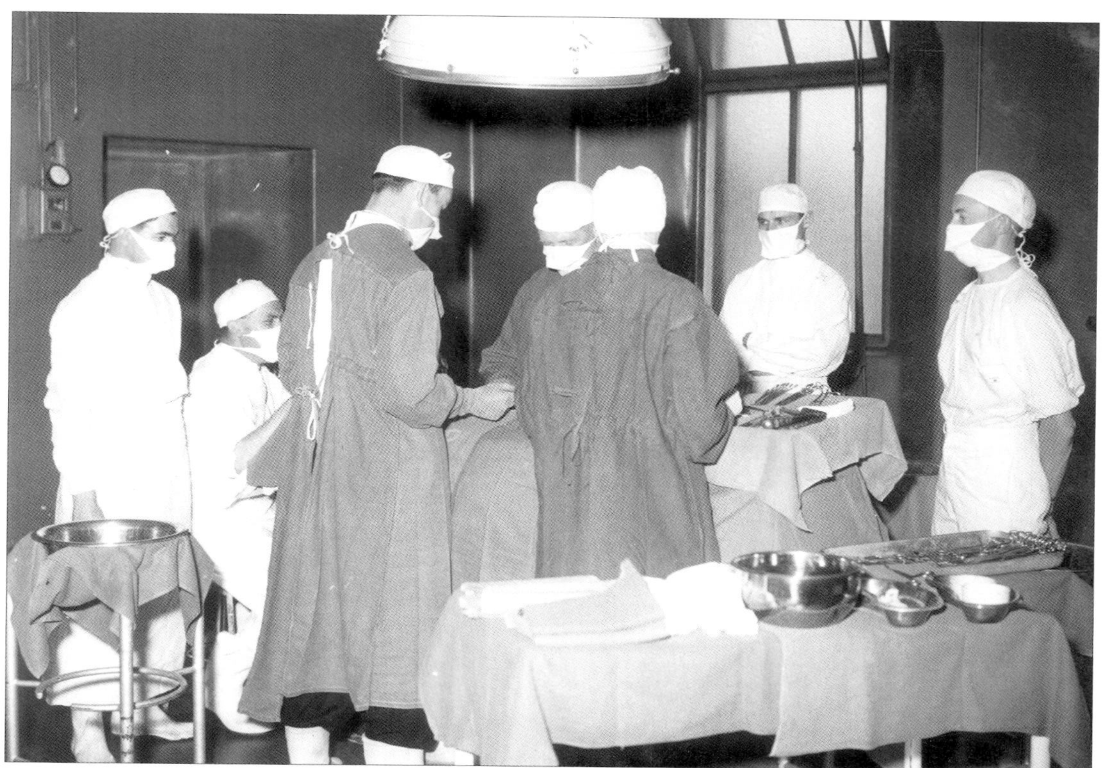

49 *The operating theatre in Sick Officers Block. This may be a recruiting picture. Surgeon Lieutenant Allan Tooley poses with SBAs Pat Smith, opposite (assisting), and left to right, George Hampton, Ron Brown, at the head of the table, and Arthur Fox, looking on with other unnamed colleagues.*

50 *The Pathology Department, 1897.*

51 *The Pharmacy, situated in the same building as the Pathology Department.*

52 *Surgeon Commander Edward Atkinson DSO, AM, Polar Medal RN 1882-1928. He joined the Royal Navy in 1908 and was appointed to Haslar as the Vaccinator in the Pathology Department. In 1910 he joined the* Terra Nova *for Captain Scott's ill-fated Antarctic expedition. Left in charge of the base camp, it was Atkinson who organised the search party that found the body of Scott. Atkinson served at Gallipoli and was awarded the DSO for conspicuous bravery at the Battle of the Somme and the Albert Medal for saving lives on board HMS* Glatton *after she caught fire in 1918.*

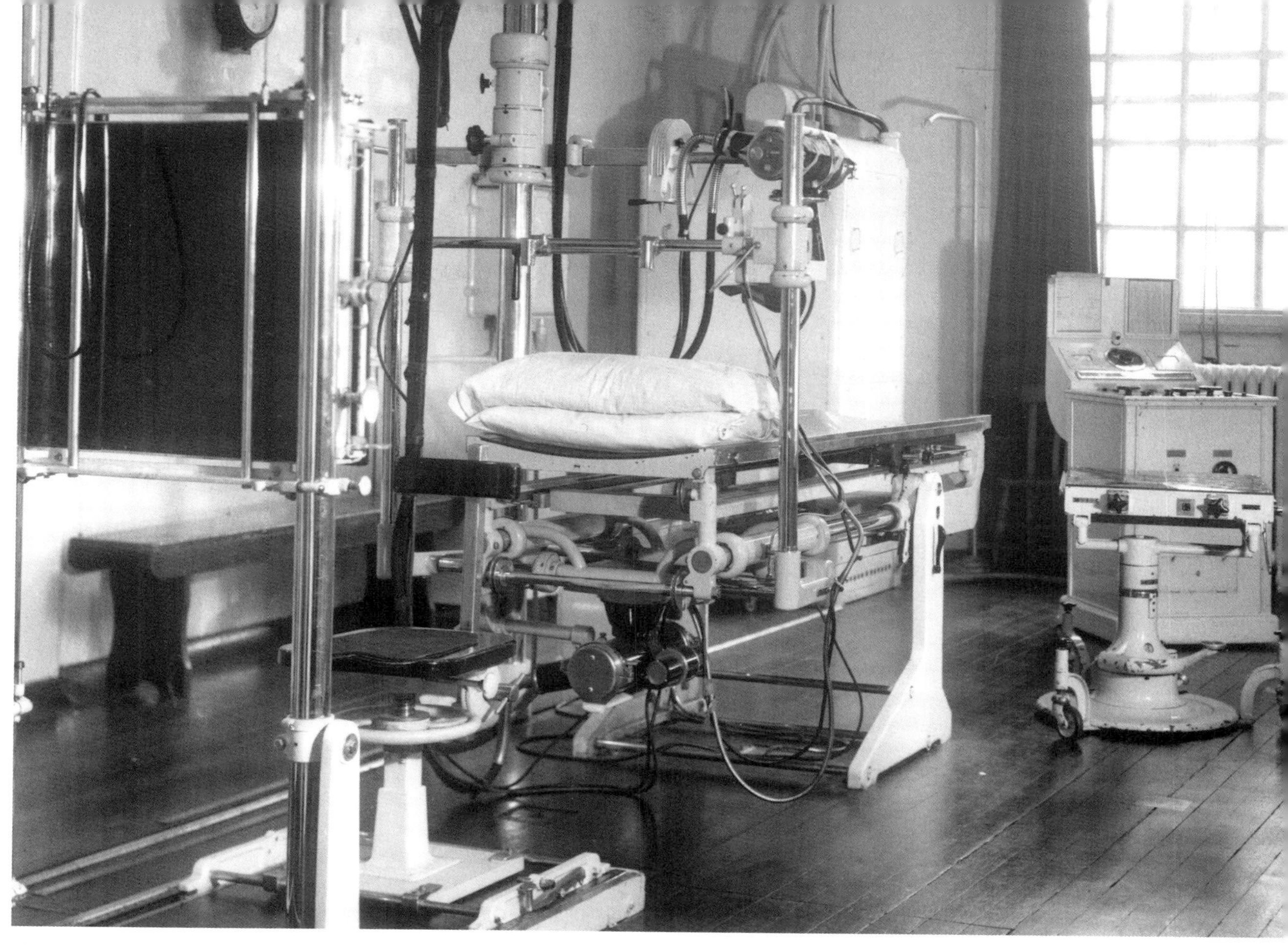

53 *The X-Ray Department in the centre block over the Arcade. This was later occupied by Nuclear Medicine following the transfer of X-Ray to the Crosslink in 1984.*

54 *The Gymnasium on the ground floor of B (previously F) Block in the 1950s.*

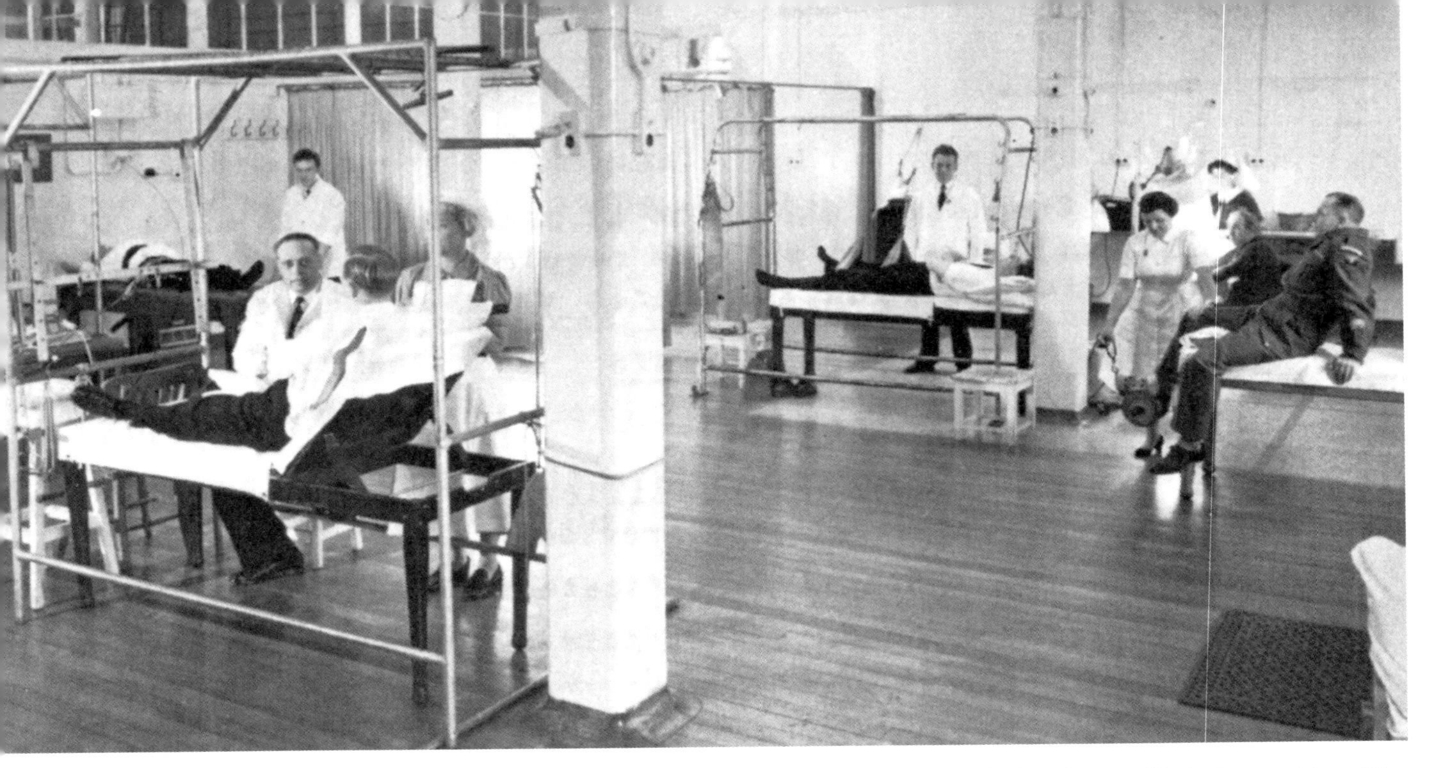

55 *The Physiotherapy Department. A posed picture taken for the first prospectus of the Royal Navy Physiotherapy School. The picture shows patients, one in battle dress, undergoing treatment. Physiotherapists, a QARNNS Nursing Sister and a Naval Nurse are in attendance.*

56 *Occupational Therapy workshop on the ground floor of E (previously C) Block. Patients stayed in hospital for many months and occupational therapy included activities such as carpentry, weaving and basket making.*

57 *A staircase in D (previously A) Block in the 1960s. This was one of the last original staircases in the block and was unpainted. After demolition during the re-build in 1969, part of the balustrade was made into the altar rail of St Luke's Church.*

58 *The last remaining original staircases are in F (previously D) Block. Their survival is because this part of the hospital was used for many years as nurses quarters. James Lind in conversation with John Howard, the prison and hospital reformer, stated in 1780, 'That in the summer he would have the windows on the stairs of the hospital nailed open for the want of fresh air'.*

59 *The supporting structure of the galley complex on the top floor above the Arcade. This area was later occupied by Sterile Services. Oak timbers taken from hulks were used alongside new wood.*

60 *The Attics were used for staff and patient accommodation. Windows opened into the inner courtyard.*

61 *In the centre block, over the main Arcade, the shaft from the ground floor to the roof was designed to admit light and fresh air.*

St Luke's and St Mary's

St Luke's was completed in 1756 and, had the fourth side of the quadrangle been completed, would have been at its centre.

Through the main doors the visitor passes under the gallery, which was reduced from its original size when the church was totally rebuilt internally in 1963-4 following infestation by death watch beetle. Much of the original undressed stonework from the floor of the church was reused in the refurbishment, which was carried out under the supervision of Mr Ken Makins, the Diocesan Surveyor. The church was rededicated on 18 October 1964 by the Right Reverend J.H.L. Phillips, Bishop of Portsmouth, and Raymond Richardson, Chaplain of the Fleet.

The area between E and D (previously C and F) Blocks originally held the Hospital Museum but this was destroyed by bombing in 1941. Later, St Mary's Roman Catholic Church was here, remaining until the construction of the Crosslink. The church was succeeded by St Mary's Chapel in C (previously B) Block, which continued to function until the closure of the hospital.

62 *St Luke's in the 1880s. Note the rendered brickwork. The iron railings enabled patients to be confined in the quadrangle. A gate permitted access to St Luke's and the railings survived until around 1905.*

63 *An Edwardian view of St Luke's. The rendering has been removed. Ivy covers the brickwork.*

64 *A view of both St Luke's and Admiral's Walk. In the foreground can be seen the main sewer grating set into the pathway. The sewers were utilised by patients for escape and by nursing staff to smuggle liquor into the hospital.*

65 *The inside of St Luke's prior to refurbishment. The balcony reaches further into the body of the church and is approached by dual staircases. Those attending church in the 18th and 19th centuries knew their place. Physicians and their patients sat to one side of the aisle, whilst the surgeons and their patients sat on the other side. Labourers sat in the balcony.*

66 *A pre-1963 view of the aisle and altar. Note the choir stalls and the Haywood Hardy painting in situ behind the altar.*

67 *A mid-refurbishment view. About a third of the original brickwork was replaced.*

68 *A mid-refurbishment view looking towards the altar end. The stained glass windows have been removed.*

69 *View of the altar from the aisle prior to refurbishment. The baldacchino over the altar was erected in 1920 as a First World War Memorial, having been designed by the architect Sir Charles Nicholson. It has octagonal Corinthian columns.*

70 *The stained glass windows on either side of the canopy depict the four evangelists and were dedicated by the Chaplain of the Fleet on 10 April 1910 to the memory of Medical Officers who had died on active service.*

71 *'The Healing of Blind Bartimaeus' was painted by Heywood Hardy RA (1842-1933) and is considered by Osbert Sitwell as one of his finest works. The painting was removed from behind the altar and placed into the side chapel under the balcony. Wrought ironwork by Mr Ken Ball, Hospital Blacksmith, can be seen to the left.*

72 *St Luke's in winter sunshine, with Sick Officers Block in the background. The ship's bell, captured at the Second Battle of Copenhagen in 1807 from the 80-gun Danish ship* King Christian VII, *stands in the foreground. The ship became a hospital hulk in the River Medway and when she was broken up in 1837 the bell was moved to Haslar. The bell has recently been returned to the Danish Navy.*

73 *The assembled clergy at the final service held on 30 March 2007. The Reverend John Hill, the last Chaplain, is third from the left.*

74 *Surgeon Captain James Campbell, Commanding Officer Royal Hospital Haslar and Fort Blockhouse, watches as the Reverend Monsignor Paul Donovan, Principal Roman Catholic Chaplain to the Navy, turns the key in the main door to mark the closure of St Luke's.*

75 *The late Commander Ian Coulton receives the key to St Luke's from Surgeon Captain Campbell.*

76 *The interior of St Mary's Roman Catholic Church.*

77 *The entrance to St Mary's Church was close to the entrance to the Nurses Quarters, with a notice on the wall that stated 'Out of Bounds to Male Personnel except on duty'. The open area in the foreground was the site of the museum and undeveloped for forty years.*

78 *St Mary's Chapel on the first floor of C (previously B) Block in the hospital replaced St Mary's Church.*

Residences

During the early years of the hospital all staff, including families and servants, were accommodated within the main range of the hospital. In March 1756 construction began on four residences, two at either end of the main façade of the hospital.

These residences face each other. For those looking at the front of the hospital, the residences to the left were later known as Houses 11 and 12 and those to the right as Houses 13 and 14.

Following a board of enquiry in 1794, the management of the hospital was, for a period of 75 years, removed from medical officers in favour of executive command by serving Naval Captains. As a result, Earl Spencer, accompanied by other Lords of the Admiralty, marked out the ground for erecting the houses for the Governor, Lieutenants and other officers on 1 October 1795.

The Terrace was built from 1796 to 1798, occupying an area to the south-west of the hospital previously used as a burial ground.

79 *James Lind (1716-94) became known as the Father of Nautical Medicine. He was the second Physician in Charge of Haslar from June 1758 to June 1783 when his son John succeeded him. James Lind's paper on Scurvy, resulting from work undertaken on board HMS* Salisbury, *preceded his time at Haslar although many of the patients he treated were suffering from scurvy. Whilst at Haslar he ensured that the fleet blockading Brest was supplied with fresh fruit and vegetables.*

80 *Houses 13 and 14 at the north-west end of the main façade of the hospital. James Lind is believed to have occupied one of these houses. Later, house 14 was the official residence of the Medical Officer in Charge of the Hospital.*

81 *Houses 11 and 12. A photograph taken in 1880. On the right-hand side can be seen the extension built by Sir John Richardson to accommodate his large family.*

82 *The south-west side of Sir John Richardson's extension overlooked the lunatics' airing ground. His son, also John, recalled his childhood much later in 1916:*

> *On the side of our garden lay the grounds of the lunatic asylum. These and their inmates had a strange fascination for me. When my father first went to Haslar, the asylum was under the charge of a medical officer who apparently held the view that lunacy could be cured or controlled only by the administration of severe disciplinary measures, and the unfortunate men were sadly knocked about by the attendants. My father's righteous soul was vexed with what he saw, for much was viewed from the verandah of our house, though hardly as much as what I could see from a perch on a ladder against the garden wall.*
>
> *As soon as the lunatics were let out of the wards in the morning, some of them took up set places in the grounds. One poor fellow for years occupied a corner under our garden wall, where he swayed incessantly from one leg to the other. The men never seemed to quarrel or interfere with each other's pitches, but they occasionally knocked down an attendant who was cruel to them, when they were, in the early days, punished with blows, solitary confinement and strait-waistcoats.*

83 *Sir John Richardson (1787-1865) entered the Royal Navy in 1807, as a surgeon's mate, becoming a full surgeon the following year. After 1815, he was on half pay in Scotland, returning to the Navy as Surgeon-Naturalist for Sir John Franklin's first and second Arctic expeditions. He was later to participate, at the age of 61, in one of the unsuccessful attempts to find the ill-fated Franklin expedition. His travels enabled him to bring many specimens to the museum in Haslar. Before Haslar, he had administered the Melville Hospital (later RNH) in Chatham. At Haslar his duties were as Physician but the arrival of another Arctic explorer, Sir William Edward Parry, as Superintendent at the hospital allowed the relationship between clinical and administrative staff to improve.*

84 *The covered balcony to the rear of Richardson's residence:*

> *The walled garden of our house was marvellous in the fruit line. I have never seen its like since. Grapes grew and generally ripened on the south wall; plums, peaches, apples, pear, and figs were produced in any quantity and of splendid quality. In those days Officers held their appointments practically for life, and consequently took much pains with their official properties. I may mention that the excellent productive qualities of our garden were deemed due to the liberal quantity of cow manure and seaweed available; the latter came in cartloads from Haslar beach.*

85 *The stable block to the rear of Richardson's residence.*

86 *The Terrace. The main residence in the centre of the Terrace was occupied initially by Governors but later by Superintendents, Inspectors General of Hospitals and Fleets, Surgeons-General, Surgeon Rear Admirals in Charge and Medical Directors General, Royal Navy.*

87 *Surgeon Rear Admiral's plaque above the door to the residence.*

88 *The Terrace in 1976.*

89 *A Victorian view of the Terrace showing the white railings at the front, later removed for wartime recycling. Officers Terraces similar to this one are also found in the dockyards at Portsmouth and Chatham.*

90 *A modern view of the houses that make up the Terrace. The pebble dash is one attempt at making the house waterproof, a problem since construction.*

91 *An 1823 engraving of Captain William Edward Parry, Naval Hydrographer and famous Arctic explorer, who came to Haslar in 1846 as Captain Superintendent. Parry was, perhaps, the most distinguished resident of the Terrace, although his introduction of compulsory sea-bathing for patients and staff may have received a mixed reaction. Sir John Richardson's son describes the effect that Parry had on the hospital:*

> *There was fairly constant friction between the fighting and healing forces – chiefly, I think, because the Captains and Lieutenants made sorties into the wards and domains of the medical staffs, sorties which were not always beneficial to the patients; or because the Captain would send for the Medical Officers in a body to his office to hear his wisdom when they were busy with visits, operations, post mortems, or instruction. But, though the governing system remained the same, all friction disappeared when Sir Edward Parry, the great Arctic explorer, became Captain Superintendent.*
>
> *He was a most genial man, and tactful, so that very soon the most excellent relations existed between him and officers of the medical staff. He affected considerable reforms in consultation with the staff – indeed, one and all in Haslar loved him and his family. Haslar became a different place officially and socially.*

92 *The rear of the Surgeon Rear Admiral's residence in summer.*

93 *The Surgeon Rear Admiral's garden looking into the walled garden and to the hospital paddock beyond.*

Victorian and Edwardian Expansion

The Georgian hospital, including the Terrace, had been constructed over a period of fifty years and was completed by the end of the 18th century. It served well the needs of the patients during the Napoleonic Wars, after which there was a period of relative calm.

The Crimean War and other later 19th-century conflicts provided the impetus for a second period of building.

94 *The Laundry was built in 1854 to replace the hospital wash house of 1756, now known as Haslar Cottages. At the top right in the roof can be seen the water tank fed from a well just inside the Gunboat Yard across Haslar Road. The tall chimney belongs to Isambard Kingdom Brunel's engine house that powered a travelator to move Gun Boats. Some washer staff caught typhus from used hospital sheets and clothing, a number dying and being buried in the hospital grounds.*

95 *A view of the Laundry from Haslar Road showing the water tank in the roof and bricked up windows and what was an original entrance through the hospital wall. The wall has in the past been scaled by escaping patients. The Guard and Police patrolled the wall and on occasion cut down the escape ropes. Sometimes up to fifty men went over the wall, returning later somewhat the worse for drink!*

96 *The Hospital Chapel of Rest (1868) with the Post Mortem Room behind and the Water Tower in the distance.*

97 *Hospitals use a lot of water. In the early 1900s the daily consumption of water in Haslar was estimated at 51gallons per head. Early shallow wells were less than satisfactory both in volume and quality of water. A new well was sunk in 1859 to a depth of 340 feet with a spring being found at 212 feet.*

The water tower was completed in 1885 and is 120 feet high, with two 125-ton water tanks each holding 50,000 gallons.

The tower is a well-known landmark and was used in the Second World War by the Luftwaffe on bombing runs heading for Portsmouth Dockyard. A former German bomber pilot visited the hospital in the 1980s and asked to see the water tower.

98 *The Sisters' Mess was built in 1899. A rose garden is in the foreground. The mess was later named after Mrs Eliza Mackenzie who, along with her clergyman husband and six trained nurses, had been sent by the Admiralty to set up a Naval Hospital at Therapia during the Crimean War.*

99 *Entrance to the Edwardian covered way that leads to the Medical and Sisters' Mess from the colonnaded area under F (previously D) Block.*

100 *The covered way looking forwards to the Medical Mess. The Sisters' Mess is to the left.*

101 *The Medical Mess was completed in 1902. The Sisters' Mess can be seen on the right. In this picture there are four grass tennis courts. There was also a croquet lawn. Two Medical Officers sit under a small tent in uniform, one reading a paper, the other dozing in the sun.*

102 *The Medical Mess with G Block (Psychiatric) and the Sentry Post in the background. Gone are the grass tennis courts and ivy-strewn walls.*

103 *The stores at the front of the hospital date from 1853. From these stores all items required to support the hospital were issued. A similar adjacent store area was used to house patients' baggage. In the 20th century the stores held medical supplies that were distributed to ships and naval units worldwide.*

104 *Building 40, as it came to be known, was built in1899 as the administrative block of the Zymotic (or Infectious) Diseases Hospital. After the closure of the Zymotics, this building supported the offices of the Surgeon Rear Admiral Medical Services and in later years became the Estate Management offices. Gone are the rail tracks that were either side of the rose beds.*

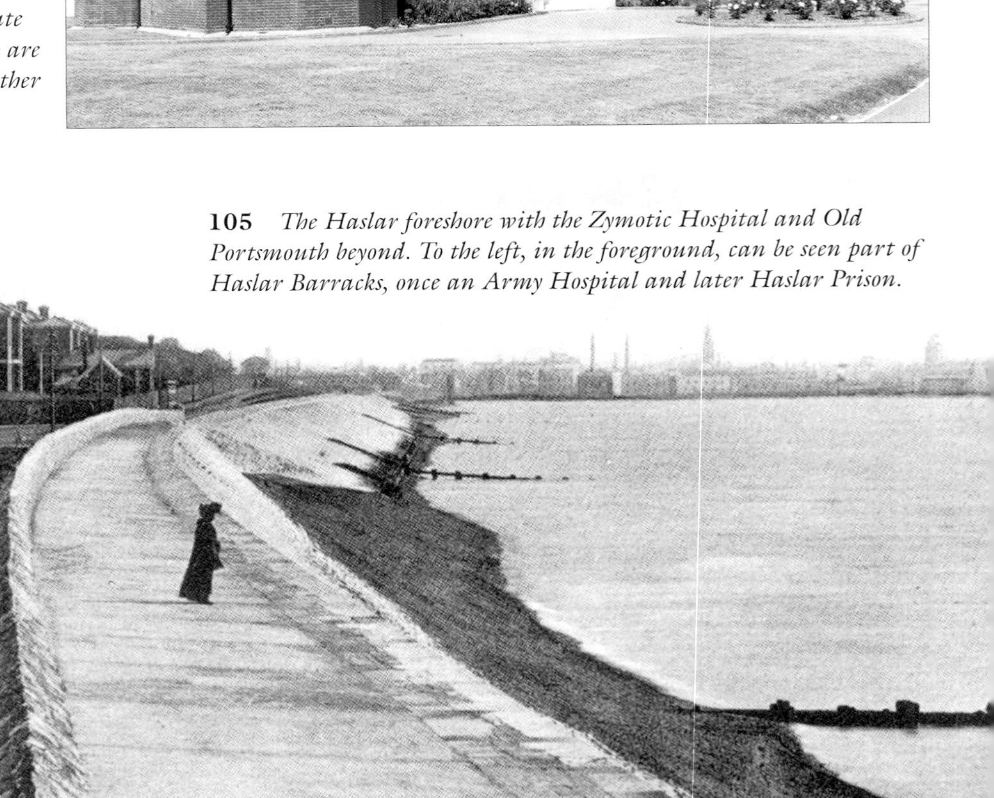

105 *The Haslar foreshore with the Zymotic Hospital and Old Portsmouth beyond. To the left, in the foreground, can be seen part of Haslar Barracks, once an Army Hospital and later Haslar Prison.*

106 *A rear view of the Zymotic Hospital with building 40 in the background. On the left is the surrounding wall that separated the Zymotics from the main hospital. To the right of the wall can be seen one of the support buildings containing the galley and stores.*

107 *Front view of the Zymotic Blocks with upper-floor verandahs where patients would sit in all weathers taking the sea air while looking out over the Solent to Spithead.*

Prior to the construction of the Zymotic Hospital, it was necessary to exhume 26 Turkish sailors who had been buried here in 1850 (including the Captain of one ship) after being admitted to Haslar with typhus. The two Turkish ships were in Portsmouth to train with the Royal Navy. After exhumation in 1899, the Turks were reburied at Clayhall in a separate Turkish Plot.

During and after the Second World War the Zymotic hospital was known as 'M' Block and became a Night Duty staff block using some ward areas for accommodation.

108 *All goods could be passed to the Zymotic Hospital through a purpose-built hole in the boundary wall in order to prevent cross-infection. Patients admitted to Zymotics were bathed on arrival and their clothes washed in Lysol.*

109 *The newly built Pathology Block, 1899. The alignment of this building is different from all others in that it faces due south to provide the best light for microscopy. In the foreground is a small fir tree, since grown in stature and now towering above the surrounding buildings.*

110 *Main Pathology Block. Built in the mid-19th century, this building served both as a laboratory and pharmacy during the Victorian era. It reverted to a pharmacy in the mid-20th century and more recently has been a Pathology administration support block.*

111 *Sick Officers Block of 1904. This view was taken in 1976 when the block was being used as Nurses Quarters.*

112 *The newly opened Sick Officers Block stands ready to receive patients. The building housed a series of four-, two- and single-bedded cabins with senior officers accommodated in the front and junior officers at the rear. The building had an operating theatre and a galley with stewards and staff to wait on the patients. The upper floor was served by a rickety iron-gated lift. Later, a series of TB cabins stood in the grounds behind the main building.*

113 *A posed photograph shows a Sub Lieutenant in a bath chair with visitors. Sick Berth Staff and nurses look on from the balcony. Most of the hospital blocks were given alphabetical identifiers and theSick Officers Block was known as Q Block.*

114 *G Psychiatric Block opened in 1910 complete with padded cell. This is the successor to the Asylum that had been on the ground floor of E (previously C) Block in the main hospital. Like many external blocks it also accommodated night duty staff. It has also been used as nurses accommodation.*

115 *G Block from the seaward side, with Eliza Mackenzie House in the background on the right. The open grounds give splendid views of Spithead.*

116 *Erroll Hall was opened in1913 following a bequest from the widow of Commander George Erroll RN, who had died in service. It was used as a library, for snooker and billiards and as a rest centre for patients.The main hall had a stage and changing rooms and up until the 1950s was regularly used for the entertainment of both patients and staff. BBC broadcasts from the Hall featured well known acts such as Flanagan and Allen, Cyril Fletcher, Arthur Askey and the Memphis Boys. At Christmas pantomimes were staged. In recent years the Hall became a staff gymnasium.*

Canada Block

When Haslar opened staff were housed within the main building. By the start of the 20th century new messes had been built for Medical Officers and Nursing Sisters. The remaining nurses eventually moved into F (previously D) Block, but it was not until 1917 that Sick Berth Staff had their own quarters.

In Canada, during the First World War, the Imperial Order of the Daughters of the Empire was keen to contribute to the war effort. The Order raised significant sums and £50,000 of this was earmarked to allow the number of beds at Haslar to be increased by 250. After consideration, it was realised that the best way to increase the number was to build staff accommodation and thus free space within the main building.

The new building was named Women of Canada Block though this was abbreviated to 'Canada Block'. The eventual cost was £38,000, the sum approved to build the original hospital in the 18th century. The remaining money was used to open two new wards at the Royal Naval Hospital, Chatham.

117 *Canada Block from the seaward side. The ground floor accommodated, in separate messes, Sick Berth Attendants (SBAs), Leading SBAs and Senior SBAs. Probationer SBAs lived in open messes in the wings of the building, many sleeping in hammocks until the late 1950s or early 1960s. A dining hall was situated on the top floor of the centre block and a galley on the ground floor. Canada Block was re-furbished in the 1980s for occupation by QARNNS nurses.*

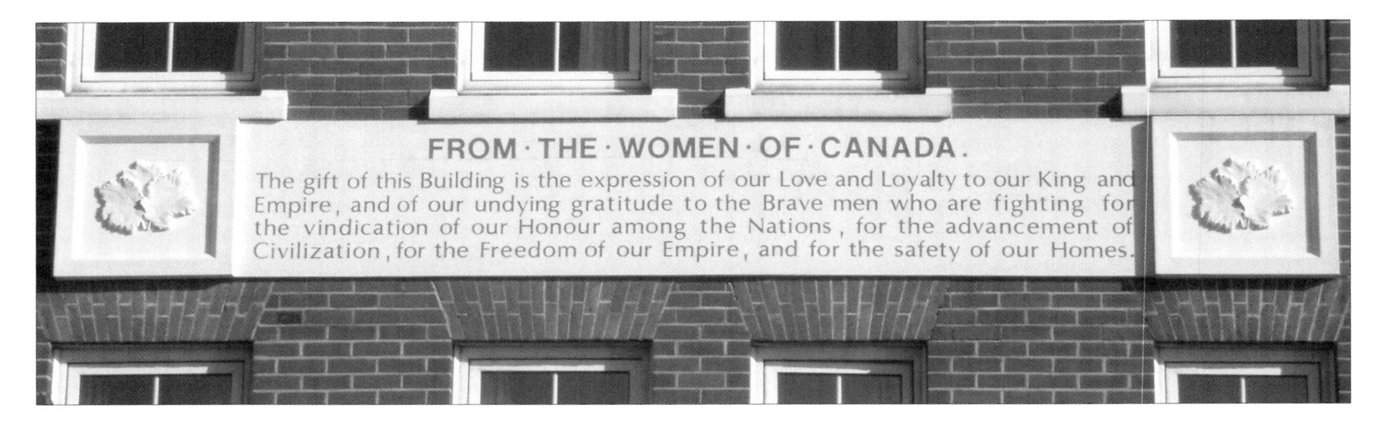

118 *'From the Women of Canada', an Expression of Love and Loyalty for King and Empire. Complete with maple leaves, this panel is situated over the first floor of the building facing out to sea and extolling undying gratitude for the brave. The Imperial Order of the Daughters of the Empire still send Christmas vouchers to all Canadian Veterans living overseas in gratitude for the service given and to show they are not forgotten. A maple tree was planted in the grounds in recent years by the Canadian Ambassador.*

119 *This is believed to be a celebration tea after the unveiling of the new Shelter presented by the Ladies Needlework Guild seen in the top right corner of the picture.*

120 *The plaque inside the Shelter, which is still in use today. Lady Colville was the wife of the Commander in Chief Portsmouth, who was to become ADC to King George V.*

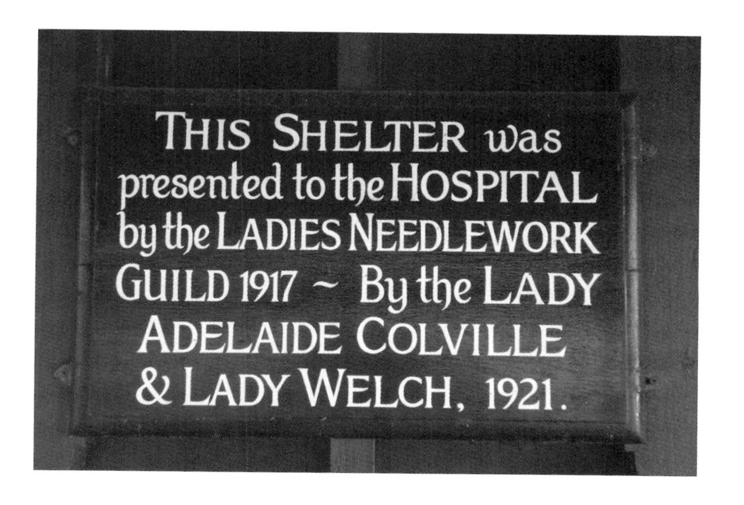

121 *The Shelter today with the plaque visible though the window. In the distance stands another shelter or pavilion facing towards the Solent and used on occasions by staff, patients and families.*

122 *The Junior Sick Berth Staff bar in the early 1960s, the scene of many a good evening, especially in 'blank week' (staff were paid fortnightly and the week before payday was known as 'blank week'). On pay day and the weekend that ensued, Gosport and Portsmouth were lively. The following week the bar was the place for a cheap beer and entertainment.*

123 *Upper Mess of Canada Block in the late 1960s. Large wardrobes were the order of the day, a change from the tin lockers previously in use. The wardrobes could be placed to give some privacy. The metal bars once supported hammocks but they became an assault course when many young SBAs challenged each other to a 'Tarzan swing' from one end of the mess to the other. Some made it, others did not!*

No pin-ups here, just a Navy News *calendar and, further over, a collection of 'Easy Rider' posters.*

124 *The top floor Junior SBA and Probationers dining room. In the 1960s a dining room assistant known as 'One Eyed Fred' worked here. At meal times he would shout, 'You lucky people' as he served out the meals. Fred had a glass eye which frequently found its way onto new joiners' plates.*

Crosslink

The advent of the National Health Service in 1948 allowed military patients to be admitted to civilian hospitals and civilian patients to be admitted to service hospitals. This arrangement was not formalised until 1967 when approval for Haslar to provide beds for between 85 and 105 civilian patients was given.

The change from a purely Royal Naval Hospital to a district general hospital, now catering for women and children, and the need for better X-ray, accident and emergency and operating theatre facilities, drove the need for expansion. After a feasibility study, the decision was taken to join the two side ranges of the original hospital at their mid-points. This improved movement within the hospital by providing an efficient functional nucleus. At the same time, replacement of the galley, stores and some staff accommodation in the older parts of the hospital could be undertaken on the former airing grounds to the south-east of the hospital towards the seawall. The main entrance to the hospital was moved to Haslar Road, with the original gates being retained for ceremonial purposes.

The foundation of the Crosslink was laid in June 1980 and the new building was opened by Admiral Sir John Fieldhouse in April 1984.

125 *A general view of the hospital quadrangle in 1979 before the bulldozers moved in to begin building the Crosslink. The photograph was taken from the top of the centre block over the Arcade. On the right are red milk crates stacked against the wall of the victualling office and next door, with the green shrubbery, is the Matrons House, all of which was to disappear with the new build. In the top section of lawn is the shrub border that once surrounded a patients' pavilion. The trees of Admiral's Walk are no longer pruned.*

126 *A JCB starts to break down the central area between E and F (previously C and D) Blocks and soon St Mary's Church would be no more. The construction of the cellars of the Crosslink is in progress and many bones are said to have been found during excavation.*

127 *The completed Crosslink prior to opening in April 1984.*

128 *A view of the Crosslink from St Luke's Church, with the five new main operating theatres on the first floor. Below are the services for the whole building. The pathway leads from the church and the design of the building was such that you could walk the route of the old Admiral's Walk towards the original (ceremonial) gates. It was intended that the Church should be visible from the gates, but in practice this was only possible if all the doors were open at the same time.*

Airing the Patients

Throughout the history of the hospital there has been an emphasis on allowing patients access to the grounds for recreation. From Victorian times ample fresh air was considered beneficial to the treatment of tuberculosis in particular. At times, sea-bathing was also encouraged. The Zymotic Hospital on the sea-wall had balconies to encourage patients to take the sea air.

129 *An Edwardian picture of patients strolling in the hospital grounds in front of the Terrace. The newly opened Sick Officers Block (1904) can be seen through the trees. The patients are dressed in Hospital Uniform, a blue shirt and blue serge jacket and trousers. This area had a patients' pathway, seen here just beyond the fence, forming a circuit around this part of the grounds. Old plans of this area show a water trough for cattle. Excavation of the area in recent years exposed the pathway and artefacts such as brass buttons from hospital uniforms and a pipe cleaning knife.*

130 *Patients and Staff, Open Air Ward. This area is in front of the old D Block, now F Block, and the remains of the open ward can still be seen. Patients suffering from tuberculosis were believed to benefit from being nursed in the open air and this area had a shelter with a screen that dropped down in inclement weather. The Wellcome Museum holds paintings of Haslar by a First World War artist. One painting is of this open air ward.*

131 *A pre-First World War postcard showing the open air ward with patients and Sick Berth Staff. One bed patient has been pushed over to join the group. The screens can be seen rolled up and tied and the patients' beds all made under the sloping roof of the ward. One wonders if the patients managed to eat their meals in the warm somewhere.*

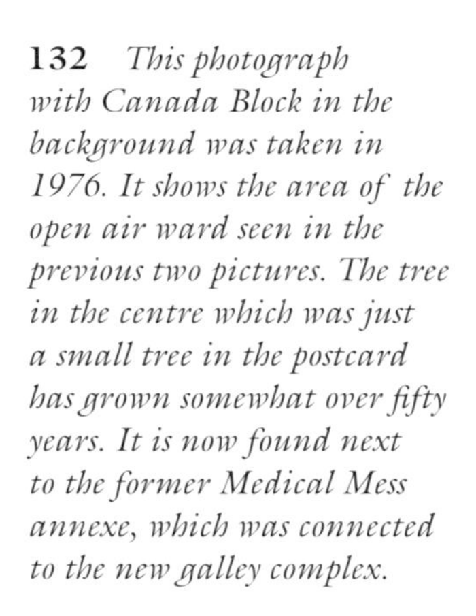

132 *This photograph with Canada Block in the background was taken in 1976. It shows the area of the open air ward seen in the previous two pictures. The tree in the centre which was just a small tree in the postcard has grown somewhat over fifty years. It is now found next to the former Medical Mess annexe, which was connected to the new galley complex.*

133 *A patients' pavilion in the area near Canada Block. Two such pavilions were built in the mid-19th century for the use of patients. This one is in the area that was near the Lunatics Airing Ground. The pavilions were raised on earth mounds and gave views over the boundary wall to Spithead. In later years the pavilion was also a popular place in the evening for courting staff, as were the airing grounds in general.*

134 *The second pavilion was built further along the sea-wall area in the open grounds opposite the sentry post. This picture, taken in the late 19th century, shows not only a huge mound of cut grass but a group of patients in hospital clothing posing for the camera. It gives a feel of a well kept country estate. By 1910 G Block was built a few yards to the left of this pavilion.*

135 *The same pavilion as in the previous photograph in a picture taken specifically for the* Navy and Army Illustrated *of 1897. Once again, patients pose and take their ease mostly in hospital uniform, but some are in naval rig and a Marine stands in the background by the pavilion.*

136 *Each block in the main body of the hospital had an open area on the ground floor facing the quadrangle. In this area patients could sit, especially in inclement weather, and chat and swap tales whilst puffing a pipe and perhaps downing a tot or two from their daily ration of rum. Most of these areas were enclosed as the demand for office and departmental space increased in the 1950s.*

137 *In the 1920s a new pavilion was built on the sea-wall in the area opposite the entrance to HMS* Dolphin.

138 *A patient in a wheel chair and a nursing attendant pose for a photograph on Admiral's Walk. With pollarded trees and neat and tidy grounds the quadrangle was the perfect place for patients and staff to stroll. St Luke's in the background is part-covered with ivy.*

139 *An Edwardian view of the quadrangle from the top of the main Arcade, or centre block, as it was also known. Either side of Admiral's Walk can be seen two patients' pavilions surrounded by hedging. Benches and seats are arranged around the outside of the pavilions.*

Around the Grounds

There is probably no other hospital in the United Kingdom as well provided with exercising grounds for the patients as Haslar, a circumstance which does great credit to the wisdom of its founders. The 'Airing ground', as it is called in old documents, is nearly a mile in circumference. The portion between the south wing and the sea is provided with two mounds, with summer houses or smoking pavilions on top, from whence delightful views are obtained of Spithead, the Isle of Wight and Southsea beach. These are popular lounges, and during smoking hours the greater part of the convalescents congregate here. A portion of the enclosure is reserved for officers, who can enjoy a stroll and a smoke under pleasanter conditions than are often vouchsafed to them afloat. The trees afford abundance of shade, or shelter from the winds, and were it not for the inevitable monotony of existence under conditions inseparable from a state of disablement, the lot of the patient at Haslar might almost seem an enviable one.

Navy and Army Illustrated Friday 19 February 1897.

140 *The Sentry Post or Gazebo in the late 1880s. It stands inside a fenced area of the grounds with entry gained through a rotating stile. St Luke's Church can be seen on the left with the newly built water tower (1885) in the distance. The Gazebo dates from the late 18th century and may have been used to provide a watch over patients. At times it was also used as a bandstand for entertainment in the First World War. Patients were able to look out over Spithead and the Solent from this vantage point.*

The Medical and Sisters' Mess had been built by 1899 and this view changed. Note the metal fence on the right that stretched across the top of the hospital quadrangle and in front of St Luke's. This design of metal bench seat can still be seen around the hospital grounds.

142 *A view from the Gazebo towards the Terrace with grass tennis courts in the foreground, 1976. These were later replaced by hard courts. Many of the large trees fell in the storm of October 1987.*

142 *A late Victorian picture of the road to the Terrace taken from the rear of St Luke's Church. A man in a bowler hat takes his ease by leaning on the fence for the photographer. A group of children are playing in the road close to the Terrace, and on either side of the picture in the distance can be seen high brick walls around the Paddock.*

143 *Taken before 1885 as the water tower is not present, this is one of the earliest photographs of St Luke's Church. A group of patients and perhaps staff pose along the iron fence over which can be seen the main hospital and the open space of the quadrangle. On the right-hand side of the quadrangle is the top of one of two patients' pavilions. In the centre is a tall post on top of which is a covered bell.*

144 *The meteorological station was situated where messes were built in 1899.*

145 *An Edwardian photograph of the ground staff tending the flower beds of the quadrangle. Haslar had a large civilian workforce who cared for the grounds, buildings and services required for the hospital. A horticultural centre was based in the present Memorial Garden with greenhouses and cold frames to produce both vegetables and flowers.*

146 *An Edwardian picture of the Medical Mess grass tennis courts. It is not easy to determine the difference between ground staff and officers.*

147 *This wonderful posed picture (c.1880) has been taken from the area of St Luke's Church looking towards the Sentry Post or Gazebo and the sea-wall. An elderly gentleman pensioner sits leaning on a cane and wearing a top hat, whilst other patients or pensioners sit in the long grass or look down from the post. In the distance is a large brick wall stretching along the sea-wall area. By 1899 this view had been changed with the building of the Zymotic (Infectious Diseases) Hospital.*

'Doc'

The establishment of a trained Sick Berth Staff for work in Naval Hospitals was authorised in 1884. In 1891 Sick Berth personnel were given new style uniforms, double-breasted jackets as worn by Chief Petty Officers, and were given the name of 'Sick Bay Tiffy'. Staff were also addressed as 'Sick Bay Stewards', especially by Officers.

The name 'Doc' has been used for all who perform medical duties in the Royal Navy. This chapter contains photographs of Medical Officers and those known as 'Doc'.

148 *Haslar, 1897. Admiral Duncan Hilston poses with his Medical Officers at the front of the Hospital. In the background can be seen the sheds of the Gunboat yard. Far left middle row sits Commander Gimlette who was to become Inspector of Fleets and Hospitals based at Haslar. The vicar sitting upright in a mortar board and collar is the Reverend Octavius Rutherford Foster Hughes BA, vicar of St Luke's.*

149 *Medical Officers in the late 19th century. Note the variety of caps, collars and facial hair.*

150 *This picture is believed to be the earliest showing Sick Berth Staff at Haslar. They pose in fine fashion with their instructors in front of the main façade of the hospital. One of the senior rates has a chest full of medal ribbons and nearly all sport a watch chain on their waistcoats. This picture was taken when the staff lived in the upper floors of the main building of the hospital. It was acquired when a person arrived at the main gate of the hospital one day with an envelope of photos and said, 'Have these, one has my Great Grandfather on, he worked at Haslar', and then left.*

151 *An interesting photograph of a member of the Sick Berth Reserve who has First World War chevrons on his right sleeve.*

152 *Night duty staff, Christmas 1928. They are not in summer rig but in white trousers over which they would have worn ward gowns. All Sick Berth Staff wore 'Tiffs' rig as worn by Naval Artificers.*

153 *Young fresh-faced Sick Berth Probationers pose with Surgeon Rear Admiral Buckeridge, Medical Officer in Charge of Haslar, and instructors, in front of Canada Block in 1937.*

154 *The first class to accept civilians into the Royal Naval Physiotherapy School at Haslar, 1960s.*

155 *Wardmaster Officers were commissioned Sick Berth Staff. This photograph was probably taken in the early 1960s at the front of the hospital. Left to right, back: E. Bishop, J. Duncan, O. Saunders, S. Saunders; E. Fay. Front: J. Lihou, A. Masters, W. Ford, J. Stockton.*

156 *Over the years many photographs were taken in front of Canada Block. Training of Sick Berth Staff took place in what was known as* Dolphin II, *now occupied by the Royal Navy Submarine Museum, and classes would march from Haslar, cross the road for instruction, and return to Canada Block for meals and to sleep.*

QARNNS AND VADs

QARNNS (by Captain Julia Massey RRC)

The 18th- and early 19th-century nurses working in Haslar were mainly widows of sailors and marines or wives of serving sailors. Instructions given by the Commissioners stated that 'there shall be one nurse to attend fourteen patients and these nurses shall be the most sober careful and diligent that can be had'. In reality the nurses were not averse to stealing patients' property and forging their wills. Living locally they imported large quantities of gin, usually 'tied around their waist and under their stays in bladders'. In some months as much as six gallons was being seized by the hospital authorities. They were also open to bribery to help patients escape, and stole hospital food and items such as bedclothes and soap. One nurse was dismissed 'for going to bed with four or five patients and infecting one of them with the foul

157 *QARNNS 1887.*

'Miss Louisa Hogg (centre), Head Sister, Royal Hospital Haslar, with Nursing Sisters. Sisters were introduced into Naval Hospitals in 1885. Miss Hogg occupied this important position for a number of years. The presence of Sisters in the wards has a restraining influence on Jack's proverbial command of words; his expressions, when in familiar converse with his chums, being marked by aptness rather than elegance, while his "terms of endearment" would grate harshly on the refined ear.'

The Navy and Army Illustrated, *1897*

disease'. The conditions of service for these women were appalling and they were liable to be dismissed at will 'upon a decrease of patients'. When the Commissioners were prompted to ask in 1755 why so many nurses quit, the response was 'being confined and imprisoned and that they never eat a hot meal, and are served with scraps left by the seamen and are badly paid having but a trifle of wages when perhaps there is four of five months due'. In 1854 the female nurses were replaced by pensioners under the direction of a female matron.

Despite the success of Mrs Eliza Mackenzie and her nurses at the Naval Hospital at Therapia during the Crimean War it was to be thirty years before female nurses returned to Haslar, by which time nurses were being trained in civilian hospitals. A number of 'experienced Naval Medical Officers' were against the introduction of female nurses. In 1884 Miss Henrietta Stewart was appointed Head Sister at Haslar together with six Sisters. Miss Stewart was found to be unsuitable and dismissed and replaced in 1885 by Miss Belle Storey. In the wards the Sisters were addressed as Madam by both staff and patients and precautions were taken to protect them from viewing the middle third of a patient's body.

An important part of the Sisters' responsibility was the practical tuition of the Sick Berth Attendants. A report from Haslar about the Sisters referred to 'their professional knowledge and skill' as being of 'incalculable benefit' and that 'the mere presence of these ladies exercises a restraining and humanizing influence over the patients and this tends directly to the preservation of order and decency on the wards'.

In 1902, HM Queen Alexandra became President of the Naval Nursing Service and it became Queen Alexandra's Royal Naval Nursing Service (QARNNS). During the First World War Sisters continued to serve in Haslar and also abroad in hospital ships and RN establishments, augmented by reserve Sisters. In 1916 the Admiralty approved the gradual increase in female nurses to free up Sick Berth Attendants (SBAs) for service at sea. The Second World War again saw an increase in Reserve Sisters serving in Haslar which, together with members of the Voluntary Aid Detachment (VAD), filled the gaps left by the deployment of the regular Sisters and SBAs. Following the war VADs continued to work in Haslar and in 1949 SBAs of the Women's Royal Naval Service (WRNS) were being trained. In 1960 the VADs and Wren SBAs were replaced by QARNNS Naval Nursing Auxiliaries (NNA). Until this time the Naval Nursing Service had been an all-officer service. In 1962 nurse training for the State Registered Nurse (SRN) and State Enrolled Nurse (SEN) qualification commenced.

Patients in Haslar were now being nursed by QARNNS Sisters and Staff Nurses together with Student (SRN) and Pupil Nurses (SEN) under training as well as Royal Navy male trained nurses (Medical Technicians (Nursing) from 1965) and those under training, and RN Medical Assistants (MAs) (formerly SBAs) trained and under training. The School of Nursing was part of the Royal Naval Medical Staff School situated in *Dolphin II* but moved in 1987 to the former Sick Officers Block. Trained QARNNS personnel were also undertaking post-basic qualifications, so continuing the highest possible professional care for patients in Haslar.

On 1 April 1983 QARNNS became a Unified Nursing Service and male nursing colleagues in the Royal Navy were in future to join QARNNS. With shortages of Naval Nurses in Haslar, due partly to the ending of the SEN qualification, QARNNS Medical Assistant Branch was formed in 1987, and civilian nurses were briefly employed to ensure the safe and high standards of care continued for patients in Haslar. QARNNS MAs transferred to the Royal Navy in 1998. QARNNS Nursing Officers and Nurses continued to provide professional patient care, alongside their Army and Royal Air Force colleagues, from 1996 to 2009 in the Royal Hospital Haslar.

158 *QARNNS Sisters look out from the Sentry Post following a Rose Bowl Tennis Tournament.*

159 *QARNNS Sisters playing in the Franklin Tennis Tournament, 1959. In 1949 Miss Olga Franklin presented to QARNNS the Rose Bowl for presentation to the winner of an annual tennis tournament. Miss Franklin and two other QARNNS Sisters spent three years as prisoners of war of the Japanese at the Civilian Internment Camp at Stanley on Hong Kong Island. They were the only Sisters of QARNNS to live under enemy rule during the war.*

160 *QARNNS Nurses outside F Block (formerly D Block) in the early 1960s, when the block provided Nurses Quarters.*

161 *Stirring the Christmas pudding, early 1960s. SRA E. Bradbury RN, MOIC, Miss C. Thompson QARNNS Principal Matron, Miss M. Fetherston-Dilke Matron-in-Chief QARNNS.*

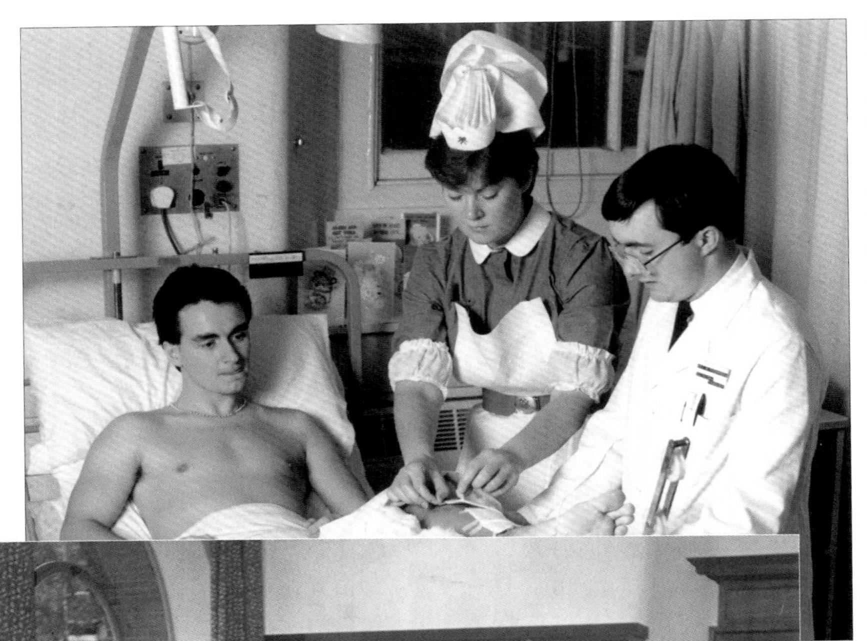

162 *Nurse Clinical Teacher with a Student Nurse on an Orthopaedic Ward, 1985. Student and Pupil Nurses gained their practical clinical experience in the wards of RNH Haslar.*

163 *QARNNS and RN Student Nurses in the Medical Library at RNH Haslar, 1962. Nurses in training undertook their formal education in the Training Division accommodation in* Dolphin II *and in June 1987 moved to the converted Officers Block which became The Royal Naval Medical Staff School.*

164 *QARNNS and RN Nurses in class in the Training Division, with Superintending Nursing Sister C. Cooke QARNNS Nurse Tutor. Nurse training began at RNH Haslar and RNH Plymouth in May 1962. In 1966 the title of Auxiliary Naval Nurse gave way to that of Naval Nurse.*

165 *HRH Princess Alexandra, QARNNS Patron since 1955, outside the Sisters' Mess with C. Thompson, Principal Matron QARNNS, and Naval Nurse Hill in 1969.*

166 *A QARNNS Nurse tending a patient at night, late 1980s.*

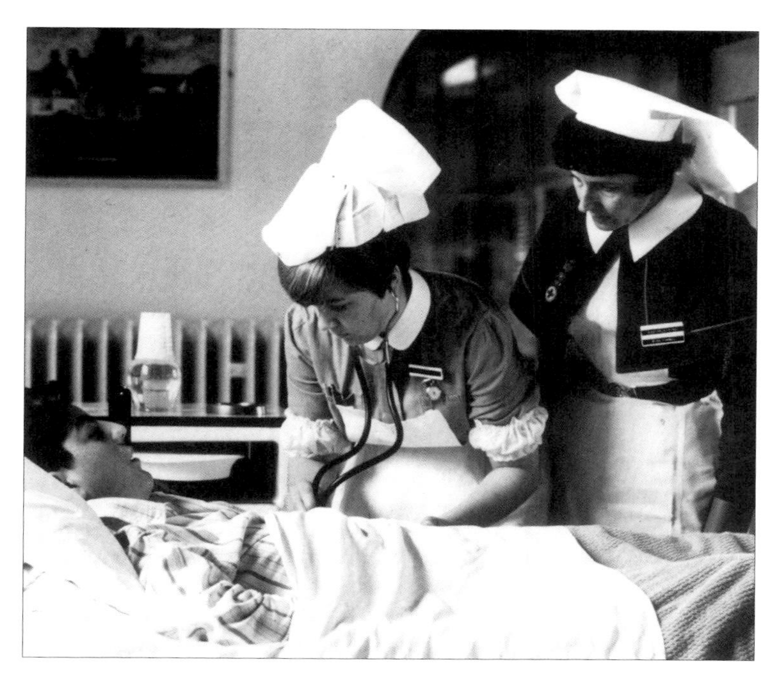

167 *QARNNS Student Nurses working under supervision in the Urology Ward. Senior Nursing Sister K. Funnell QARNNS was formerly a Wren SBA who transferred to QARNNS for nurse training, and was the first QARNNS Rating to become a QARNNS Nursing Sister.*

168 *QARNNS Medical Assistant in front of the hospital in 1989. Female Medical Assistants served in QARNNS on their inception in 1987 and were fully integrated into the RN Medical Branch in 1999.*

VADs (by Mrs Sylvia Bell)

In 1909 it was decided to form a Voluntary Aid Detachment to provide medical assistance in time of war. Volunteers were drawn from the Red Cross, St John's and St Andrew's. When the WRNS were formed in1917, VADs were also invited to opt for service with the Royal Navy and the VAD (RN) came into being. They became part of the Reserved Forces of the Crown and mobile members were committed to serve anywhere: at home, on ships or in naval establishments overseas. At the outbreak of war in 1939 there were some 5,000 members enlisted in the VAD (RN) and most served at least part of their time in Haslar before going on to serve in other theatres of war, some even going to sea on carriers to transfer prisoners of war from the Far East to Australia and Canada.

VADs came from all walks of life. They bought their own uniforms both for nursing and for 'walking out'. Financial reward was minimal at £10 a month – less a sizeable deduction for messing but plus a small allowance for the upkeep of their uniforms.

The majority of VADs were employed as ward nurses, but others covered a wide range of duties including X-ray, operating theatre, dental assistant, laboratory technician, blood bank, pharmacist, medical secretary, clerks and cooks, and where necessary additional training was provided by the Navy.

While on duty each VAD took orders from her immediate superior, usually a QARRNS sister, but all were presided over by a Red Cross Commandant. Throughout the war this post was filled at Haslar by Miss Irene Waistall. She was a strict disciplinarian (she needed to be!) but always had the welfare of her VADs in mind and was highly respected.

VADs were accommodated in M Block (Zymotics) with any 'overspill' allocated to billets, mostly in Alverstoke about a mile away. Those living outside the hospital were issued with naval bicycles to facilitate their journeys to and from work at all hours of the day and night. These were heavy machines with fixed wheels, spiked pedals and hooded lights (for the blackout) and not easily managed, especially over Pneumonia Bridge!

Life in hospital could be very rewarding but also extremely tiring and, at times, intensely distressing. Most of the patients were young men, many with horrendous wounds, and not all survived. It was essential that VADs could enjoy some degree of recreation and the dances and shows in the Errol Hall were very popular. On one memorable occasion, Bud Flanagan gave a show to mark his appreciation of the way the hospital had cared for his son. For anyone lucky enough to obtain a late pass until 11pm, Gosport and Portsmouth offered wider scope for entertainment but such excursions usually involved walking 'home' in the blackout.

No doubt each VAD carried back to civilian life memories of one or more special incidents which had affected her deeply but all those present at the time will remember air-raid measures and the intense pressure following D-Day.

Although Portsmouth and Gosport were heavily bombed, Haslar Hospital escaped damage apart from one raid which hit the library and made a large hole in the 'quarter deck'. However, air-raid warnings were not infrequent and these required all patients – other than those who could not be moved for medical reasons – to be transported from the wards to the cellars where they remained with appropriate nursing staff until the 'all clear' was sounded.

So far as D-Day was concerned, staff were confined to the hospital before the event and, if possible, patients were moved to other hospitals to make room for the expected heavy intake of wounded personnel. The foreseen rush began on 7 June and there was no respite for many weeks. The patients were from all three British Services, from the allies and even from the German forces. The scale of the operation was awesome and, for many, brought home the dreadful human cost of war.

When they were able to find a brief respite from the wards, many VADs found solace in St Luke's Church. The organist would often play soothing music and one could pray for the patients and ask for strength to carry on, however tired one felt. It was with deep gratitude that a number of ex-VADs attended the last service at St Luke's in 2007.

VADs at Haslar felt specially privileged and the experience of serving there was unforgettable. The architecture was impressive; the history was remarkable – where else could one nurse in a ward once used by the wounded from Trafalgar? – and the location was wonderful. The Navy's premier base was just across the harbour and there were views of the Solent where naval activities seemed unceasing. The VADs were engulfed in the Senior Service and proud to be part of it.

VADs continued to serve with the Royal Navy until 1960 when they were disbanded. An Association was formed, with Lady Mountbatten of Burma as its patron. The Association held its inaugural meeting at Haslar and its final meeting at the Institute of Naval Medicine in Alverstoke, thereby enabling members to visit Haslar for conducted tours of the updated facilities and some of the wartime features, such as the underground operating theatres. What memories were evoked, some sad, some joyful, but all unforgettable!

169 *VADs in an operating theatre, preparing instrument trays and surgical apparatus in the 1940s.*

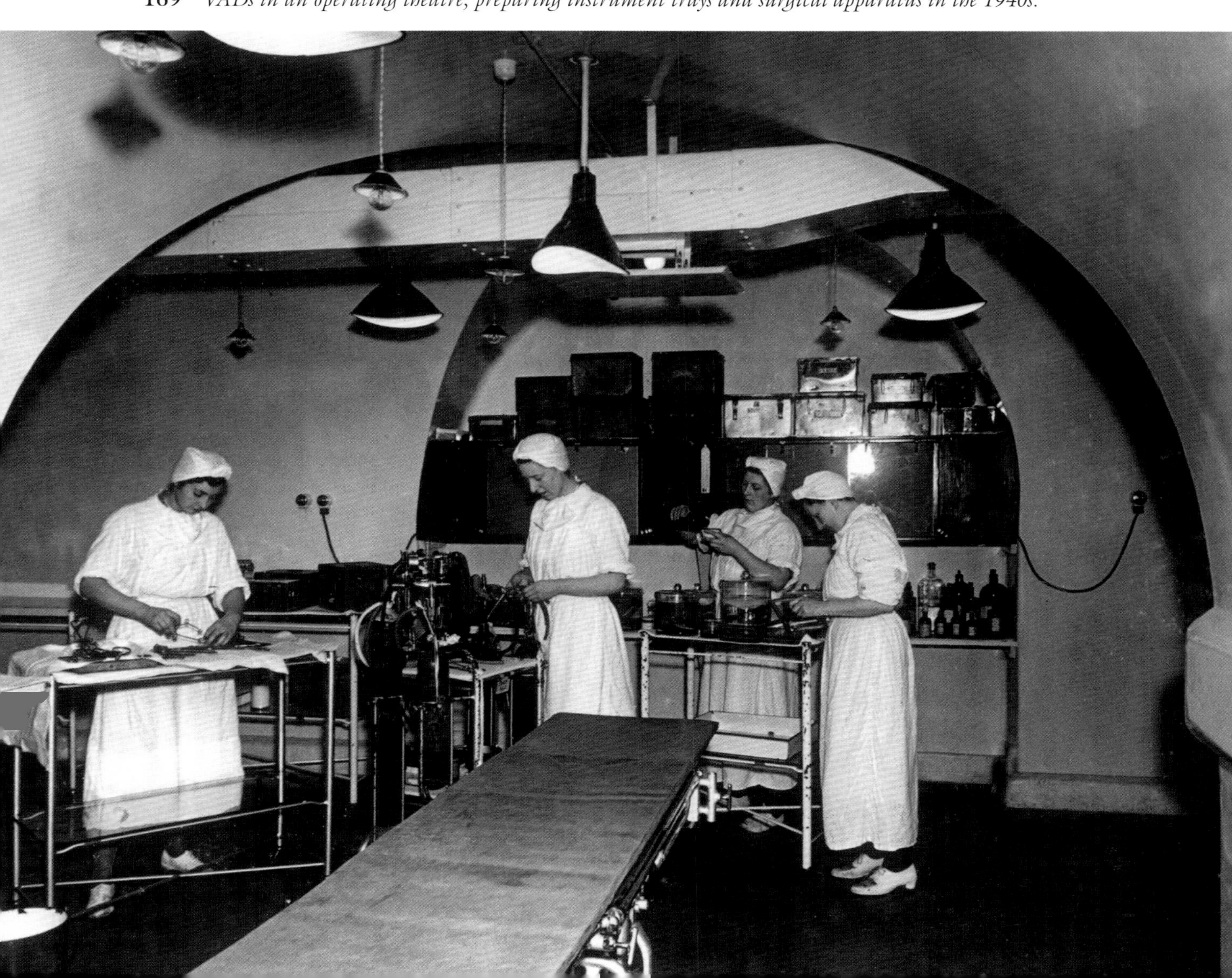

170 *New recruits to the VADs with Miss I.M. Wastell VAD Commandant, 1940s. Miss Wastell retired in 1946.*

171 *VADs outside their Quarters, D Block (later F Block) with VAD Commandant Miss Beazley.*

172 *Midday meal for the VADs.*

173 *VADs in their sitting room.*

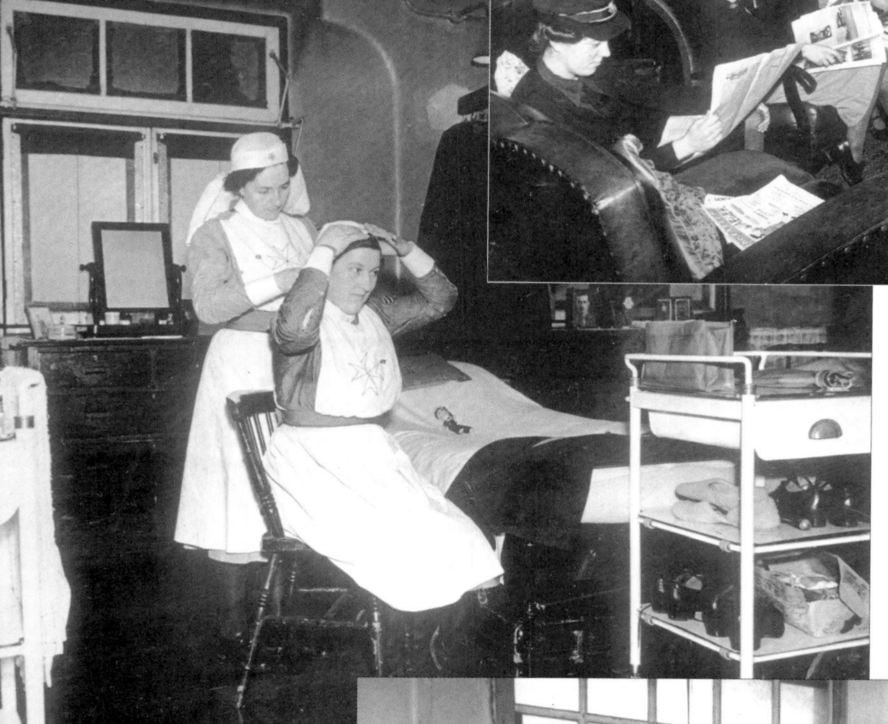

174 *Instruction from a Supervising VAD on how to wear a cap.*

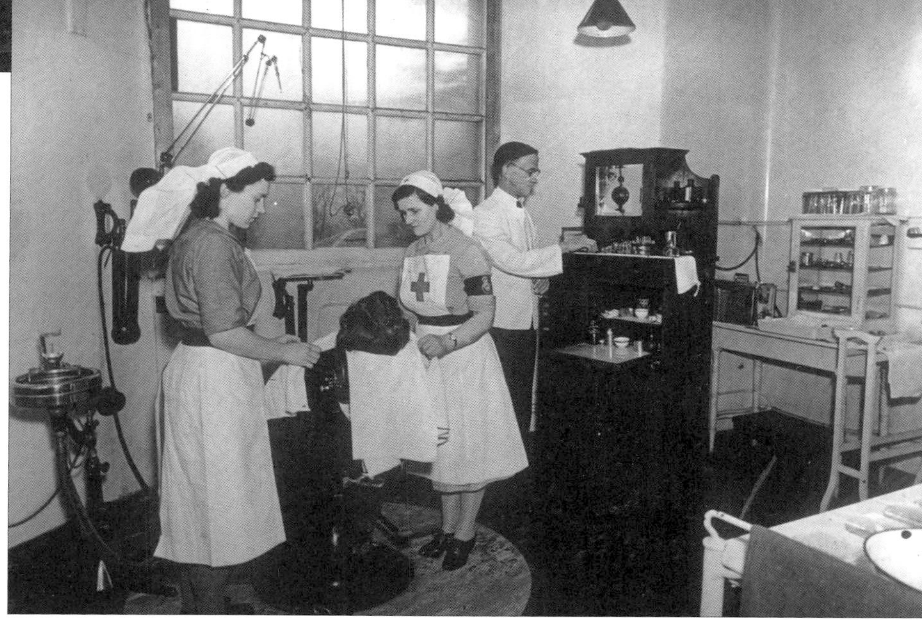

175 *VADs assisting the dentist.*

176 *QARNNS Nursing Officers and ratings on the balcony of Building 80, formerly Officers Block and later the Royal Naval Medical Staff School in 1999. In 1995 QARNNS Officers adopted Naval titles and rank insignia. The crossed As, the insignia of Queen Alexandra, has been retained as part of QARNNS uniform.*

Royal Visits

In August 1855 Queen Victoria and Prince Albert visited the hospital. The Queen spent an hour touring the hospital, commenting favourably on the views of the Solent and the Isle of Wight.

A second visit 27 years later came close to being cancelled due to fog in the Solent. As the weather improved, the Queen arrived with little notice and presented campaign medals to those recently returned from Egypt. A young sailor called MacGuire who had lost a leg in action made to rise from his bed to meet the Queen but she gently placed her hand on his head and with a regal but motherly smile made him lay back on his pillow, and then pinned his medal to his bed jacket. Following this visit the Queen commented, 'Haslar Hospital was unquestionably the noblest of institutions of the kind in the Kingdom.' After the Queen's death Haslar was mentioned in her memorial published in the press: 'Haslar hospital testifies to her [the Queen's] loving thoughts for her seamen, for its wards and by her kind words and beneficent actions the Queen eased the pain of the sick and wounded from her ships.'

The future King George V, then the Duke of York, visited Haslar in March 1897 to speak to members of the Benin expedition. and he also toured the hospital and took lunch with the officers, with some of whom he had served whilst in the Navy. The King and Queen Mary returned in 1910.

On 9 May 1917 Queen Mary attended Haslar to open the newly built Canada Block and to tour the hospital, meeting both staff and patients and finally presenting service awards, amongst others, to those Royal Marines who had been awarded the Military Medal.

177 *Queen Victoria presents Commander Purvis with the Egypt Medal during her visit to RH Haslar on 23 December 1882.*

Queen Mary's daughter, Princess Mary the Princess Royal, visited Haslar in January 1943 as part of a visit to Portsmouth and was presented to QARNNS, VAD and Sick Berth staff and also took time to tour the hospital.

After the Second World War, Princess Alexandra visited Haslar on many occasions as Patron of Queen Alexandra's Royal Naval Nursing Service.

Lord Mountbatten was a regular visitor. His powder-blue Jaguar, with Naval Signalman radiator mount, would be parked in front of the Arcade and became a familiar sight. Staff who had the pleasure of meeting him were often struck by his ability to remember their names.

In 1982 the Prince of Wales visited those injured in the Falklands Campaign. He toured wards and departments, taking time to chat with both staff and patients, and on leaving through the Arcade stopped and chatted with staff and families.

178 *Queen Mary attended Haslar to open Canada Block on 9 May 1917 and, following the opening ceremony, she walked through the hospital and in front of the Arcade she presented Distinguished Service Medals to sailors and the Military Medal to two Royal Marines.*

179 *A summer's day and everyone is well dressed to greet King George V on an official visit to RH Haslar. He arrived in a hospital tram. There is a spare tram in the siding, whilst a Sick Berth Branch Chief looks on with many hospital officers and civil staff in attendance. A QARNNS Nursing Sister can be seen in the crowd by the King's right shoulder. A group of hospital Sick Berth Staff wait in the Arcade.*

180 *King George V and Queen Mary alight from a hospital tram, 23 July 1910. All present are wearing Cowes Rig, white trousers and uniform jackets, the tradition when the Royal Family were at Cowes on the Royal Yacht* Victoria and Albert. *During their tour of the hospital they visited the wards, St Luke's Church and the Operating Theatre situated over the Arcade.*

181 *VADs are presented to Princess Mary, the Princess Royal, during her visit to Haslar in January 1943.*

182 *Princess Mary passes C (previously F) Block whilst talking with a QARNNS Sister and accompanied by Surgeon Rear Admiral Eric Bradbury. Commandant Wastell VAD walks behind.*

183 *Princess Alexandra, Patron QARNNS, meets Naval Nursing Auxiliaries during a visit to Haslar.*

184 *The Prince of Wales arrives in the Arcade in 1982 and is greeted by Miss Wade, Matron, and Surgeon Rear Admiral Houghton before visiting patients from the Falklands Campaign.*

185 *The Prince of Wales with QARNNS Senior Nursing Sister Christina Arnold and John Strange, an injured crew member from HMS* Sheffield. *John had been repatriated from the Falklands onboard the Hospital Ship* Uganda.

186 *Surgeon Captain John Richardson, Medical Officer in Charge at Haslar, leads the Prince of Wales through a ward accompanied by Senior Nursing Officer Arnold.*

Haslar 250

The Haslar Heritage Group was formed in 2001 to plan events to mark the hospital's 250th birthday in 2003. The events were spread throughout the year although this was not the original intention. It became necessary as many of the hospital staff spent some months in Kuwait and Iraq.

In June 2003 the BBC Antiques Roadshow visited, with well-known stalwarts including Michael Aspel and Henry Sandon. A few days later a visit by former QARNNS and VAD Nurses allowed the Heritage Group to gather information to complete the boards hung in the main corridor of the Crosslink building. The display boards ultimately provided the idea to produce this book.

187 *Michael Aspel discusses Arms and Militaria with expert Bill Harriman, whilst an attentive audience looks on.*

188 *Having taken a break from discussing his favourite subject, 'Pots', Henry Sandon has his pulse taken by Lt Fletcher QARNNS. No doubt it had been raised by the sight of so many Nurses, dressed in their ward uniform, acting as Stewards for the day.*

189 *On a perfect June day Michael Aspel pulls a pint of 'Haslar Celebration Ale' in the beer tent, watched by Lt Col Phil Ward and Eric Birbeck, with Dave Pickersgill of Oakleaf Brewery who brewed the special edition ale. The label carried the story of beer issue to patients at Haslar.*

190 *The public wait in orderly line to present their antiques to a specialist. The queues continued until late afternoon.*

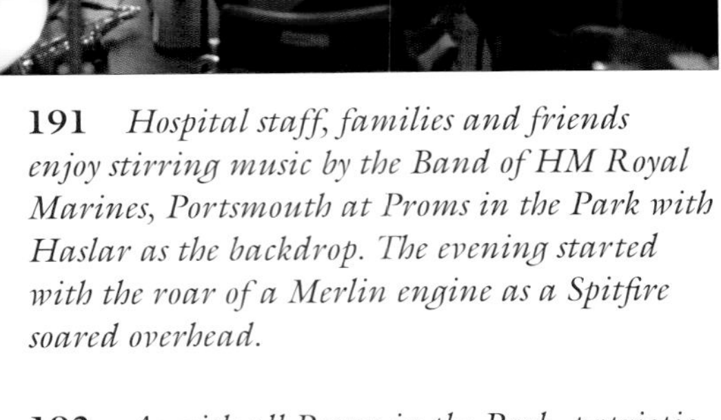

191 *Hospital staff, families and friends enjoy stirring music by the Band of HM Royal Marines, Portsmouth at Proms in the Park with Haslar as the backdrop. The evening started with the roar of a Merlin engine as a Spitfire soared overhead.*

192 *As with all Proms in the Park, patriotic music and fireworks brought a splendid summer's evening to a close.*

An Historical Meeting and Dinner was held in May 2004, with many past Commanding Officers and Matrons attending. The atmosphere of the day is best conveyed by the speech made by Surgeon Captain Ray Radford CBE, a former Medical Officer in Charge of Haslar:

7 May 2004

Mr President, Distinguished Guests, Ladies and Gentlemen.
What a marvellous day we have had and most of us present have sufficient experience to know that it does not happen by magic. We thank again today's presenters, they must have spent many hours honing their talks to reach the superb level that they achieved and we thank MDG for his courtesy in hosting us for lunch. I regret that in his otherwise superb talk Commander Jeff Tall reminded us that you join Haslar by Pneumonia Bridge and leave by Dead Man's Mile.

I must point out that due to increased efficiency and moving the main gate it is now only three-quarters of a mile. It is a privilege to have been invited today and our thanks go to the Haslar 250 Committee and in particular to that indefatigable group, Col Phil Ward and Mr Eric Birbeck and not forgetting Mrs Ann Ryder as well, who have all contributed so much, not only to today, but to the whole year's memorable functions.

We are dining in a historic mess and, by the way we have been looked after, the standards traditional to the Submarine Service and to the Haslar Medical Mess are in good hands and are being well maintained. The front of the menu stimulates me to ask a favour of Eric, namely that he will convey to the department of Medical Illustration the delight that their beautiful art works, in so many formats, have given during the year. They are a joy to look at.

We will shortly be toasting 250 years of Service by Haslar to the Armed Forces, the civilian population of Gosport and, by its research and training, to British Medicine in general. Haslar's name has permanently entered national history and national vocabulary and for my part I am specially honoured to have been asked to propose the toast in such distinguished company. (I hope there are no people here so mean minded as to be hoping that I will slip up over the hospital's name or for that matter the name of Fort Blockhouse.)

What do we mean by Haslar? A fine building. They built well in those days and I do not need to remind one certain person here tonight that only diamond drills could persuade it to be connected to the Crosslink. The walls may have been rigid but Haslar has been just the opposite. Over its 250 years it has been noted for its flexibility, constantly adjusting itself both architecturally and functionally to the demands of the Service in Peace and War, keeping in the forefront of Medical advances, giving its patients the care and treatment they rightly deserved and, last but not least, launching on their lifetime careers, generations of Nurses, Doctors in Specialist disciplines, Technicians, Medical Branch Personnel, Radiographers, Physiotherapists and Civil Staff, along with many others.

In a way the most dramatic developments have taken place in the last fifty or so years and many of the people here tonight experienced them, or even instigated them. We have seen Haslar change from a post-war, half-day, sleepy hollow to a first-class comprehensive District General Hospital for the Navy and Gosport Population and then to a Triservice Hospital and base.

Whatever turf wars took place in the higher Single Service ranks, the young soldiers, sailors and airmen at the workface put them to shame, with no loss of their own service's identity by their concentration on the task in hand and their friendly relations both in the hospital and on deployment. The Haslar-based esprit-de-corps was summed up by a notice I saw in the Theatre coffee room. It read, 'Thursday, Army Run Ashore'.

I have mentioned the civilian population specially, because they have always supported Haslar and Haslar has always supported them. Certainly a gratifying feature in the recent years of uncertainty has been the resounding toast to Haslar sounded by the civilian population in its tireless efforts to save it.

Many here are ex-Matrons and MOICs, and one thing you quickly learn is that there is more to a hospital than Doctors and Nurses. How humbling it is, on taking charge, to visit areas that you have hardly entered before and have taken for granted – stores, kitchens, workshops, offices, greenhouses, boiler rooms, CSSD, laundry (notice padre, I didn't say the church) – and find them staffed by desperately loyal, unassuming people who have given their working lives to Haslar, serving totally out of the limelight. Their predecessors, often quaintly and intriguingly titled, have run through its 250 years of history and we will not forget them all when we toast the hospital.

Perhaps for Freudian reasons, because I cannot totally believe it will ever happen, I have skated around the threat of closure, but we all know that the final step in the reorganisation of the Defence Medical Services, financially and administratively, is planned to be the closure in a few years time of Haslar as a military unit. It is poignant at a time when Haslar still runs nine, arguably ten, operating theatres and even more Army and Navy Units are moving to Gosport. We do recognise that the decision was not taken lightly but it still grieves us greatly. It is no consolation to be following the path of the other great service hospitals such as Woolwich, Wroughton, The Cambridge at Aldershot, Plymouth, or, for that matter, of many famous civilian hospitals. We all hope that if Haslar ceases to be a Service establishment its facilities will be retained in some form by the NHS. And even more, that its historic name will be perpetuated in some way.

What is also important is that before Haslar fully closes, freely available, high quality, local hospital services are guaranteed for the many servicemen and families based in this area on a long- or possibly even more important, short-term basis. The planning and negotiating required places a great burden on those responsible, not least the Surgeon General, Surgeon Vice Admiral Ian Jenkins, and the new CO, Surgeon Captain James Campbell. We would like to express our confidence in their wisdom and judgement and to extend to James our congratulations and best wishes on his joining the prestigious list of people who have had the honour of leading this great establishment over 250 years.

I come now to the toast itself. I shall be asking you to rise and drink a toast to this great historic hospital, to all that it has achieved and to all, great and small, who served it over 250 years. Please rise, Ladies and Gentlemen, to toast:

THE ROYAL HOSPITAL HASLAR.

Happy Christmas

Christmas in hospital was always a special time. Many patients would be given home sick leave but staff did their best to ensure that the patients remaining enjoyed the festive season as much as they were able. On Christmas Day visits might come from Santa, with presents, the Surgeon Rear Admiral in Charge, Matron and the Mayor. Wards were decorated and carol services were held in St Luke's. Staff would also sing carols around the wards. In the late 1940s and the 1950s lights were strung between the trees in front of the Arcade. A large Christmas star was placed on the bell cupola of St Luke's until 2006.

The war years were no exception and staff did their best to carry on the Christmas tradition. Despite rationing, the food was good and one VAD, who served at Haslar at the time, remembers how VAD Commandant Wastell 'grasped things out of Heaven' in order to ensure that staff had special treats. A special treat for 'Jack' was a beer ration, not just at Christmas but on a daily basis, Doctor's orders permitting. Stacks of Brickwoods Brewery crates could always be seen at the entrance to Victualling Office store, delivered daily. Officers were permitted wine and spirits.

193 *The snow lies deep, crisp and even in the winter of 1954 and there is not a footprint to be seen. The pollarded trees of Admiral's Walk stand like sentinels across the hospital quadrangle.*

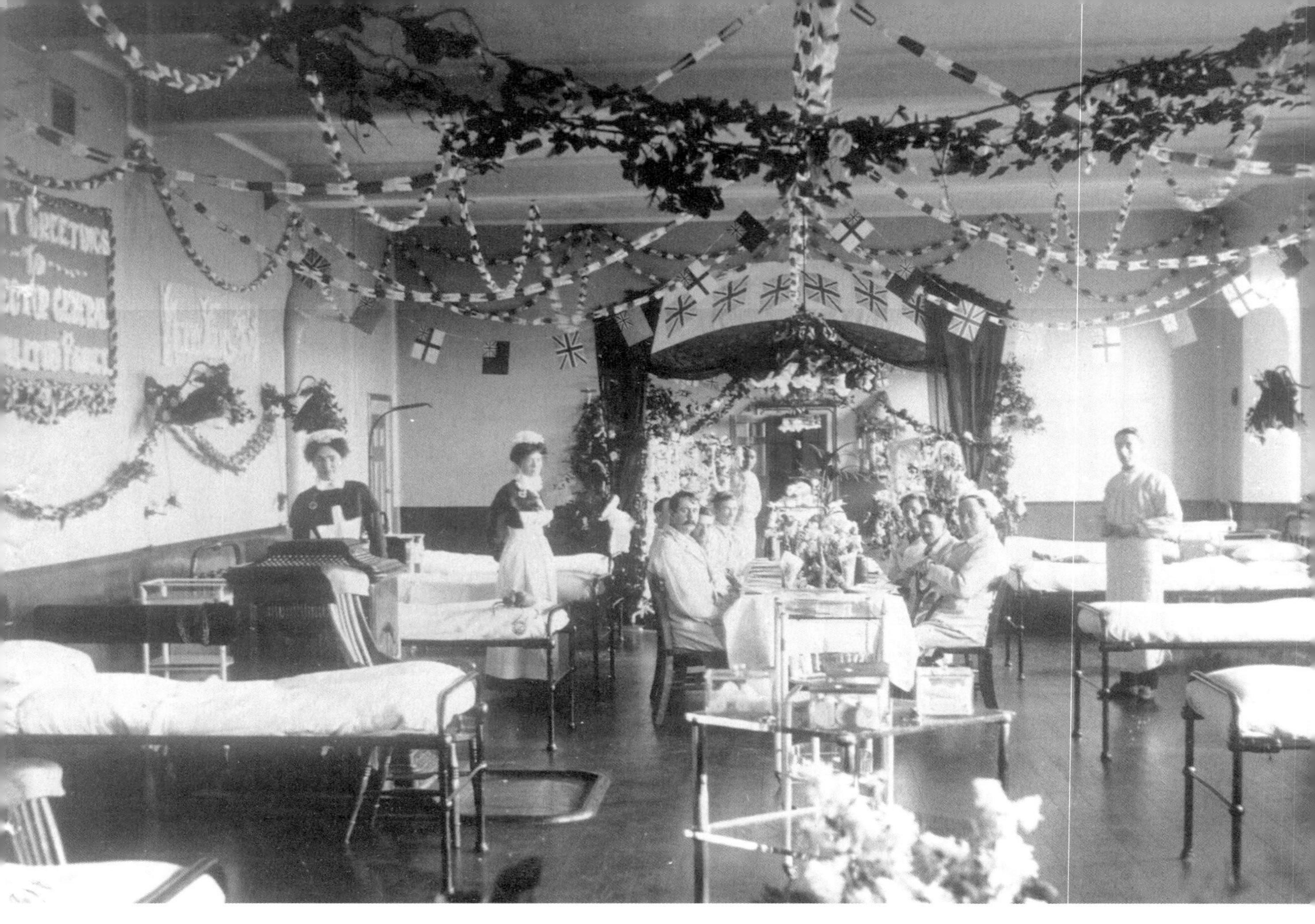

194 *An Edwardian Christmas. QARNNS Nursing Sisters, Sick Berth Staff and patients await a visit from Inspector General of Hospitals and Fleets, T.D. Gimlette CB. The 'Hearty Welcome' sign on the wall behind the ward stove has been made from cotton wool and no doubt the Christmas decorations were also hand-made by the patients. It appears that the patients await lunch, and perhaps the Inspector to carve the turkey?*

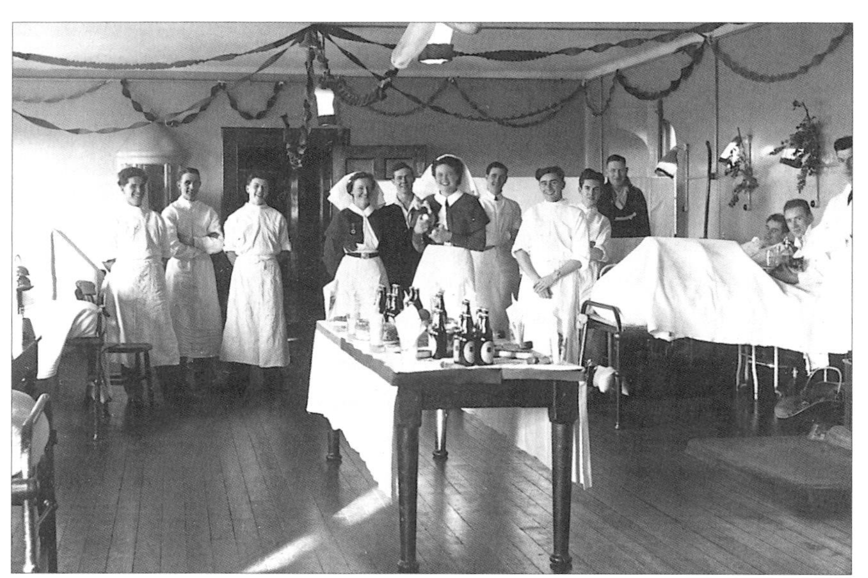

195 *The coal scuttle stands full by the ward fire in this festive picture and again QARNNS Nursing Sisters and Sick Berth Staff pose for the camera with patients who were to spend Christmas in hospital. The table is laden with bottled beer, dates, nuts and crackers. This picture shows the teak floor of the ward. Once a week the beds were pushed back so that the Nurses and Sick Berth Staff could lay down tea leaves and sweep through collecting the dust.*

196 *Christmas 1949 and Sister Joyce Cattermole, Dr Crouch, L/SBA Bannister and SBA Packham and other staff and patients pose for J.C. Lawrence, the well-known Gosport photographer.*

RN HOSPITAL
HASLAR

1968

Christmas Menu

a very
Happy Christmas

MENU

Christmas Day, 1968

Breakfast

Fruit Juice
Grilled Bacon and Fried Egg
Chipolatas
Rolls, Butter, Marmalade

Dinner

Tomato Soup
Roast Turkey Forcemeat Stuffing
York Ham
Roast Potatoes
Cauliflower Brussels Sprouts
Christmas Pudding and Rum Sauce
Mixed Nuts Fruit
Dates and Figs

Tea

Sherry Trifle
Chrismas Cake Fancy Biscuits

Supper

Giblet Soup
Cold Roast Pork Apple Sauce
Creamed Potatoes Green Salad
Mince Pies
Biscuits and Cheese

197 *The Christmas menu for 1968.*

198 *This simple and evocative line drawn card by E.G. Tucker portrays the life of the VADs in Haslar during 1943. Warships and the forts in the Solent, Portsmouth and a small ferry are on the left with the front of Haslar on the right. In the centre, QARNNs, VADs and Sick Berth Staff go about their duties with the Admiral's Walk and St Luke's in the background. At the centre left, the VADs enjoy Christmas lunch in their mess, cats and all. Centre right, a dormitory scene shows VADS unpacking and fixing their uniform and hats with stockings drying on hangers at the end of the beds. The emblems at the bottom of the card are for the Red Cross, VADs and St John's.*

In reality, the life of all staff at Haslar during the war meant hard work caring for the injured. Staff often worked long 12-hour shifts with short six-hour breaks.

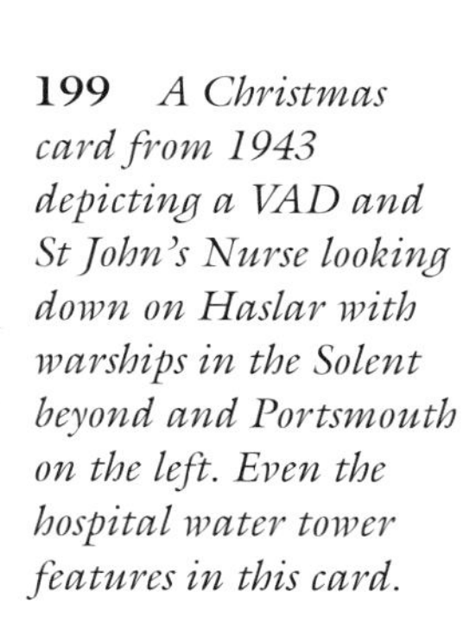

199 *A Christmas card from 1943 depicting a VAD and St John's Nurse looking down on Haslar with warships in the Solent beyond and Portsmouth on the left. Even the hospital water tower features in this card.*

Burials, Excavations and Memorials

Much of the land to the south-west of the hospital was used for burials. This includes the area now known as the 'Paddock', on which The Terrace was built and the Memorial Garden. The number of burials in Haslar is likely to amount to tens of thousands but it is difficult to establish an exact figure. During the years 1779-80, James Lind reported 1,716 deaths and burials in the hospital. In 1782, following the capsize of the *Royal George* at Spithead, 600 sailors, possibly including Admiral Kempenfelt, were interred at Haslar.

During the Napoleonic Wars Haslar was busy, not just with Naval patients but also with Army patients, especially after the closure of the Army General Hospital in Gosport which had a brief life on the site of what is now St Vincent College. In the years 1808 and 1809 there were 1,256 burials. A significant number of these were soldiers of Sir John Moore's Army who were admitted suffering from typhus and dysentery following the retreat from Corunna. Others were sailors, soldiers with Walcheren fever, Russian sailors whose ships had been impounded, and some hospital staff.

Records from 1825 show that grave robbers were active in the grounds of Haslar. Three were caught and sentenced to imprisonment at the Lentern Assizes held at Winchester. In 1826 the north corner of the paddock was enclosed. Headstones from other parts of the paddock were moved to line the wall of this area. During the next 33 years it was used for burials. Many staff and their families were interred here, including Lieutenant Alexander Forsyth Parr who, following service with Nelson at the battles of the Nile, Trafalgar and Copenhagen, was Lieutenant of the hospital for 25 years. Among the patients buried here are a sailor from the USS *Niagara* and a sailor from HMY *Victoria and Albert*. This burial area is now known as the Memorial Garden.

From 1859 burials continued at the newly established Naval Cemetery in Clayhall Road. Funeral processions started from the hospital, continued along Haslar Road and then into Clayhall Road. The route became known as 'Dead Man's Mile'. Bands playing funeral marches were asked not to strike up until some distance from the hospital.

In 2005 the first formal archaeological dig was undertaken in the Paddock area, resulting in interesting finds, and further digs were carried out in subsequent years as a joint MoD, Defence Estates, Cranfield University project. Results have shown that bodies were interred sequentially, with one grave dug, the body buried, and then the next grave dug. The bodies were found to be aligned northwest-southeast, whereas east-west is more usual. It is possible that space was a constraint, or that the burials were aligned with the main hospital axis. Over the period of excavation coffin nails were

200 *The Haslar Paddock looking towards the Terrace. From 1753 until 1826 this was the main burial area.*

found along with surviving wood from coffins (pine). Records show that funerals cost seven shillings and sixpence, but many people could not meet the cost from their meagre estate. Sometimes it was met by friends or from the sale of the deceased's belongings (a naval custom). A number of skeletons were removed for further analysis and all of these are likely to be male and under 35 years of age, with two being assessed as under 20 years of age.

The Haslar Heritage Group noted that many graves were unmarked and arranged for a memorial plaque to be unveiled and dedicated to all who served their country and ended their days at Haslar and were buried in the hospital. On 10 June 2005 Admiral Sir Alan West GCB, DSC, ADC, First Sea Lord, unveiled the memorial plaque.

201 *The Paddock looking towards Clayhall. In the foreground is an area recently excavated. Until 1826 headstones marked burials in these grounds but they were later transferred into what is now the Memorial Garden, which served the hospital from 1826 to 1859 when Clayhall Naval Cemetery opened.*

202 *A view from the top floor of the Surgeon Rear Admiral's Residence showing the Paddock and the gardens to the rear of the Terrace. Bodies were also buried in the area now occupied by the walled gardens. Top left is the old HM Detention Centre, previously a Borstal, which in the 19th century had been an Army hospital and camp for the troops returning from the retreat from Corunna in 1809.*

203 *Excavation of the Paddock area was first undertaken in 2005. This picture shows Surgeon Captain Campbell, Lt Col Jones and Mrs Frances Allan viewing an excavated grave with the archaeologist.*

204 *This is the grave seen in the previous picture, showing three skeletons with excavation markers in place. It was believed that they were buried in hammocks but excavation has revealed that bodies were often buried in pine coffins. Over time, the coffins collapsed within the grave.*

205 *Modern forensic archaeology has allowed archaeologists to take tooth enamel samples in order to find out where the person was born and lived.*

206 *The Memorial Garden. A peaceful and tranquil area with many hospital staff buried alongside patients of the hospital from 1826 to 1859. Sir John Richardson's first wife and son Kendal were buried here. Some trees within the garden are dedicated to personnel who served both at Haslar and in the Naval Medical Services and whose ashes are scattered in the gardens.*

207 *10 June 2005. Admiral Sir Alan West GCB, DSC, ADC, First Sea Lord, admires the Plaque unveiled to commemorate those who served their country in both the Navy and Army and who died from wounds and disease and were buried in the Paddock with no marked grave.*

208 *In Memoriam. The Plaque and ceremony were paid for by the Haslar Heritage Group.*

Royal Hospital Haslar Burial Ground

In Memoriam

From 1753 until 1826 the area beyond this wall, known as the Paddock was used as a burial ground to lay to rest many thousands of sick and wounded who ended their days in Haslar Hospital.
Amongst those interred here are soldiers and sailors who gave their lives for their country during the turbulent days of Trafalgar, Corunna and Waterloo.
They lie side by side, Hammocks their shrouds and coffins, brothers in arms in death as in life.

This plaque was unveiled by
Admiral Sir Alan West GCB, DSC, ADC
First Sea Lord
10 June 2005

209 *Members of the Queen Alexandra's Royal Naval Nursing Service and Queen Alexandra's Royal Army Nursing Service stand heads bowed ready to lay the wreaths.*

210 *Admiral Sir Alan West lays a wreath on behalf of the Royal Navy.*

211 *Surgeon Captain J. Campbell lays a wreath on behalf of the Royal Hospital Haslar.*

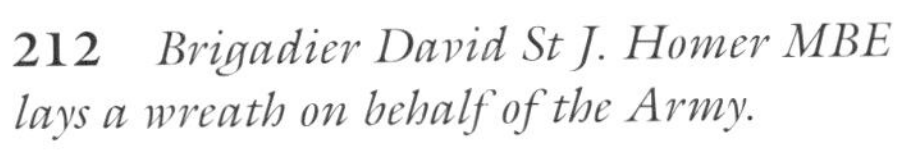

212 *Brigadier David St J. Homer MBE lays a wreath on behalf of the Army.*

213 *Admiral Sir Alan West with Ann Ryder, Eric Birbeck and Lt Col Ward RAMC, the Haslar Heritage Group.*

214 *Admiral Sir Alan West poses with past and present members of Queen Alexandra's Royal Naval Nursing Service and Mrs Sylvia Bell of the Voluntary Aid Detachment that served at Haslar during the Second World War.*

215 *The First World War Memorial to Medical Officers and QARNNS Nursing Staff who lost their lives during the war is dedicated on Thursday 17 August 1922 with Surgeon Rear Admiral W. Bett CB, MVO, Medical Officer in Charge of Haslar, in attendance.*

216 *The War Memorial dedicated to members of the Sick Berth Branch and Sick Berth Reserve who gave their lives in both World Wars. This memorial was initially placed in the area between Canada Block and G block, then moved to face Canada Block and finally to the front of Haslar.*

217 *Dr Andrew Shortland of Cranfield University, Bedford and Phil Harding of* Time Team *discuss the archaeological excavation for a documentary broadcast in 2009.*

218 *Students from Cranfield Forensic Institute prepare to lift a skeleton for achaeological research.*

219 Time Team *filming in the Paddock.*

Getting to Haslar

Haslar has never been the simplest of places to get to. Those who served and worked at Haslar a few decades ago remember the PAS (Port Auxiliary Service) boats calling at numerous Naval Establishments on both sides of Portsmouth Harbour and at the Haslar Jetty. Alternatively, the Gosport Provincial Bus Company's No. 11 bus could be taken from near the ferry in Gosport via Alverstoke, down 'Dead Man's Mile' to the gates of the hospital, before turning on the sea-wall at the gates of HMS *Dolphin*.

When the hospital opened the principal access was by boat to Haslar Jetty. Some of those travelling to and from ships at Spithead landed on the Haslar foreshore. In the 18th century, a doctor from the hospital tasked with visiting the sick floating at Spithead complained that his rower was repeatedly press ganged! Early access from Gosport was either a long journey by horse or carriage via Alverstoke, or via the ferry across Haslar Creek near where bridges were later built.

The ferryman was an employee of the hospital and was not pleased when a Mr Forbes built the first bridge across Haslar Creek in 1795. The ferryman built a house on the Gosport side of the bridge and irritated the Governor and Council of the hospital by obtaining a licence to sell liquor at a time when drunkenness was a great problem in Haslar. The problem was solved in 1807 when the bridge was destroyed. The circumstances of the destruction are unclear.

A temporary timber footbridge built by the Royal Engineers in 1811 lasted until 1814 when it collapsed. In 1833 four men drowned while attempting to cross Haslar Creek during gales. This may have encouraged the

220 *With the main gate open, two members of the Metropolitan Police are on duty and ready to receive an ambulance tram car from the Haslar Jetty. The main entrance had three gates, one to the right of the tramway gate that allowed people on foot to enter the hospital, the night bell having to be rung in the silent hours when the gate was closed. To the left of the centre gate was a larger gate for road traffic. It was not until 1984 that the new gate was put in place on the Haslar road in order to cope with larger vehicles.*

construction of a road bridge in 1835. During the Second World War the centre of this bridge was removed to allow boats access to the Gun Boat yard. A steep pedestrian bridge was built over and across the gap which soon became known as 'Pneumonia Bridge'. Such was the height of the bridge that in winter, in a full-blown westerly or easterly gale, getting to Haslar was no fun at all!

Pneumonia Bridge holds many memories for Haslar staff, including late night walks back from Gosport and a last pint in the *Haslar Tavern* that stood opposite Trinity Church. Staff walked over the bridge late at night in the other direction on a duty run from the Juniors Mess with a 'Pussers Ditty Box' (small hand case) to collect an order of egg banjos (sandwiches) from the Cartoon Café in Squeeze Gut Alley (Bemisters Lane).

In 1877 a tramway was built from the Haslar Jetty through the main gate to the Arcade, where the patients receiving room was situated. Three tram cars were built by The Midland Railway Carriage and Wagon Company (Saltley). The cars were hand-propelled, a handrail being placed on either side of the car which was pushed by staff to and from the Jetty. There were points at each end of the tramway. King George V was just one important visitor propelled back and forth on his official visits to the hospital. An 18-inch gauge track also ran parallel, using the left-hand rail of the tram track up to the main gate of Haslar. It then veered left towards Fort Blockhouse (later HMS *Dolphin*). At the sea-wall the line also turned right and ran along the hospital sea front, allowing patients to be delivered to Zymotics (infectious diseases, Isolation) Hospital. It then continued past Fort Monkton and Gilkicker to the pier at Stokes Bay, allowing munitions, mines and torpedoes to be delivered from Blockhouse to ships in the Solent. Both the tramway and railway became derelict in the 1920s.

221 *A tram with patient is pushed into the hospital, 3 January 1907. This method was labour-intensive, hence the number of sailors in a variety of Naval rigs required for one tram. The patient's stretcher was mounted in the middle of the tram and this patient was from a fire at the Gunwharf (HMS* Vernon*).*

222 *The railhead at the front of Zymotic Hospital. Patients were entrained at the Haslar Jetty and taken on a short ride along the sea front and then admitted for what could be a lengthy stay of up to six months.*

223 *A remnant of track remaining in the Arcade. From the opening of the hospital until the late 20th century patients were unloaded here from handcarts, trams or ambulances.*

224 *Hospital staff leave Haslar Jetty on a PAS boat en route for either Portsmouth Station, HMS* Vernon, *Kings Stairs or HMS* Excellent. *Doctors, QARNNS Sisters and Wardmasters were allocated the comfort of the stern section, all other staff having to sit on the sides in all weathers. Submariners from HM Submarine* Grampus *look down from the conning tower.*

225 *Haslar from the Gosport foreshore, a fine picture believed to have been taken around 1880. Through the masts of the boats on the far side of the bridge can be seen the turrets of the Police Post that stood in front of the main gate of the hospital.*

226 *Haslar Bridge. This is the third Haslar Bridge, completed in 1835. The bridge was to lose the centre section during the Second World War so that MTBs and MGBs could enter Haslar Creek. The bridge was not replaced until the mid-1980s.*

227 *Haslar Bridge Toll Booth. An ambulance waits to pass the toll booth into Gosport. Haslar staff were exempt from payment. This site is now occupied by yacht chandlers in Haslar Marina.*

229 *Pneumonia Bridge, c.1970s. This bridge was aptly named as in winter, with a westerly or easterly gale and rain, nobody got to the other side dry. The bridge was meant to be temporary but it stayed in place until the late 1970s. The original bridge can be seen below and was an ideal fishing point. On one occasion Sick Berth Staff from Haslar managed to get an Austin 7 across – some feat! Many staff tried to swim this point and at least one life was lost.*

230 *A hospital barge of 1866 with the Royal Victoria Hospital Netley in the background. This vessel was used to transfer patients from troop transports anchored in the Solent to either Haslar or Netley hospitals.*

Closure and Freedom Ceremonies

The number of sick in Gosport forced the opening of the hospital in October 1753, the main range being completed in 1754. The title Royal Naval Hospital Haslar was used informally at first, but became the formal title of the hospital in the 20th century.

Just two years after it became a Tri-Service hospital in 1996, the Commanding Officer of the now Royal Hospital Haslar, Brigadier Guy Ratcliffe, addressed the staff in St Luke's Church to inform them that Haslar was expected to close in 2001 or 2002. It continued as a military hospital until 2007, operated in partnership with the Portsmouth Hospitals NHS Trust, and then for a further two years remained in use by the NHS while the redevelopment of the Queen Alexandra Hospital at Cosham proceeded.

230 *After 242 years of continuous service as a Naval hospital the white ensign is lowered for the last time in April 1996. The Royal Naval Hospital Haslar transfers into a new era as a Tri-Service hospital including continuing service to the civilian population of the surrounding area.*

231 *The Band of HM Royal Marines, Portsmouth marches away from the handover ceremony with a Guard of Naval Medical Branch Staff, QARNNS, RAMC, QARANC and PMRAFNS lining the road.*

232 *The Royal Marines Band Plymouth stands ready to lead the Parade of Hospital Staff through the ceremonial gate to Gosport for the Freedom of Gosport Ceremony 29 March 2007. The first march of the parade was to 'Haslar Farewell', a march commissioned by the Haslar Heritage Group and composed by Captain Peter Curtis RM.*

233 *Royal Naval Medical Branch Staff and Queen Alexandra's Royal Naval Nursing Service led by Lt Jason Davies, Medical Services.*

234 *Royal Army Medical Corps, Queen Alexandra Royal Army Nursing Corps and Royal Army Dental Corps led by Captain Ian Treveil RAMC.*

235 *Royal Air Force Medical Staff and Princess Mary's Royal Air Force Nursing Service Staff led by Warrant Officer George Cuthbert RAF.*

236 *Royal Hospital Haslar MOD Civilian Staff march proudly with their service colleagues led by Mrs Ann Ryder.*

237 *The Standard of the Royal Naval Sick Berth and Medical Branch Association leads retired members of the Branch, many having trained and served at Haslar. Retired members of the QARNNS followed.*

238 *The RH Haslar Closure Ceremony, 30 March 2007. Surgeon Captain James Campbell, the outgoing Commanding Officer in Charge of RH Haslar, pauses to reflect with a member of the RN Medical Branch under the watchful eye of WO George Cuthbert.*

239 *The Union Flag lowered for the last time as part of the RH Haslar Closure Ceremony watched by both the media and Haslar Staff.*

240 *The well-known Naval hymn 'Eternal Father Strong to Save' rings out across a wet gathering. This was a different day weather-wise from the Freedom Ceremony held in bright spring sunlight the day before.*

241 *True to tradition, the Commanding Officer and his wife are about to be drawn out of the Hospital through the Haslar Ceremonial gate on a Gun Carriage pulled by hospital staff.*

242 *'How did we do?' asks Captain Campbell, watched by staff and Commander Ian Coulton, Officer Commanding Fort Blockhouse.*

243 *Queen Alexandra's Royal Naval Nursing Service Matrons and Sisters. From left to right: Commander Jean Bancroft, Miss Pamela Graystone RRC, Miss Pat Gould CBE RRC, Captain Julia Massey RRC, Captain Trish Hambling OBE, ARRC and Miss Eileen Northway CBE, RRC.*

244 *To the applause of gathered staff and friends, Mrs Frances Allan, Hospital Director, cuts the decommissioning cake with Surgeon Captain Campbell's Naval Sword.*

Royal Hospital Haslar Commanding Officer's Decommissioning Speech 30 March 2007

In a few short minutes we will haul down the flag for the last time, and the Royal Hospital Haslar will cease to be a military unit. It is an appropriate time to reflect and give thanks for all those who work here now and all those who went before us:

254 years
73 Commanding Officers and as many matrons
Thousands upon thousands of doctors
Tens of thousands of nurses, technicians and other essential military staff
An army of civilian workers
Millions of patients
A host of smiles and a river of tears, in equal numbers
Great triumphs and breakthroughs, plus a few disasters
A seat of teaching and learning
A home to many and a lifetime's work to others

Since this great institution first graced the skyline of Gosport in the 1750s, she has found a place in the hearts and memories of so many people. She has experienced times of fame and high praise, neglect at other times, bombing by the enemy; coveted jealously by some, mocked by others – but never ignored.

She was already a mature lady at the time of Trafalgar, took in the sick and wounded from Corunna, maintained the health of the Fleet during the Pax Britannica, shone during World War 1, excelled during World War 2 and D-Day, took in some of the wounded after their long journey home from the Falklands, now 25 years ago.

We are military medical people working in a fine medical institution. For us, it's all about the patients. We must be able to respond to their needs. We live in a changing world with different and challenging wounds of war. Our casualties now survive with complex multiple injuries which would, and do, tax the most advanced of hospitals. I myself have seen and treated these wounds in Iraq and the Afghan plains, where our wounded soldiers, sailors, marines and airmen and women get the top class treatment they deserve.

However, back here in the UK, we no longer see the survivors of a distant battle brought home after a long sea journey, which was the model that the Royal Hospital Haslar was built to serve. They now fly home swiftly and need immediate high level care from a legion of top specialists. Throughout her long history, the Royal Hospital Haslar has adapted to the demands placed upon her. We can no longer respond to these demands here.

The Royal Hospital Haslar was noble in concept, elegant in design and robust of build. She is the Alma Mater to generations and has been the salvation of many.

> She was charged with providing help and succour
> to the sick and wounded of the Fleet.
> She has discharged her duty.
> That is all.
>
> Surgeon Captain J.K. Campbell Royal Navy

246 *Haslar, taken from the tramway.*

Royal Hospital Haslar Staff

Commanding Officers

The following is a list of Commanding Officers and other senior officers of the Royal Hospital Haslar from October 1753 to the hospital's closure in 2009. The listing has been taken from available information within Royal Hospital Haslar using name and title boards.The information has been transcribed directly from the title boards and apologies are offered if names are missing, or if errors have occurred. The fault lies with the sign writer who held the brush at the time and whose brush has long lain idle.

Physicians and Council

10 October 1753 George Cuthbert MD
1 June 1758 James Lind MD
'Father of Naval Medicine'
24 June 1783 John Lind MD

Governors

26 August 1795 William Yeo Captain
(Buried in the Paddock of RH Haslar)
1 July 1808 Charles Craven Captain

Superintendents

24 February 1820 H. Garrett Rear Admiral
5 April 1838 Sir E. Chetham Kt KCH Captain
2 December 1841 J. Carter Captain
2 December 1846 Sir W.E. Parry Kt FRS Captain
26 July 1852 W.J. Hope-Johnstone Captain
6 May 1853 G.W.C. Courtney Captain
14 December 1854 H. Smith CB Captain
10 July 1855 S.C. Dacres Captain
5 June1858 Hon G.F. Hastings CB Captain
27 April 1863 H.E. Edgell CB Captain
20 June 1864 C.F.A. Shadwell CB Captain
25 January 1869 G. Wodehouse Captain

Inspectors General of Hospitals and Fleets

12 April 1869 J. Salmon MD
18 April 1873 W.R.E. Smart CB MD
13 November 1877 W.T. Domiville CB MD
25 November 1879 J.W. Reid MD
1 April 1880 D.L. Morgan CB MD
8 June 1883 A. Irwin CB MD
2 June 1884 J. Dick
7 June 1887 J. Breakey MD
25 April 1889 D.M. Shaw CB
2 January 1894 D. Hilston MD
2 January 1897 A. Turnbull MD
9 March 1898 H. McDonald CB
12 July 1899 H.D. Stanistreet
18 March 1901 R.W. Coppinger MD
15 March 1904 H.M. Ellis
1 July 1907 J. Porter CB MD
1 May 1908 T.D. Gimlette CB

Surgeons-General

1 May 1911 H. Todd CB KHS
5 June 1913 J.J. Dennis CB MD

Surgeon Rear Admirals

26 June 1916 C. Welch CB
4 October 1918 A.G. Wildey CB
5 May 1920 W. Bett CB MVO
26 April 1923 A. Maclean CB MB KHS
26 April 1926 D.W. Hewitt CB CMG MB FRCS
9 May 1929 H.C. Whiteside CB
7 May 1932 W.W. Keir CMG KHS
1 May 1935 C.L. Buckeridge CB OBE KHS
25 November 1937 T. Creaser MD BCh DTM&H KHP
25 November 1940 W. Bradbury CBE DSO MB BCh
27 January 1945 H.R.B. Hull CB KHS
27 October 1946 J.A. O'Flyn CB KHP
21 March 1948 J.A. Maxwell CB CVO CBE KHS
15 June 1949 F.G. Hunt CB CBE QHP
30 October 1952 J. Hamilton CB CBE QHS

30 June 1955	E.T. Rudd CB CBE QHS
30 June 1958	G. Phillips CB QHS
30 June 1961	D.D. Steel-Perkins CB CVO QHS
8 June 1963	J.M. Holford CB OBE FRCP
1 April 1966	E.B. Bradbury CB QHP
7 July 1969	N.S. Hepburn CB CBE QHS
30 June 1972	C.L.T. McClintock CB CBE QHS

Surgeon Captains

30 June 1975	A.P.M. Nicol MVO CBE FFARCS
4 May 1976	F.A.F. Mckenzie QHP FRCR
9 May 1978	P.W. Head OBE QHS FRCS
8 January 1982	J.W. Richardson OBE QHS FRCS
26 April 1983	J.B. Drinkwater QHS FRCS
3 April 1984	R. Radford QHS FFARCS
11 November 1986	D.A. Lammiman LVO FFARCS QHS
13 December 1988	F. St C. Golden OBE PhD MB Bch
4 September 1990	I.L. Jenkins QHS FRCS

Surgeon Commodore

1 December 1994	I.L. Jenkins QHS FRCS

Commanding Officers Royal Hospital Haslar

following Royal Hospital Haslar becoming a Tri-Service hospital on 1 April 1996.

2 April 1996	Brigadier G.E. Ratcliffe QHP FRCP
15 March 2000	Air Commodore T.W. Negus OBE FDSRCS

Commanding Officer Royal Hospital Haslar and Ministry of Defence Hospital Unit (MDHU) Portsmouth

following Royal Hospital Haslar entering into partnership with Portsmouth Hospitals NHS Trust.

30 March 2001	Surgeon Captain L.J. Jarvis MBBS FRCR
1 March 2003	Lt Col F. Tredgett RAMC
6 May 2003	Surgeon Captain L.J. Jarvis MBBS FRCR
9 December 2003	Surgeon Captain J. Campbell FRCS (Ed) FRCS (En)

On 31 March 2007, and following 253 years and 169 days of continuous service as a hospital, military command ceased.

Hospital Director

Haslar remained under MOD control until closure and a Hospital Director was appointed.

1 April 2007	Mrs Frances Allan BSc(Eng) Hons

Matrons Royal Hospital Haslar

Past Head Sisters and Matrons of RH Haslar

Head Sister

1885	Miss H. Stewart
1886	Miss B. Storey
1889	Miss L. Hogg
1901	Miss G.H. Mackay
1903	Miss F. Cadenham
1909	Miss E.E. Hart RRC
1912	Miss K.M. Hickey RRC
1922	Miss M.C. Clark RRC
1929	Miss C.C. Renwick RRC and Head Sister-in-Chief QARNNS 1934

Matron

1937	Miss D.W. Beale ARRC
1939	Miss M. Goodrich RRC
1944	Miss J. Gillanders RRC

Principal Matron

1946	Miss K. Baker RRC
1950	Miss G. Martin RRC
1953	Miss M.E. Gawston OBE RRC
1957	Miss K. Greenwood RRC
1959	Miss J. Woodgate RRC
1961	Miss S.K.E. Richards RRC
1962	Miss A.A.E. Burman RRC
1964	Miss A.I. Mitchell RRC
1967	Miss C. Thompson RRC
1970	Miss C. Cook RRC
1973	Miss P. Gould RRC

Matron

1975	Miss S.R.R. Barton ARRC

Matron

1976	Miss H.M. Scott ARRC
1978	Miss H.E.K. Gander ARRC
1979	Miss E.M. Northway ARRC
1980	Miss E. Wade ARRC
1982	Miss P. Greystone ARRC

Chief Nursing Officer

1986	Miss J. Titley ARRC
1988	Miss J. Massey ARRC
1989	Miss V.C. Fisher ARRC
1991	Miss C.M. Poole ARRC
1995	Miss J. Bancroft

Commander

1995	Commander J. Bancroft

Director of Nursing

following Royal Hospital Haslar becoming a Tri-Service hospital on 1 April 1996.

2 April 1996	Group Captain B.J. Forward ARRC PMRAFNS
9 March 1999	Colonel K. George RRC L/QARANC
9 October 2000	Commander E.M. Weall ARRC QARNNS

Senior Nursing Officer
following Royal Hospital Haslar entering into partnership with Portsmouth Hospitals NHS Trust.

30 March 2002	Commander E.M. Weall RRC QARNNS
15 September 2003	Commander N. Howes QARNNS

St Luke's Church Chaplains

Name	Date of Service
Mr Ritchie	1758-1763
Lewis Boisdaune	1763-1770
R. Hudson	1772-1797
J. Hall BA	1798-1812
Henry Lloyd DD	- 1813
David Evans	- 1813
Thomas Morgan	- 1815
A. Lawrence	- 1816
David Lloyd	- 1821
James Dunne MA	7 Jul 1828
William George Tucker MA	11 Mar 1853
George Jackson MA	7 Nov 1865
Robert Picton	18 Mar 1871
John James Harrison MA	15 Dec 1875
Frederick William Nickoll MA	27 Feb 1878
Bartholomew King LLD	3 Nov 1881
Alfred James Whistler BA	Mar 1884
George Mahon Sutton BA	Jul 1885
Charles Clark AKC	20 Aug 1885
James Payton BA	8 Apr 1887
Henry Barnett Harper BA	4 Sep1890
Arthur Price Hill BA	18 Aug 1893
Octavius Rutherford Foster Hughes MA	7 Apr 1896
William Stuart Harris BA	12 Jul 1896
Charles Robert Mullins BA	6 Jun 1890
Hugh Keys Moore BA	1 Aug 1905
Henry Backwell MA	16 Sep 1908
Ralph Granby Sadier BA	12 Jan 1918
Thomas Wilfred L. Caspersz MA	15 Oct 1918
Christopher Graham BA	25 Nov 1920
Christopher Philip Godwin Rose BD MA	3 Sep 1925
John Archibald BA	1 Jan 1929
Noel Cyril Jones BA	27 Apr 1933
Vernon Kyrke MA	11 Aug 1933
Norman Braund Kent OBE MA	20 Sep 1936
John Wilfred Evans BA	28 Sep 1938
William Henry Stanley Chapman BA	1 Jul 1941
John Wiltshier MA	1 Feb 1944
Cyril Owen Amos Darby OBE	17 Jun 1946
Perry Malby Dodwell BD MA	24 Sep 1949
Charles Patrick de Candole	31 Jul 1953
Cuthbert Guy Desormeaux Long MA	9 Nov 1955
John Stanton Jeans AKC	1 Jan 1958
Julian James Andrew Newman BA	23 Sep 1960
Evelyn Hugh Jenoyr Levinge AKC	18 Oct 1964
Martin Kitchener Orme BD AKC	2 Mar 1967
David Vincent Evans MA	27 Jan 1970
Leslie John De Groose	17 Oct 1971
Peter Woodhall	9 Jan 1974
Anthony Arthur Upton	8 Mar 1976
Peter John Gregson BSc	13 May 1976
John Edmund Frank Rawlings AKC	3 Dec 1978
John Edward Goodband Clark	18 Jun 1981
Anthony John Francis Metters AKC	20 Aug 1982
Richard Francis Buckley	14 Jan 1985
Michael John Smith DipTh	23 Sep 1987
Stephen Philip Pickering SSC	23 May 1990
Steven David Brookes BA	20 Aug 1992
David Barlow QHC MA	4 Mar 1994
Christopher John Luckraft BA AKC	18 Feb 1997
Jeremy Peter Ames QHC BD AKC	27 Apr 2000
John Hill	12 Oct 2004

Index

Figures in **bold** refer to illustration page numbers.